The Cambridge Introduction to
Theatre Studies

Providing thorough coverage of the methods and tools required in
studying historical and contemporary theatre, this introduction
examines the complexities of a rapidly changing and dynamic discipline.
Following a cross-cultural perspective, the book surveys the ways theatre
and performance are studied by looking initially at key elements such as
performers, spectators and space. The central focus is on methodology,
with sections covering theatre theory, historiography, and textual and
performance analysis. The book covers all the main theatrical genres –
drama, opera and dance – providing students with a comparative,
integrated perspective. Designed to guide students through the
academic dimension of the discipline, the volume emphasizes questions
of methodology, research techniques and approaches, and will therefore
be relevant for a wide variety of theatre studies courses. Informative
textboxes provide background on key topics, and suggestions for further
reading are included at the end of each chapter.

Christopher B. Balme is Professor of Theatre Studies at the University
of Munich.

The Cambridge Introduction to
Theatre Studies

CHRISTOPHER B. BALME

CAMBRIDGE
UNIVERSITY PRESS

CAMBRIDGE UNIVERSITY PRESS
Cambridge, New York, Melbourne, Madrid, Cape Town, Singapore, São Paulo, Delhi

Cambridge University Press
The Edinburgh Building, Cambridge CB2 8RU, UK

Published in the United States of America by Cambridge University Press, New York

www.cambridge.org
Information on this title: www.cambridge.org/9780521672238

First published 2008

Printed in the United Kingdom at the University Press, Cambridge

A catalogue record for this publication is available from the British Library

Library of Congress Cataloguing in Publication data
Balme, Christopher B.
The Cambridge introduction to theatre studies / Christopher B. Balme.
   p.   cm.
Includes bibliographical references and index.
ISBN 978-0-521-85622-5
1. Theater.   I. Title.
PN2037.B25   2008
792 – dc22   2008026920

ISBN 978-0-521-85622-5 hardback
ISBN 978-0-521-67223-8 paperback

Contents

Plates

Figures

Tables

Preface

Students embarking on the discipline of theatre studies at the beginning of the twenty-first century are confronted by a wealth of perspectives that the founders of the discipline at the beginning of the twentieth century could have scarcely imagined. They will find themselves situated in an academic discipline that is unique in a number of ways. Firstly, it links practice and theory in a manner that is still unusual within university study but which is slowly becoming a model for other subjects. Secondly, it offers a choice of perspectives and emphases ranging from the historical to the philosophical, from the purely aesthetic to the explicitly political. Thirdly, the student will find a subject that is by definition comparative and international in outlook.

The potential flipside of such variety is of course disorientation and lack of focus. Because the discipline of theatre studies has developed in so many different directions, it is often difficult to orientate oneself and situate what one is actually studying within the 'wider picture'. It is the aim of this introduction to provide an initial orientation. It is structured in such a way that will be of interest to students at different levels of study, both undergraduate and graduate. It seeks to provide information and answers to questions that may be posed at various stages of university study.

The first point to be emphasized is that this book focuses on theatre studies as an academic university discipline. It does not address issues of purely practical relevance such as acting skills, voice training, lighting technology, etc. The second point is that it will emphasize questions of methodology, research techniques and approaches, rather than provide in-depth information and facts on the subjects themselves. The reader will search in vain for a detailed discussion of Greek or political theatre, but will find information on the sort of sources theatre historians consult to create their accounts of the subject. In addition, there can be found at the end of each section numerous directions for further reading.

The book is structured so that it approximates very generally the way the subject is taught and researched at English-speaking universities. However, because all academic disciplines are in a constant state of (mostly productive) flux, any attempt to delineate sharply specific subject areas is ultimately doomed to failure. Shifts in accentuation and the redefinition of disciplinary focus are unavoidable and indispensable. Departments are forever changing course structures to keep up with perceived shifts in research, or simply in response to local administrative exigencies. What is attempted here is a cross-section or a set of broadly defined common denominators that will probably not mirror any departmental course structure but rather resonate in many different places.

Like any discipline, theatre studies has and is being subjected to processes of differentiation and specialization, which force university courses to find a happy medium between imparting normative, canonized knowledge on the one hand, and following the vagaries of contemporary research trends on the other. The structure of the book also tries to define basic fields of knowledge in Parts I and II, and provide perspectives on current research in Part III. Theatre studies is today no longer synonymous with the study of dramatic texts in various periods of European history, and this book tries to take account of different theatrical practices in a variety of cultural and historical contexts.

The book is divided into three parts, preceded by an introduction. In the introduction, I argue for the necessity of an *integrated* approach to theatre, meaning the incorporation of intercultural and interdisciplinary perspectives on drama, music theatre, dance, puppet theatre and performance art. Within each part, the order of the chapters is not binding. It may be useful for students to tackle the chapters on theatre theory quite early on, as a number of terms and concepts are explained that are used throughout the book. Each chapter concludes with suggestions for further reading. From the huge number of books and articles potentially available, I have focused on up-to-date English-language publications that are most probably readily available in a university or departmental library. The main body of the text contains, of course, many more references, which are listed in the bibliography. The book concludes with a list of reference works, periodicals and websites that students should find useful for pursuing more specific questions.

A book of this kind is principally indebted to the scholars of the field, past and present, whose endeavours have made theatre studies into one of the most vibrant disciplines in the humanities. On a more personal note, I would like to thank those colleagues who read the book or parts or it at different stages. Peter Boenisch (University of Kent), Martin Revermann and Stephen Johnston (both at the University of Toronto) all took the trouble to read most of the manuscript at a late stage, making many valuable comments and drawing my attention to many errors, some more egregious than others. Nicola Shaughnessy (University of Kent) also provided constructive feedback on a field not my own, for which

I am very grateful. At Cambridge University Press, Vicki Cooper supported the project from the outset and Rebecca Jones kept me on track throughout. Most of this book was written at the universities of Amsterdam and Munich. The superb departmental libraries of both institutions made what at times appeared to be a Sisyphean task much more manageable. At Amsterdam, Peter Eversmann and Nienke Meeter helped expedite the project in ways they are probably not aware of. At Munich, Julia Friedenberger provided efficient assistance in the final stages.

Introduction: theatre and theatre studies

The term 'theatre' has its origins in the Greek word *theatron*, meaning a 'place for looking'. Thus, originally, theatre referred to both a place as well as to a particular form of sense perception. Today, the concept of 'theatre' can refer to: (1) a building; (2) an activity ('going to' or 'doing' theatre); (3) an institution; and, (4) more narrowly, an art form. In the past, theatre was often used as a synonym for drama, a usage that can be still be found in the names of some university departments. The terminological complexity of the term means that the object of theatre studies is multi-dimensional and composed of many different fields of enquiry and scholarly perspectives. These areas of study can be grouped under the following broad categories:

- historical
- aesthetic/theoretical
- social/cultural.

If we examine our four definitions, we can see they correspond to these categories in one or more ways. Theatre buildings are, for example, of historical interest, the extant Greek theatres being over 2,000 years old. Those of particular architectural significance may also be of aesthetic interest, and, depending on where they are located, theatre buildings occupy a variety of social and cultural functions ranging from high-class political and economic representation to covert demonstrations of counter-cultural resistance. As an activity for the spectators, theatre-going may encompass a similar mix of social and aesthetic processes ranging from conspicuous consumption (the box at the opera) to semi-religious observance. Most makers of theatre (actors, directors, designers, writers) regard their craft primarily as an aesthetic activity, although its highly collaborative nature might even be of interest to a sociologist or anthropologist. This self-image has of course changed over time: the job of the director scarcely existed before 1900 as a separate artistic function; and before 1750 acting was seldom, if ever, regarded as an art form.

1

Theatre as an activity is probably the most complex aspect of the medium, and certainly the dimension that has given rise to the greatest degree of theoretical commentary. Theatre does not require specialized buildings, but they are certainly the norm. As we shall see later in Chap. 2, it does demand the imaginative collusion of spectators and performers to function. In the 1960s, the theatre critic and translator Eric Bentley described this collusion by means of a famous formula: 'A impersonates B while C looks on' (1965: 150). This bedrock equation is predicated on the assumption that the performer's activity is essentially role-playing (impersonation), pretending to be another person. The spectator's activity is the 'willing suspension of disbelief' and acceptance of the make-believe. As we shall see in the course of this book, theatre can no longer be reduced to this basic activity, although it certainly holds true for most of its historical manifestations. What is important is the description of the basic aesthetic activity involved in theatre – the active role played by the spectator to make the theatrical experience happen.

These examples should suffice to demonstrate the highly complex nature of theatre and its potential to be studied from a variety of perspectives. It can be an object of study for social and cultural historians, for psychologists and sociologists as well as for students of architecture and town-planning. Before the advent of a specialized discipline, however, the bulk of theatre research was undertaken by literary historians concerned with the 'golden ages' of European drama and dramatists such as classical Greece, Shakespeare, Molière or Weimar classicism. This is especially true of classical philology and Shakespeare studies, which boast over 150 years of intense research into all aspects of the stage surrounding the dramatic texts. In light of such competition, it was not always easy for theatre studies to assert its claim to legitimacy as an independent discipline. Such disciplinary demarcation disputes and territorial squabbles were part and parcel of the emergence of theatre studies as an autonomous academic discipline in most countries, as we shall see below. At the same time, the discipline retains strong historical interests and has in turn influenced different branches of literary studies. A great amount of work has been carried out in the past two decades on the history of performance reception, for example. In the field of Greek drama, the Archive of Performances of Greek and Roman Drama (www.apgrd.ox.ac.uk) should be noted, both in terms of its book publications and its online searchable database. Performance reception is strongly represented in Shakespeare studies (the Cambridge 'Shakespeare in Production' series) and more generally in Cambridge University Press's 'Plays in Production' series.

Today, the fields of enquiry are manifold and continually changing. There are, of course, considerable national differences as well. *Theaterwissenschaft* in

Germany, which has one of the oldest traditions of independent research, is still more theoretically orientated and suspicious of practical work than courses in the UK or the USA. The important point is, however, that a subject which began in most countries as a discipline devoted to historical research and the study of dramatic texts appears to have left this legacy largely behind. Today, theatre studies has a strong focus on *live performance*, in all its artistic, cultural and generic variety.

Integrated theatre studies

While theatre studies has until recently focused attention on dramatic texts and their productions (both past and present), this isolation of one aspect or genre of the theatrical medium is increasingly coming under scrutiny and criticism.

The European theatre tradition is characterized by a high degree of specialization, which has seen the development of specific and highly autonomous theatre forms. Since the Renaissance, we can observe the evolution and institutionalization of dramatic, music, dance and puppet theatre. The distinction between these four genres or forms is based on the activity of the central performer, who predominantly speaks, sings, dances or mimes, or is non-human. It is erroneous to assume that these theatre forms have always existed in splendid isolation. Dramatic theatre without musical accompaniment, for example, was only introduced in the late nineteenth century. There are countless historical genres that mixed, in various combinations, speech, song and dance. Forms such as the *opéra comique*, the operetta and the musical employ the acting and dancing singer. The strict licensing of dramatic theatres in the eighteenth century (only a few theatres in Paris and London were permitted to perform 'straight plays') encouraged mixed genres such as pantomimes and melodramas, which emphasized singing, dancing, mime and even occasionally puppetry. Most forms of classical Asian theatre make no distinction between dance, drama and musical theatre on the level of performance.

As already mentioned, the origins of theatre studies as a branch of literary criticism or history meant that scholars focused almost exclusively on dramatic theatre, and a highly selective cross-section at that. Even today, students must prepare themselves for courses of study that emphasize, almost exclusively, spoken theatre. Other forms, such as opera or dance, and very seldom puppet theatre, are, unless there are specialized departments, often marginalized. The study of opera is usually delegated to music departments with the result that research has often emphasized questions of musical style or biographical detail, neglecting opera's place in the theatre culture of a period or indeed the analysis of operatic performances. Needless to say, subgenres such as operetta or musicals were accorded even less attention. Dance as an area of academic research had an even more difficult task to legitimize itself. It established itself sometimes in music, sometimes in theatre departments and often in connection with dance training.

Since the middle of the 1980s, the call for an integrated approach to theatre studies has become increasingly audible. There are a number of reasons for this. An important one is the necessity to accommodate new works that transcend conventional generic boundaries. Dance works may include spoken text, operas employ pantomime, puppets 'perform' alongside actors or singers: a growing number of such works require from scholars at least a working knowledge of all major theatre genres. For this reason, the main theatre forms will be outlined below to provide a basic orientation for the later chapters, which will draw freely on these forms.

Dramatic theatre

The terms 'drama', 'dramatic theatre' and 'spoken theatre' are often used interchangeably. Although strictly speaking the term 'drama' refers to a form of literature (along with prose and poetry), it is also employed as a synonym for theatre in general, which is, however, both historically restricting and highly ethnocentric. Etymologically, the word 'drama' comes from a Greek noun δρᾶμα, meaning originally an action and then a play for the stage. Most European languages have adopted the Greek word in this sense, although the English usage is far more encompassing than, say, the French or German equivalents. As a field of study, 'drama' in the English-speaking world is often used as a synonym for theatre. In this book, 'dramatic theatre' will be used to encompass those forms of theatre that employ exclusively or predominantly the spoken word. The predominance of the spoken voice as a defining characteristic means that a large number of other genres could be included as well, for example:

- stand-up comedy and satirical revues
- children's and young people's theatre
- devised theatre
- improvisational theatre.

With the exception of devised theatre (which is understood here to mean pieces not based on a pre-existing dramatic text), these forms will not be dealt with in any depth for space reasons, but they are still important manifestations of dramatic theatre nonetheless. If one were to look to other media, then it would also be necessary to include radio and television drama, which certainly constitute branches of drama but not of theatre. In recent years, the equation of theatre studies with dramatic theatre has come under criticism because of the almost exclusive focus on 'highbrow' canonized works. On the one hand, this focus reflects the practice of most subsidized and university theatres, which attempt to strike a balance between classics and new dramas. On the other, it has led to a neglect of marginalized forms, both in the past and in the present.

Music theatre

Music theatre as an area of theatre studies is marked by a curious paradox. Its dominant form, the opera, has for two centuries been the paramount manifestation of theatrical culture, commanding the most economic support and occupying central functions of political representation. Yet, until recently, it has been largely neglected by theatre studies, which accorded it at best a marginal place in its field of study. The term itself is also somewhat contested. 'Music theatre' can be employed as an overall concept encompassing all forms of theatre with a musical predominance. This would necessarily include everything from grand opera to the 'lowly' musical revue. In the English-speaking world, it would also include the musical as a specific genre of great economic importance, but which has, until recently, played only a very marginal role in the theatre cultures of continental Europe. Most research attention has been focused, not surprisingly, on the opera, a manifestation of music theatre that enjoys extremely high cultural status.

Research into opera has long been a subdiscipline of musicology. Its incorporation into theatre studies is a relatively recent phenomenon, which has grown in importance owing to the spread of interdisciplinary perspectives. A musicological approach to opera focusing primarily on the score or questions of musical style and genre tends to eschew major dimensions of the operatic experience. From a historical perspective, these would include questions of economics and political representation as well as the importance of virtuosic performance as a central component of the star system. Contemporary questions of staging and theatre design (scenography) can today often be better studied in the opera than in the dramatic theatre, as directors and designers switch between theatrical genres and, equipped with bigger budgets in the former, appear to experiment more freely.

The study of opera within theatre studies nevertheless poses certain problems, the most important of which is the necessity for some kind of specialized musical knowledge. Whereas comprehension of spoken language is more or less innate, musical competence is not. It requires special training and acquaintance with a multitude of conventions that can only be acquired over time. This requirement was clearly a hindrance to including music theatre, and especially opera, within the purview of theatre studies. It was not until the 1970s that musicology and theatre studies began to focus on the same research questions. They included questions on:

- stage technology
- history of staging
- the working methods of composers, librettists and ballet masters
- history of reception
- history of operatic subjets
- the economic conditions of opera production over the past centuries.

These are, of course, questions that have been the staple fare of theatre historians for the past century. We would need to add to the list, somewhat later, the field of performance analysis. These are also questions that do not require, in the first instance, specialized musical knowledge. On this level, co-operation is indeed possible, and an increasing number of publications are documenting such new perspectives, as we shall see in Chap. 9.

There are a number of good reasons for including music theatre in an integrative theatre studies:

- Performative dimension: works of music and dramatic theatre are made manifest by a performer; they are transitory and rely on dramaturgy and staging to achieve completion. In a narrower sense, we can say that the human voice is another common factor: the singing voice on the one hand, the speaking voice on the other.
- Historical dimension: in certain periods, music theatre is the dominant aesthetic and cultural medium. Any examination of nineteenth-century 'theatre' history in any number of countries – including Germany, Italy and France – is distorted if forms of music theatre are not given appropriate attention. The beginnings of modern directorial theatre and design are also inextricably linked with opera.
- Individual artists: many leading directors and designers work in both genres. In addition, no discussion of experimental theatre is complete without knowledge of the theories and works of composers like John Cage or Mauricio Kagel. A new type of composer-director is also emerging, represented by artists such as Steve Reich and Heiner Goebbels.

Dance theatre

The terms 'dance theatre' and 'theatre dance' are of recent coinage and encompass dance forms that are performed primarily in a theatrical context. The best known of these is, of course, classical ballet, which in the twentieth century was followed by developments such as modern dance, *Ausdruckstanz*, postmodern dance and *Tanztheater* to name just a few. Technically speaking, any form of dance can be made 'theatrical' simply by performing it in front of an audience. In this book, 'dance theatre' and 'theatre dance' will be used interchangeably as overall concepts. In recent years, these terms have been extended by concepts and genres such as 'movement' or 'physical' theatre. These have arisen to designate an increasing number of groups and experiments that seem to fall between dramatic and dance theatre, but where the moving (rather than the speaking) human body is clearly the dominant mode of expression. Physical theatre could also be used to encompass older forms of primarily movement-based theatre, such as pantomime and/or mime, which have their roots in classical antiquity.

The wider field of dance as a cultural phenomenon encompasses a myriad of manifestations ranging from folk dance to ritual. The study of these forms is often delegated to other disciplines such as folklore studies, cultural anthropology or even sport, and does not strictly fall in the remit of theatre studies. In those departments where dance is studied within its own institutional framework (and is not part of another discipline), dance as cultural expression and theatre dance may well be studied together. Because of the close institutional connections between dance and music theatre – well into the nineteenth century, operas and operettas almost always included dance scenes and interludes – the study of dance theatre was often conducted as a marginalized wing of musicology. The contributions of major composers such as Tchaikovsky or Stravinsky required at least a passing acquaintance with the history and conventions of ballet. In the Anglo-American world, academic dance research emerged either as a support discipline for the training of dancers or as a field in its own right, but often under the institutional umbrella of theatre studies. Particularly in the USA, dance studies is regarded as an interdisciplinary field of research combining aesthetic as well as broader cultural perspectives.

Like music theatre, theatre dance shares many features with dramatic theatre. Hence dance theatre research also has many perspectives in common with theatre research. On the level of performance, it deals with a complex aesthetic object. Like theatre studies, it has to deal with an ephemeral art form whose 'texts' are even more intangible than those of music or dramatic theatre. Ultimately the spectator is confronted with bodies moving in space whose movements may or may not be recorded on paper (choreography) for future dancers or generations. Nevertheless, these works constituted by physical movement can be studied from historical, theoretical and aesthetic perspectives. Historically oriented dance research concerns itself with individual choreographies, periodization, major dancers and choreographies.

Theoretical research is focused primarily on questions of analyzing the body and movement (see Chap. 10).

Puppet and mask theatre

Puppet theatre looks back on manifold traditions and artistic forms. It ranges from simple hand-held glove puppets to highly complex performances integrating objects, marionettes, masks and live performers. One can distinguish between two-dimensional figures, employed mainly in shadow theatre, and three-dimensional, plastic figures used in hand, rod and string puppetry. Today, it is becoming increasingly difficult to sustain the traditional distinction between puppets and live theatre. Because of the historical, aesthetic and cultural significance of puppet theatre through history and across cultures, it must come into the purview of an integrated approach to theatre studies.

In Western theatre traditions, puppet theatre has always been a relatively marginalized genre, associated principally with children's entertainment. A glance at other theatrical cultures reveals a completely different status. Javanese *Wayang Kulit*, for example, a form of shadow theatre using transparent rod puppets, is the most widespread theatre form in Indonesia, whose origins go back to the eighth century AD. Equally widespread among the Turkish people is *Karagöz*, which is also a form of shadow puppetry with beginnings around the sixteenth century and which has sustained its appeal until today, where it can be found on television as well as on the stage. Of high cultural status is the Japanese *Bunraku*, which achieved great prominence in the seventeenth and eighteenth centuries and today is considered to be one of the great classical theatre forms of Japan, together with *Nô*, *Kabuki* and *Kyôgen*.

In the European context, puppet theatre has only sporadically gained recognition as being of aesthetic value. Nevertheless, as a wider cultural phenomenon, it is ubiquitous and can be found in many historical and cultural contexts. Apart from theatrical performances of all kinds, these include commercial uses in fairground booths, religious contexts and even juridical applications such as the carrying out of punishments on effigies.

Modern puppet theatre does not emerge until around 1900, when puppets, particularly marionettes, were seized on by a number of representatives of the avantgarde as a means to reform realistic, text-based dramatic theatre. In Russia, Germany, Austria and France, artists emerged who proclaimed a new kind of puppet theatre distinct from fairground and children's entertainment. The reception of Asian theatre in this period also had a decisive influence on many of these artists, although their aims transcended a mere imitation of exotic forms.

After 1945, puppet theatre developed rapidly in a number of directions. Perhaps the major advance was the increasing 'visibility' of the manipulator and finally the incorporation of live performers into productions. The major influence here was probably *bunraku*, which uses three black-clad manipulators who are supposed to be 'invisible'. Groups such as the South African Handspring Puppet Company work primarily with *bunraku*-type puppets, but also include human actors (see Plate 1). Another development has seen the introduction of puppets into productions with live performers, such as in the work of Ariane Mnouchkine, Tadeusz Kantor and Robert Lepage. Although puppet theatre has only received marginal attention from mainstream theatre studies because of its association with children's entertainment, indifference is today changing to fascination. In light of an increasing number of complex productions and theories that explore and cross the boundaries between human and puppet theatre, this marginal position can no longer be justified historically, aesthetically or culturally.

Like puppet theatre, masks and masking are deeply embedded in the history of the medium. The Greek theatre used masks, and the mask has in fact come to be a symbol of the medium, embodying as it does central metaphors such as concealment and the distinction between art (the mask) and life (the living actor). The masked *Commedia dell'arte* character has also assumed something of a synecdochal function as a representation of theatre as a whole.

Masks also draw attention to theatre's ritual origins and are often studied in intercultural contexts. This usage can be seen as a point of comparison or even tension within the Western tradition because the status of mask-use in Western theatre is controversial. It oscillates between vehement rejection and passionate advocacy. The absence of masks from mainstream theatre is linked to the dominance of psychological drama, while their reappearance in theory and practice at the beginning of the twentieth century is motivated by dissatisfaction with precisely this tradition. Masks provide one of the foundations for Edward Gordon Craig's 'Theatre of the Future' and represent for Vsevolod Meyerhold in the middle phase of his work a 'symbol of theatre' itself. Among leading contemporary directors there is similar dissent. On the one hand we find advocates such as Giorgio Strehler and Ariane Mnouchkine, who seek to draw on the tradition of masking in popular culture, and on the other Peter Brook's sceptical attitude to reintroducing to 'Western art theatre' what he calls the 'morbid mask' (Brook 1988: 218), which is representative for a widespread view that Western culture has lost any kind of functional masking tradition. As theatre historian Susan Smith puts it: 'The modern Western world is

Plate 1. *Bunraku*-style puppets used by the Handspring Puppet Company in their production of Monteverdi's *Il Ritorno d'Ulisse* (1998). In this production, one of the manipulators is also a singer. Note the difference between costumed and black-clad manipulators.

mask-poor. The areas where masks retain their cultural and religious meanings are all outside the boundaries of Western tradition' (Smith 1984: 3). Recent developments in postcolonial and intercultural theatre are overcoming this dichotomy, however, as indigenous masking traditions are fused with experimental approaches, which are usually outside the psychological mainstream.

From theatre studies to performance studies

If we look at the development of theatre studies in the UK and North America, we can observe three major stages of evolution. On both sides of the Atlantic, the discipline was defined as the study of drama, albeit with a strong performative focus. The first theatre studies degree programme in the USA was established in 1914 at the Carnegie Institute of Technology, with others soon to follow (Jackson 2004). In the UK, the first department was established at the University of Bristol in 1947, which provided a model for many others throughout the English-speaking world. The essential difference between the two countries was the degree of professional training involved. In 1926, George Pierce Baker established a degree programme at Yale University that aimed to provide training for the theatrical professions. Dramatic analysis and theatre history were adjuncts to a primarily vocational orientation. In the UK, drama was studied very much like any other arts subject, with a view to providing critical and historical perspectives on a central cultural phenomenon.

A second phase can be identified in the 1970s, which saw a renaming of some (but not all) drama departments as departments of theatre studies. This change in nomenclature reflected a shift in focus towards the theatrical performance as the central object of study, from both contemporary and historical perspectives. The name change also signalled a break away from literary studies, of which drama was seen as a part. This did not mean that dramatic texts were no longer studied (on the contrary), but it did indicate that they were just one – and perhaps not even the most important – part of a more complex cultural phenomenon. Scholars studied theatre buildings, the evolution of acting, and the complex dynamics of the performance itself. However, it would be over-simplifying the matter to suggest that these changes followed such neat categories. From the outset, first-generation scholars working in drama departments conducted theatre historical research, and even today the study of dramatic texts continues to be a central part of the discipline. The central shift, however, concerns the concept of performance and its study.

The third and most recent phase in the discipline's development refers to the rise of performance studies in the 1980s. Since the mid 1960s, Richard

Schechner, a New York-based academic and director, had been advocating a concept of performance transcending text-based drama and embracing interconnections between play, games, sports, theatre and ritual. In the following years, Schechner demonstrated in numerous publications the interdisciplinary potential of such a concept, and emphasized its status as a social science rather than as a branch of the humanities. The definition of performance within the broader parameters of the social sciences implied a departure from aesthetic and historical paradigms that had until then dominated theatre studies. In this understanding, dramatic theatre is just one possible manifestation of performance. In performance studies, one is more likely to study the performance aspects of a church service or a political rally than a dramatic text. Although the institutionalization of performance studies as an independent discipline has been relatively slow – even in the USA there are still only very few independent departments of performance studies – its ideas have been tremendously influential. Research and teaching using a performance studies methodology and objects of study or research are now widespread in many theatre departments, especially at graduate level. A low degree of specific institutionalization has not prevented a spread of courses and research into the subject. Although this book is devoted to theatre studies as the discipline has evolved since 1945, and not performance studies, it takes cognizance of the fact that now the two disciplines are merging and intermingling in many ways. For this reason, I will often speak of 'theatre and performance', in which case the wider cultural definition of the term 'performance' (see Chap. 5) is meant.

Outline

In the first part of this book, we shall look at the constitutive elements of theatre. Reduced to the simplest common denominator, theatre, or more precisely a theatrical event, consists of a simultaneous and mutually conditioning act of playing and watching by performers and spectators gathered together in a common space. All additional elements – set design, costumes, dramatic text, direction, etc. – can be regarded as more or less important or unimportant accessories, which can be dispensed with as need be without actually endangering theatrical performance. The precise nature of the interaction of these elements remains a matter of dispute amongst theatre scholars. Should we call it 'playing' as in a game, or should we regard it as a form of 'communication' as in normal human interaction? Or is theatrical performance something different again, a unique and ineffable combination of play and communication, or even an exchange of energies? Each ascription has its own disciplinary pedigree: theatre as play is strongly influenced by sociology and anthropology; theatre as communication by semiotics and communication theory; theatre as energy exchange appears in more recent post-semiotic philosophy but is also discussed in acting theory. On closer inspection, it becomes clear that a theatrical performance involves all these elements: it is play in the sense that the participants, performers and spectators usually obey pre-assigned roles and interact accordingly, but the parallels are ultimately limiting because games do not normally transport narratives or other aesthetic content.

Theatre also involves communication, both on stage within the fiction being enacted and between stage and audience. Theatre scholars are interested principally in questions pertaining to the outer communication system, i.e. between stage and audience (see Chap. 2). Internal communication within the fictional world (e.g. Hamlet's relationship to Ophelia) on the purely textual level is the traditional domain of dramatic and literary criticism. When this relationship is translated into theatrical signs (gesture, costume, intonation, etc.) then we are dealing with performance analysis and it is of central interest for our discipline (see Chap. 8). For the time being, however, we shall examine the three fundamental elements – performer, spectator, space – in isolation, but always conscious of the fact that in a performance situation they exist in a dynamic triadic relationship to one another. There are historical and pragmatic reasons for doing this. Traditionally, scholars have studied them in 'splendid isolation', so, initially at least, it is necessary to follow these lines of enquiry.

Part II – Subjects and methods – will look at the central perspectives of theatre studies, as outlined above. These are in main theoretical, historical or analytical in orientation, and are based in turn on substantial bodies of knowledge and scholarly methodologies. The central methodological focus in Part II is devoted to performance analysis (see Chaps. 7–10), which has grown to become perhaps the central area of study of the discipline. While other subjects may examine the textual (literary criticism), musical (musicology) or visual (art history) aspects of theatre, the performance remains the key differentiator of theatre studies. For reasons of terminological clarification, the part begins with two chapters dealing with theatre theory. Chapter 4 will look at the long and rich history of theatre theory, beginning with the arguments first developed by Greek philosophers. Chapter 5 will focus on contemporary developments in theatre theory as they intersect with wider discussions such as semiotics, poststructuralism and performance theory. The next chapter in this part will discuss theatre history from a methodological point of view. From being the undisputed foundation of theatre studies, theatre history has developed into a highly contested and complex field of theoretical and even ideological debate. Our focus will be historiographical, i.e. we shall look at how theatre history is researched and written, and not at the development of theatre itself.

Part III will examine how theatre studies intersects with other disciplines. Due to theatre's multifarious functions over different periods of time and in different cultural contexts, it has been the object of investigation by a variety of disciplines. There are, of course, many potential points of contact, and for reasons of space I have had to focus on only two. Chapter 11 will be devoted to the relatively new but rapidly expanding field known as 'applied theatre', which is concerned with the application of theatrical techniques in various therapeutic, pedagogical and developmental contexts. Chapter 12 will look at theatre's interfaces with other media, ranging from cinema to the internet.

Further reading

There are many studies that engage with the fundamental question of what constitutes theatre. Richard Southern's *The Seven Ages of the Theatre* (1962) provides, like Eric Bentley, an essentialist definition. Peter Brook's *The Empty Space* (1968) remains a canonical statement by one of the leading directors of the post-war period, although the minimalist concept suggested by the title has been challenged. A more recent and stimulating reformulation of the same question is provided by the Brazilian director and theatre pedagogue Augusto Boal in *The Rainbow of Desire: The Boal Method of Theatre and Therapy* (1995: 13–29). A succinct and perceptive discussion of the concepts 'drama' and 'theatre' in their wider cultural context can be found in William B. Worthen's introduction to the *Harcourt Brace Anthology of Drama* (1999: 1–10).

For accounts of the development of the discipline, see Shepherd and Wallis (2004) for the UK, and Jackson (2004) for the USA.

Part I

Elements of theatre

Chapter 1

Performers and actors

If I may be allowed to conjecture what is the nature of that mysterious power by which a player really is the character which he represents, my notion is, that he must have a kind of double feeling. He must assume in a strong degree the character which he represents, while he at the same time retains the consciousness of his own character.

(James Boswell 1770: 469)

The study of performers and actors has not always been a central and systematic concern of theatre studies. At various times, buildings, social organization, dramatic texts and then performance analysis have seemed to occupy more attention than what we would normally consider the defining element of theatre, the performer. There are many reasons for this periodic disregard. An important one is simply the question of definition. Are we speaking about the actor (the reciter of dramatic texts) or should we widen our purview to include other types of performer: the dancer, singer even circus clown or acrobat? Theatre studies has traditionally not opted for the wider definition, although the growth of performance studies in the past decade is beginning to change this exclusive interest in the 'actor'. There are, of course, very good historical reasons for focusing on the actor. The European theatre tradition is characterized by a high degree of specialization within the performing arts. This is by no means the case in other theatrical cultures, where there may not even be different words for actor and dancer, for example. But even in the European context we can find in certain historical periods theatre traditions where the differentiation is by no means entirely accurate. The professional performers of the *Commedia dell'arte* troupes, for example, were accomplished actors, singer and dancers.

If we restrict ourselves for the time being to the actor, then we can ask if there is a minimal definition of this activity upon which all can agree? The usual definition – the actor seems to speak and act, not as him or herself, but in a role that he or she pretends to be – becomes questionable on closer inspection. For example, it does not address the question of the means the actor employs to create this state, nor does it define when a person is actually

a commonplace of rhetorical theory and practice that a speaker had to first feel emotions himself (Roman orators were almost exclusively men) before being able to impart the same on his listeners. For rhetors, the main problem was one of affective correlation between speakers and listeners. Within the context of acting theory proper, it became an internal problem within the actor: how to manage genuine and 'affected', i.e. played, emotions.

The 'scientific' basis of this understanding of the relationship between body and emotions was the so-called 'theory of the passions'. Until well into the seventeenth century, acting and public speaking were considered to be linked activities distinguished by three abilities:

- to exercise emotional control over their bodies
- to act on a wide physical space
- to emotionally affect listeners sharing the same space (Roach 1985: 27–8).

Because of this protean quality, the actor in particular was increasingly regarded as a moral and philosophical 'problem'. The ability to disguise one's own emotions while at same time affecting those of the spectators became increasingly incompatible with prevailing notions of ethical integrity and sincerity, as we shall see below.

A visual canonization of the passions was provided by the French court painter Charles Le Brun in the late seventeenth century, in his illustrated treatise *Méthode pour apprendre à dessiner les passions* (1702) (see Plate 2). Although the exact number of passions, or emotional states, was never finally fixed, Le Brun provided forty-three illustrations with commentaries. They show different passions in their variations and mixed forms (the so-called mixed passions). The basic passions include: astonishment, rapture, simple love, desire, hope, sorrow and despondency. Originally conceived as an aid for painters, Le Brun's systematization was used extensively by actors in the eighteenth century. It was not until the eighteenth century that acting began to be discussed and theorized separately from rhetoric. Nevertheless, the theory of the passions remained influential throughout the century and even into the nineteenth century. What did change in the eighteenth century, however, was the physiological explanation for the corporeal side of acting.

Although it gradually died out on the professional stage, the link between acting and rhetoric remained strong in the education sector. In the late eighteenth century, rhetoric was redefined as 'elocution', thereby losing its pejorative overtones of insincerity and dissembling. The teaching of elocution in schools and universities in the English-speaking world retained the bond between public speaking on the one hand and speaking for the stage on the

Plate 2. The passions according to Charles Lebrun. Top: left to right: horror, revulsion, simple physical pain. Bottom: left to right: awe, delight, admiration.

other. Promulgated in the British empire through graded examinations from Trinity College (LTCL), in the USA through university departments of speech and communication, the rhetorical tradition continued to exercise an influence as an educational 'skill' that is today being redefined as one of the key qualifications necessary for professional advancement. The transformational power of elocution is demonstrated most famously in George Bernard Shaw's play *Pygmalion* (and in its later musical adaptation, *My Fair Lady*), where a professor of phonetics and elocution teacher, Henry Higgins, 'improves' not only the speech of the working-class girl, Eliza Doolittle, but her whole social being.

The rise of acting theory in the eighteenth century forms a central field of research for theatre studies. Theories and manuals of acting that begin to appear in large numbers throughout the century vary a few basic questions, the most important of which is whether the actor should try and consciously feel the emotions he/she is supposed to be playing or not. More important than the various positions taken, however, are the theoretical and philosophical concerns motivating this debate. They transcend, in fact, purely theatrical problems and touch on the fundamental question of how human beings think, act and feel. During the Enlightenment, this broader field became known as 'anthropology', a term that in the eighteenth century did not just mean the study of distant cultures, but that of the human species as a whole. The key question was one that still concerns us today: to what extent is human behaviour naturally determined, and to what extent the result of social or cultural conditioning?

Interestingly enough, the actor became one of the examples used to discuss what is obviously not a purely aesthetic problem. It was an ideal of the Enlightenment that human beings should strive to achieve a kind of balance between their internal emotional life and its outward expression in social intercourse. All forms of 'dissembling' were viewed negatively as dishonest or as vestiges of 'courtly' behaviour. Against this background, the actor's art was discussed in controversial terms. On the one hand, it was a necessary vehicle for the performance of dramatic poetry (and for that reason alone was socially acceptable). On the other hand, the actor as a professional dissembler was at odds with the ideal of emotional transparency. He/she seemed to be equipped with double emotions. The key text in this debate is by the French philosopher Denis Diderot (1713–84). His *Paradox of Acting*, written around 1770 but only published posthumously in 1830, provides the most sophisticated discussion of the problem. Diderot 'solves' the problem by separating the actor's emotional life from her art (his key examples are actresses). Diderot argues that the actor's art is a purely aesthetic matter, comparable to that of the painter who, Diderot claims, does create directly from life but by mediation through an aesthetic ideal, which he calls the *modèle idéal*. According to Diderot, acting is an analogous but even more complex aesthetic process in which four levels of production or mediation can be distinguished:

- private person
- artist
- *modèle idéal*
- acted character.

Because the actor has to consciously control all these levels it is inconceivable that he or she can simply reproduce genuinely or authentically felt feelings on stage.

Because of its delayed publication, Diderot's essay was not discussed intensively until the end of the nineteenth century, where it provided a bridge, as it were, to twentieth-century theories.

Pedagogy of acting

The study of acting theory begins at most departments and acting schools with the major theories of the twentieth century, to which we shall return below. This is not to say, however, that the nineteenth century remained disinterested in the art of acting from a theoretical point of view. On the contrary: in this period we see the rise of major stars and the spread of the European theatre tradition to all continents including Asia, which of course had its own deeply rooted forms of acting. The ubiquity of acting necessarily gave rise to discussion of its principles. Diderot's 'paradox' sparked off a drawn-out controversy initiated by the French actor Constant Coquelin, which drew replies from (among others) Henry Irving and William Archer (Matthews 1958).

Perhaps the most influential attempt to systematize acting for pedagogical purposes was the famous Delsarte system. After training as a singer, François Delsarte (1811–71) developed his method not just for the stage actor but also for the singer and dancer. It emphasizes the interdependence of body and emotion (or the 'spiritual act' as Delsarte termed it), in fact giving priority to physical movement over speech. Through intermediaries, Delsarte's strongly corporeal understanding of performance influenced artists such as Isadora Duncan and Jerzy Grotowski.

In the twentieth century, we can identify three broad theoretical tendencies. They can be summarized under the following schematic headings in connection with their founders, with the headings referring in each case to the relationship between actor and role:

- involvement (Stanislavsky)
- detachment (Brecht; Meyerhold)
- self-renunciation (Grotowski).

Involvement

The most influential theoretical and pedagogical model of the twentieth century has been, without doubt, Konstantin Stanislavsky's (1863–1938) 'method' or 'system', which in one respect at least goes back to mid-eighteenth-century discussions. One of his most famous tenets requires that the actor draw on his or her own emotional experience (the so-called emotional or affective memory) to create a role. The concept of 'emotional memory' establishes a congruence between the actor's actual emotional makeup and the requirements of the fictional role without, however, simply repeating the old idea of identification. Stanislavsky developed complex exercises to achieve a level of

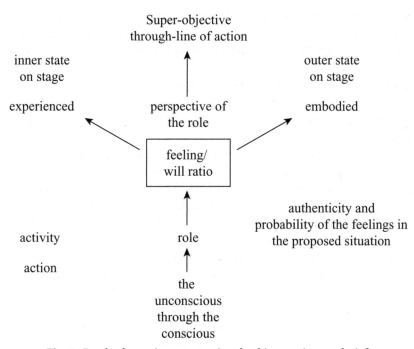

Fig. 1. Psychodynamic processes involved in creating a role (after Konstantin Stanislavsky's *Rabota Aktera nad Soboi* [The Actor's Work on Oneself]).

conscious control demanded by Diderot and others. These exercises require that the actor break up the role into units and objectives that together provide a kind of score. Despite focus on the individual part, the individual actor is never supposed to lose sight of the 'super-objective'. This refers to the overall goal of the play as defined by actors and director, which provides a culmination point for the 'through-line of action' and all roles in the play. The super-objective only usually emerges during the rehearsal process.

Over several decades, Stanislavsky continued to develop his system. Although exceptionally complex and detailed in its parts, the system is essentially the attempt to systematize the emotional/psychological (inner) and physical (outer) components of acting. Figure 1 is adapted from the 1950 Russian edition of Stanislavsky's magnum opus, *The Actor's Work on Oneself*, partially translated into English as *An Actor Prepares* in 1936, two years before the first Russian version. It reflects this late stage of the system's development. Particularly in his later years, Stanislavsky emphasized the importance of balancing the physical and vocal aspects with the emotional. The diagram illustrates the psychodynamic processes involved in creating a role. He illustrates how the process of acting moves through several stages involving a complex interaction of physicality, cognitive and affective states plus intellectual study of the dramatic text itself. These processes finally culminate on the level of 'through-line of action' and 'super-objective'. This highly schematic representation of the 'art of acting' represents an attempt by Stanislavsky in later life to systematize the training imposed on the actors of the Moscow Art Theatre and their famous ensemble technique.

Because of the huge influence exerted by Stanislavsky's 'system', the writings that underpin them – principally his autobiography *My Life in Art* (1924) plus the three volumes on acting – have themselves become the subject of research. Scholars have investigated the differences between Stanislavsky's own writings and their reception in the USA under the influential acting teacher Lee Strasberg (1901–82), where it became known as *method acting*. Of particular interest in this history are the English translations by Elizabeth Hapgood, who provided substantial abridgements rather than literal translations, and whose terminology has been accused of obfuscating rather than clarifying the admittedly verbose originals. It is hard to overestimate the influence of Stanislavsky's legacy in the twentieth century, which continues to impact on acting pedagogy and to be a subject of academic research (see Pitches 2006).

Detachment

Bertolt Brecht's theory of *gestic acting* is usually regarded as a counter-model to Stanislavsky. Brecht approached acting less from an emotional and hence psychological angle than from its ability to demonstrate social relationships. Gestic or *gestus* stems from gesture and refers in the first instance to physical movements that accompany speech. Gestus in this sense should not be seen as an expression of an actor's personal experience but rather as supra-individual and thus symptomatic of larger, social contexts. This means that the actor's relationship to his or her role is a detached one. Role enactment should serve as an alienation or distancing effect (*Verfremdungseffekt*),[1] whose goal is to endow the spectator with a searching, critical attitude towards the action on stage.

Brecht's essay 'A New Technique of Acting' contains a succinct summary of his acting theory. To achieve the desired alienation effect, Brecht suggested that the actor employ the following devices:

- perform in the third person
- transpose the action into the past
- speak the stage directions and commentaries:

> Using the third person and the past tense allows the actor to adopt the
> right attitude of detachment . . . Speaking the stage directions out loud
> in the third person results in a clash between two tones of voice,
> alienating the second of them, the text proper.   (Brecht 1964: 138)

The fundamental idea behind gestic acting is that emotions and thoughts are
externalized as in traditional rhetoric. However, purely individual expression
is not gestic in the Brechtian sense. Gestus is also not restricted just to acting
but is a wider concept in his theory. Whether expressed in linguistic, musical
or corporeal signs, gestus must always refer to intersubjective relations by
illustrating or commenting on them.

Generally speaking, one can observe after 1945 a growing interest in the
physical component of acting and a reduction of focus on the 'emotional
problem'. All body-oriented acting theories belong in the broadest sense to
the 'detachment' school. They emphasize the 'outside-in' approach, meaning
that movement and gesture are the starting point for performance. One must,
however, further differentiate between theories aimed at acting in dramatic
theatre and those deriving from non-verbal performance forms such as dance
or pantomime.

The first major movement-centred acting technique of the twentieth century is Vsevolod Meyerhold's (1874–1940) theory of *bio-mechanics*, which he
developed after 1918 as a counter-model to Stanislavsky. Bio-mechanics is
based on the idea that mechanical laws of motion as developed in assembly-
line production could be applied to the human body. In Meyerhold's words,
the actor should not be guided by 'inner experience', but by faith in a precise
performance technique: 'The art of the actor consists in organizing his material; that is in his capacity to utilize correctly his body's means of expression'
(Meyerhold 1969: 198). Not surprisingly, Brecht often drew attention to the
importance of Meyerhold's technique for the development of his own theory
of gestic acting.

Self-renunciation

Jerzy Grotowski's (1933–69) acting theory is less a theory in the strict sense
of the word than a technique and philosophy of acting. Its sources are also
very eclectic. Grotowski drew heavily on Stanislavsky's system, but intensified
even more the demands he placed on the physical and psychological resources
of the individual actor. He also experimented with Asian performance techniques, as we shall see in the section on cross-cultural perspectives below.
More than any of his predecessors, Grotowski defined acting as a communicative process with spectators and not just as a production problem of the
actor.

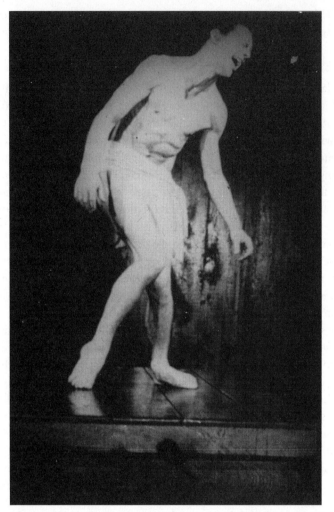

Plate 3. Ryszard Ciéslak in the first version of *The Constant Prince*, Teatr Laboratorium, 13 Rzędów, Wrocław, 1965.

According to Grotowski, the central vehicle of theatrical action is the human performer, above all the expressive means of body and mind, which can be drawn upon to the point of total and utter self-renunciation. An impressive expression of the intensity demanded of the actor was demostrated in the legendary production of *The Constant Prince* (1965) with Ryszard Ciéslak in the title role. Plate 3 shows the moment of 'translumination', the most intense state in the process of self-renunciation.

Between these three basic tendencies there are many hybrids and variations, particularly in the area of acting pedagogy. On closer inspection, most are revisions or further developments of these three. In fact, the area of pedagogy is a field of theatre studies where various areas of research intersect: theories of acting, general theories of the theatre and acting pedagogy proper, especially when the latter is part of a more general programme of theatre reform. One can say that all attempts to theorize or systematize acting are implicitly or explicitly pedagogical in nature, as these ideas are invariably intended for theatre practice.

As mentioned above, specialized acting manuals do not begin to appear in Europe until the eighteenth century. Before that, very little thought had gone into the problem of defining and prescribing acting in a normative fashion. For one thing, the teaching of acting in a formal, institutionalized sense does not really begin on a wide scale until the twentieth century. Before that, instruction took place 'on the job' through an informal apprentice system, or in the form of private instruction. This made it very difficult to study acting pedagogy before the twentieth century. Theatre studies has concentrated its interest, therefore, on the concepts that have influenced contemporary acting practices. Most work has been done on Stanislavsky's 'system' and its particular development in the USA. A variation of this school can be found in the acting method developed by Michael Chekhov, one of Stanislavsky's pupils, which is in turn becoming a subject of research. A lot of research has also been focused on Meyerhold's system of bio-mechanics. In the tradition of body-centred methods, the famous school of Jacques Lecoq and the mime tradition of Étienne Ducroux must also be placed, both of which are now being studied academically to ascertain their impact on contemporary performance practices. Outside the established schools, the pedagogical form of the workshop has done much to disseminate methods and techniques.

From the point of view of theatre studies, acting pedagogy is an important and potentially very fruitful area of research. Despite the rise of workshops and other non-formalized instruction contexts, acting schools are still the most important point of entry into the profession. Their methods and philosophies of instruction seem to be increasingly eclectic, a mixture of 'tradition' and individual preferences. An area of research would be not only the (often unconscious) premises and discourses underlying instruction, but also a comparative perspective across national borders. National traditions in theatrical cultures seem to manifest themselves nowhere more strongly than in the area of acting pedagogy.

Acting pedagogy can also be found in non-professional contexts, especially in the area of 'applied theatre' (see Chapter 11), where the aim is less to achieve professional-level virtuosity than to foster integrative and consciousness-widening skills. In this context, acting can be seen as an empowering and participatory activity, which emphasizes interpersonal interaction. Acting's combination of physicality and cognitive abilities, especially role-playing, make it a crucial element of many kinds of group-building activities.

Cross-cultural perspectives

A crucial influence on contemporary performance pedagogy has been the widespread reception of non-European – in the main Asian – performance techniques. Bertolt Brecht was one of the first twentieth-century theorists to point to Asian (in his case Chinese) acting practices as a means of reforming Western psychological realism (Brecht 1964). In point of fact, most major theatre reformers of the early twentieth century (Adolphe Appia, Edward Gordon Craig, Max Reinhardt, Vsevolod Meyerhold and Jacques Copeau to name just a few) responded in some way to Asian theatre (see Pronko 1967). The major influence on acting, however, is a post-war phenomenon. Jerzy Grotowski studied, albeit briefly, Asian performance forms. More important than Grotowski himself has been his disciple Eugenio Barba (Barba and Savarese 1991), whose concept and practice of 'theatre anthropology' has contributed to an internationally recognized awareness and exploration of performance techniques from disparate cultural backgrounds (see below). Peter Brook has made substantial use of acting techniques from a variety of cultural backgrounds by incorporating cultural diversity into his research. Western acting schools regularly include Eastern martial arts such as Aikido or Tai Chi in their programmes, as an integral part of movement training. Asian performance traditions appear to the West to be particularly 'body-centred' rather than mind- or emotion-focused. Particularly influential have been the techniques developed by the Japanese director Tadashi Suzuki, whose 'method' combines traditional Japanese performance techniques with his own personal philosophy.

Studies of acting techniques are by no means a Western invention. Both Indian and Japanese cultures have produced substantial treatises on acting as well as other aspects of theatre production. The *Nātyashāstra*, compiled between 200 BC and 200 AD by Bharata Muni, is an important compendium of practice and aesthetics of Indian Sanskrit theatre combining drama, dance and music. The text has often been compared to Aristotle's *Poetics* because it distinguishes between the emotions produced by the text and actors (*bhāva*) and the feelings they elicit in the spectators (*rasa*). The eight principal *rasa* – love, pity, anger, disgust, heroism, awe, terror and humour – can also be compared to the rhetorical system of affects. Contemporary Japanese *Nō* theatre still draws on the principles outlined by its founding master Zeami in the fourteenth century (see box, p. 32).

Excerpts from The *Nātyashāstra* on *bhāva* and *rasa*

Rasa is the cumulative result of *vibhāva* (stimulus), *anubhāva* (involuntary reaction) and *Vyabhicārī bhāva* (voluntary reaction). For example, just as when various condiments and sauces and herbs and other materials are mixed, a taste (different from the individual tastes of the components) is felt, or when the mixing of materials like molasses with other materials produces six kinds of tastes, so also along with the different *bhāva*-s (emotions) the *Sthāyī bhāva* becomes a 'taste' (*rasa*, flavour, feeling). But what is this thing called *rasa*? Here is the reply. Because it is enjoyably tasted, it is called *rasa*. How does the enjoyment come? Persons who eat prepared food mixed with different condiments and sauces, etc., if they are sensitive, enjoy the different tastes and then feel pleasure (or satisfaction); likewise, sensitive spectators, after enjoying the various emotions expressed by the actors through words, gestures and feelings feel pleasure, etc. This (final) feeling by the spectators is here explained as (various) *rasa*-s of *nātya* . . .

Relation between *rasa* and *bhāva*

A question is asked here. Are the *bhāva*-s produced by *rasa*-s, or *rasa*-s produced by *bhāva*-s? Some are of the opinion that their relation is symbiotic. That however is not correct. It can be clearly seen that *rasa* is produced from *bhāva*-s and not vice versa. Here are the verses in support of the above.

(1) Theatre-producers say that a *bhāva* is called as such because it leads to (*bhū*-) a *rasa* arising out of various kinds of acting.
(2) Many materials of different kinds produce a distinctive flavour; likewise, a flavour is produced by the *bhāva*-s through acting.
(3) There is no *rasa* (flavour) without a *bhāva* and there is no *bhāva* without *rasa*. Through acting, mutually they lead to a distinct result. (Rangacharya 1996: 55)

A special case of cross-cultural acting is theatre anthropology, as defined and practised by Eugenio Barba. An Italian educated in Norway and Poland, where he worked with Jerzy Grotowski, and now resident in Denmark, Barba is a theatre director, pedagogue and researcher. His research is conducted within the framework of the International School of Theatre Anthropology (ISTA), which has convened since 1980 in different countries.

In Barba's understanding, theatre anthropology is the study of the physiological and cultural factors determining the human being in a performance situation.

In terms of his research programme, Barba is interested in identifying universal principles underpinning performance, irrespective of cultural origin. His approach is intercultural and comparative; he includes the Western operatic tradition as well as Peking opera and *Nō* theatre. To enable such comparisons he has developed a terminology and perspective that make such comparisons productive.

His primary interest is the human body and the way different performance cultures determine and shape it through specific training practices as well as wider cultural conventions. One point of departure is the famous essay 'Les techniques du corps' by the French ethnologist Marcel Mauss ([1934] 1973), who argues that culture influences fundamental bodily practices such as walking, sitting, running, etc. Body techniques are socially or culturally determined facts, not physiological givens.

Following on from Mauss, Barba argues that the culturally determined nature of bodily techniques manifests itself most clearly in the performance traditions. A fundamental distinction can first be made between performance traditions that emphasize *daily* or *extra-daily* techniques. Western theatre acting, especially since the nineteenth century, has emphasized daily techniques, i.e. the performer's attempts to emulate the bodily techniques of everyday life. Traditional Asian forms such as *Kabuki* in Japan or *Kathakali* in India, on the other hand, have developed highly elaborate kinaesthetic conventions that require extended training, sometimes from early childhood, and which bear little resemblance to everyday movement; hence they are termed extra-daily techniques. Classical ballet would be an example of a Western performance form utilizing extra-daily techniques. Other examples would be acrobatics, mime and highly stylized theatre forms such as the *Commedia dell'arte*. According to Barba, the goal of realist theatre is to imitate daily bodily techniques with a maximum degree of accuracy, a goal that is realized most completely in Stanislavsky's acting pedagogy.

The cultural differences in performance traditions are easy to identify. A more difficult task, however, is the identification of common principles. How can one compare, Barba asks, the ballet dancer with the *Kabuki* actor? To do this, one must proceed to a second level of analysis that Barba terms the 'pre-expressive'. This refers to 'a basic level of organization common to all performers' (Barba and Savarese 1991: 187). The pre-expressive level of bodily techniques pre-exists specific cultural semanticization or conventionalization. The pre-expressive dimension includes elements such as balance, weight, position of the backbone, eye movement, etc. that are utilized to produce perceivable energy. This physically engendered energy can be termed 'presence', a quality that certain performers have or can produce and which attracts spectatorial attention even though they may not have said a word. According to Barba's theory, this ability has little to do with conscious intention or expressivity but with unconscious techniques that are the result of long training: 'above all in the traditions of codified theatre . . . the performers mould their body according to specific tensions and forms and it is these very tensions and forms which create lightning in the spectator' (Barba and Savarese 1991: 186).

Despite the international traffic in performance traditions such as Barba's ISTA project, which have very little in common with psychological character-based acting, our present concepts of acting are still oriented essentially along the three axes outlined above and, irrespective of whether we are looking at methods emphasizing involvement, detachment, or self-renunciation, all three work with the idea that the performer will be enacting a role. Whether it is Stanislavsky's division between the 'actor's work on himself' and his 'work on the role', or Brecht's requirement that the actor make the division between actor and role visible, or even Grotowski's insistence on the intensification of the actor's enactment of the role, in all cases there remains a relationship between these two entities. All proceed from the notion that the actor's task is primarily to realize a figure or character sketched out in words by an author.

The equation of role-enactment with acting is, however, a predominantly Western perspective. Although this structure may be residually present in Asian theatre forms, the two citations from *The Nātyashāstra* and Zeami's Treatises (see box, p. 32) suggest that role-enactment is not the dominant function of the actor. In Sanskrit theatre – and this is certainly true for traditional forms such as *Kathakali* – the task of the actor is to evoke a certain response from the spectator. In *Nō* theatre, the skill of the performer lies in carrying out and fusing highly codified sequences of movement (*kata*) and chants. Even in the West, the traditional equation has been questioned. In the 1960s, and chiefly in response to the performances of the New York happenings, the performer and theorist Michael Kirby coined the term 'non-matrixed acting' (Kirby 1972) to account for performances that made no attempt to create and inhabit a fictional role. In view of the most recent tendencies in theatre, however, and especially in the area between experimental theatre and performance art, we can say that the category of 'character' is, if not at the end of its tether, certainly in a crisis, productive or otherwise. Recent tendencies towards a 'postdramatic' theatre (Lehmann 2006) or a theatre without 'characters' (Fuchs 1996) that we find in the texts of Heiner Müller, the productions of Robert Wilson or the British group Forced Entertainment, require completely new skills and tasks of the actor. It would seem too that acting theory needs new parameters and terms to keep step with developments on the stage.

Excerpts from Zeami's Treatises on *Nō* Theatre

QUESTION: What is the relation between movement and text in a *Nō* performance?

ANSWER: This matter can only be grasped through intricate rehearsal. All the various kinds of movement in the *Nō* involved in the performance depend on the text. Such things as bodily posture and carriage follow from this, as well. Specifically, one must project feelings that are in accord with the words being spoken. For example, when the idea of observing some object is suggested in the text, the actor performs a gesture of looking; if such matters as pointing or pulling are mentioned, then the appropriate gesture is made; when a sound is to be heard, the actor assumes an attitude of listening. As the body is used in the service of all that is suggested by the text, these gestures will of their own accord constitute the appropriate acting style. The most important aspect of movement concerns the use of the actor's entire body. The second most important aspect concerns the use of his hands, and the third, the use of his feet. The movements of the body must be planned in accordance with the chant and context expressed in the *Nō* text. It is hard to describe this effect in writing. It is best to observe and learn during actual rehearsals. When one has practiced thoroughly with respect to the text of a play, then the actor's chant and gesture will partake alike of the same spirit. And indeed, the genuine union of music and movement represents a command by the actor over the most profound principles of the art of the *Nō*. When one speaks of real mastery, it is to this principle that one refers. This is a fundamental point: as music and movement are two differing skills, the artist who can truly fuse them into one shows the greatest, highest talent of all. Such a fusion will constitute a really strong performance. (Rimer and Masakazu 1984: 27)

Further reading

An excellent introduction to theories and approaches to acting across the centuries is *Actors on Acting: The Theories, Techniques, and Practices of the Great Actors of All Times as Told in Their Own Words*, compiled by Toby Cole and Helen Krich Chinoy (1970); *The Player's Passion: Studies in the Science of Acting* by Joseph Roach (1985) remains the best discussion of the changing scientific paradigms underlying acting theory and practice, from the rhetorical tradition to Stanislavsky; William B. Worthen's *Idea of the Actor: Drama and the Ethics of Performance* (1984) discusses actors and acting in relation to drama, with examples from Elizabethan, eighteenth- and twentieth-century drama. Mel Gordon's *The Stanislavsky Technique* (1987) provides an accessible introduction to the complex genesis and developments of the Stanislavsky 'system'. Bella Merlin's *The Complete Stanislavsky Toolkit* (2007) can be used as a hands-on coursebook for learning and applying the key terms. *Acting (Re)Considered: A Theoretical and Practical Guide,* edited by Phillip B. Zarrilli (2002), contains an excellent collection of essays by scholars and practitioners discussing acting and performing from practical, philosophical and cross-cultural perspectives. Its extensive bibliography can direct students to specialized areas. Daniel Meyer-Dinkgrafe's *Approaches to Acting: Past and Present* (2001) brings Western and Indian traditions into dialogue with one another. For more advanced students, Hollis Huston's *The Actor's Instrument: Body, Theory, Stage* (1992) discusses acting in relation to contemporary critical theory.

Chapter 2

Spectators and audiences

In theatre, the audience regulates the performance.

(Bertolt Brecht, *Arbeitsjournal*)

An audience without a history is not an audience.

(Herbert Blau, *The Audience*)

It has become something of a commonplace in theatre studies to state that the spectator is at the centre of the theatrical event and hence of theatre itself. On one level, the statement is self-evident: a theatrical performance without an audience is at best a rehearsal, at worst a hypothetical construct. Few scholars today would argue against the proposition. Claims regarding the spectator's centrality are ubiquitous in most fields of theatre studies: they figure in performance analysis as well as theatre theory and history. This assumed centrality is not, however, matched by a corresponding quantity of research. As the annotated bibliography at the end of this chapter indicates, major books on the subject can be counted on the fingers of one hand. There are a number of reasons for this. The most important is that theatre studies by tradition has defined itself, like literature or art history, as a discipline investigating an aesthetic object: initially the drama, then the theatrical performance. As we shall see in different sections of this book, there are many different ways to investigate this object: all the different interpretive strategies elaborated by the humanities to study texts, images and musical scores can and have been applied to theatre as well. A second reason can be located in the lack of engagement displayed by theatre semiotics in the spectator question, as Susan Bennett has argued in her important book *Theatre Audiences: A Theory of Production and Reception* (1990: 72). Because semiotics dominated theatre theory and analysis in the 1970s and 1980s, spectator research remained sidelined. A third reason can be found in the obvious methodological difficulty that audience research poses. To study the spectator individually or collectively implies a shift from interpreting an aesthetic object to studying the cognitive and emotional responses of actual human beings. This is the field of empirical psychology and sociology, and most theatre scholars do not possess this kind of scholarly background and

34

training. The gulf is not, however, unbridgeable, as this chapter endeavours to show. The fact remains, however, that it is much easier to insist on the importance of theatre spectators than to actually investigate their contribution to a performance in a given historical or contemporary case. Today, many scholars are of the opinion that there is, in fact, little point in separating out the spectator from, for example, the larger performance event or questions of performance space. Both questions will be dealt with in later chapters, where issues relating to spectatorship will re-emerge.[1]

As already mentioned, the insistence on spectator response as a crucial element of theatre has always been recognized in theory as well as practice. Aristotle's concept of 'catharsis' (see Chap. 4) placed the question of the effects of theatrical performance at the heart of dramatic and theatre theory. Similarly, for the last two centuries, it has been an almost unquestioned assumption that production and reception work together to produce 'identification' between spectator and characters represented on stage (see Chap. 4), a concept elaborated theoretically and dramaturgically in the eighteenth century (but, it could be argued, already implied by the idea of catharsis). Identification assumes also 'the suspension of disbelief', as Samuel Taylor Coleridge so famously put it in his *Biographia Literaria* (1817): the acceptance by the reader or spectator of the fictional or virtual world on the page or stage. All these are familiar terms, even outside theatre studies. They also constitute central questions for spectator and reception research.

Thinking about the spectator's function and contribution to the theatrical performance is by no means an invention of theatre studies. In the prologues to plays, where the audience is addressed directly, we find numerous admonitions and injunctions. Shakespeare's appeal to the audience in the prologue to *Henry V* (1599) – 'piece out our imperfections with your thoughts' – stipulates the cognitive activity necessary to make the performance work. Ben Jonson's contract between audience and playwright enacted in the induction to *Bartholomew Fair* (1614) – in which the playwright agrees to provide a play and the audience agree to pay their money, be quiet and exercise criticism – can be seen quite literally as an example of the *contrat théâtral* that most theatre scholars would agree is at the heart of theatrical performance.

It could be claimed that there is, therefore, no case for investigating a discrete category, 'spectator', independent of the performance as a whole. This could indeed be argued, and as the field of theatre and performance studies continues to develop, this may indeed become the case. Indeed, in this book, spectatorship will also be treated in various other contexts: in theatre theory (Chap. 4), in performance analysis (Chap. 8) and in the chapter on applied theatre (Chap. 11). But for the meantime, theatre studies has tried to define fields of investigation revolving around spectatorship, audience research and reception. Each term designates not only a discrete object of research but different research practices and disciplinary alliances. While not coterminous, these concepts can certainly overlap. The following categories highlight basic differences, both conceptually and in terms of disciplinary approaches:

Term	Definition	Field/approach
Spectator	(a) the individualized, actual recipient; micro-aspect	psychological, cognitive, emotional
	(b) ideal or hypothetical recipient	semiotics, aesthetics, reception theory
Audience/public	collective group(s) of spectators either for a particular performance or historical period; macro-aspect	sociological, historical, psychoanalytical, economical

While these categories indicate possible fields of enquiry and methodological approaches, they do not answer the question of how we can actually study spectators and audiences. These are questions of theory and method, some of which are outlined below. Broadly speaking, we can say that most research to date has concentrated on (a) the individualized, actual recipient; (b) the hypothetical recipient; and (c) on the macro-aspect of audiences as collective groups.

Spectator response

Questions of spectator response can be broadly subdivided into cognitive and affective fields. The mental activity required to follow and respond to a theatre performance is a cognitive one. The emotional effects theatre can have on spectators (being proverbially moved to tears) belong to the affective realm. In actuality, the two are inextricably intertwined, but for heuristic reasons it is useful to deal with the two types of responses separately because they highlight two different fields of enquiry.

The cognitive activities required to participate in a theatre performance are manifold and do not begin when the curtain goes up and lights go down, but long before. In his influential study, *Frame Analysis: An Essay on the Organization of Experience* (1974), the sociologist Erving Goffman elaborates a complex theory to explain how individuals utilize different forms of behaviour, which he terms 'frames', in different situations. Frames are 'principles of organization which govern [social] events and our subjective involvement in them' (Goffman 1974: 10). The act of playing requires, for example, a different attitude and set of behaviours than when answering questions at a job interview. These behaviours and attitudes, or 'frames', are socially acquired cognitive abilities and competences. They consist of a set of more or less fixed rules and conventions. The theatrical frame is especially important because Goffman uses it to exemplify many aspects of his theory. Theatre-going is defined by a series of complex behaviours that regulate the way spectators behave to each other and to the performance and performers on stage. These behaviours are culturally and class-specific to a high degree, even within Euro-American theatre culture. Frames do not remain inviolate or immutable; in fact, Goffman devotes most of his book to showing what happens when frames are broken, transgressed and redefined. Socially functional behaviour requires also that we change frames as the situation demands. Goffman also studies what happens when the conventions governing one kind of frame are applied to another kind of activity not normally defined by that frame, a process he calls 'keying'. An attempt to ritualize theatre, for example (a favourite strategy of theatre reformers throughout the twentieth century), would involve the performers and spectators keying the conventions of ritual and its associated behaviours into a theatre frame.

Goffman's frame theory has been adapted for the theatre by the Dutch theatre scholar Henri Schoenmakers (Schoenmakers 1990). He proposes four hypotheses on the theatrical frame:

(1) Frame competence must be developed. The relevant conventions and behaviours are not innate, but have to be learned.
(2) Frames are contingent. This means they are subject to historical change.
(3) Contingency refers also to cultural differences. The elements, norms and behaviours that make up the theatrical frame are not homogeneous but appear in culturally specific combinations.
(4) The theatrical frame determines the cognitive and emotional reactions of the spectators. All actions on stage, even if they are identical with actions in the real world, are governed by the rules of the theatrical frame.

In her standard work on the spectator and the theatre, *Theatre Audiences*, Susan Bennett divides the theatrical frame into two: an inner and outer one. The outer frame Bennett defines as a 'cultural construct' that involves the production of the theatrical event: the work of the performers and the audience's expectations of a performance. The inner frame is the theatrical performance itself, 'the spectator's experience of a fictional stage world' (Bennett 1990: 1). Bennett's use of the term 'frame' is not exactly identical with Goffman's, but it still identifies the need to differentiate between two different levels of the theatrical event, a differentiation that is crucial for spectator and audience research. The next section will be devoted to reviewing the ways the inner frame has been studied.

Reception and response

The approaches looked at so far derive their methodology almost exclusively from the social sciences. This is not surprising considering the dominance of the social sciences in the 1960s and 1970s, when theatre studies itself was expanding. The call to place 'the spectator in the leading role' was widely supported, and the social sciences, especially sociology and psychology, seemed to have the methods at hand to answer the questions. Yet the humanities also developed approaches to the same questions but using methods that were compatible with their conventional hermeneutic practices. Within literary studies in the late 1960s the reader was also pushed into the limelight and declared to be, if not the real creator of the text, at least as important as the actual author. In France, Roland Barthes's pronouncement of the death of the author became a rallying point for reception research, as did his call for an almost eroticized relationship (*jouissance*) between reader and text in *The Pleasure of the Text* (1975), which challenged older ideas of texts possessing stable meanings implanted intentionally by an author. In Barthes's view, the reader produces the meaning, not the author.

A similar idea, although founded on different theoretical premises, was proposed by art historian Ernst Gombrich for the visual arts. Gombrich emphasized the 'beholder's share' in constructing meaning from a seemingly complete visual image in his influential study, *Art and Illusion: A study in the Psychology of Pictorial Representation* (1960). Gombrich argued that an image is always only partial, and the beholder effectively reconstructs or 'completes' a perceived image through a combination of past experience, mental schemas and inferential interpretation. This theory was widely discussed in theatre studies in the early phase of reception studies, where the idea of inferential completion dovetailed with similar ideas on the spectator's share in constructing the meaning of a performance.

Equally influential on the continent were the writings of a group of literary scholars based at the University of Constance in Germany. Wolfgang Iser and Hans Robert Jauss also challenged the idea of a fixed text whose sedimented meanings had to be extracted by hermeneutical interpretation. They argued instead for increased recognition of the reader's work in 'completing' the literary text, of filling in the gaps or blanks (*Leerstellen*) that every text by definition contains. This work of completion changes by definition over time as each generation of readers creates its own text, particularly of the classical canon. Each reader brings a certain 'horizon of expectation', as Jauss called it, to the act of reading, which is conditioned by previous experience on the one hand and textual signals such as genre on the other. To describe the interplay between text and reader in the production of meaning, Wolfgang Iser coined the term 'implied reader' to designate a reader who is neither empirical nor historical but whose responses are built into the structure of the text (Iser 1978). This concept avoids the danger of losing contact with the work itself. Although individual readers' responses will be different, they can still be measured against structural elements located in the text.

Although reader-response theory began to lose prominence by the late 1980s in the area of critical theory, as Susan Bennett points out (Bennett 1990: 36), it still left a legacy within theatre studies. There have been a number of attempts to adapt reader-response theories to theatre studies. Patrice Pavis, for example, has applied Iser's concept of the implied reader and posited an 'implied spectator'. He argues that a theatre production, like a literary text, contains networks of 'response-inviting structures'. Reception aesthetics assumes that aesthetic communication functions by merging the response-inviting structures of the text with the expectation and knowledge of the spectator/reader in *concretizations*. These are, according to Pavis, quite literally the moments when production and reception coalesce as spectators ascribe meanings to the signs produced on stage. Pavis does not regard the spectator simply as a passive recipient of a constant stream of signals emitted from the performance area. The spectator brings to bear a number of different receptive codes that are simultaneously active. They include:

Psychological codes that determine:

- the perception of space (see Chap. 3) and influence the interactive nature of space and reception. Factors such as location within the auditorium have a decisive influence on receptive attitudes.
- identification with and pleasure in illusion and the creation of fictional worlds. This process is strongly influenced by unconscious mechanisms.
- the 'horizon of expectation' that is determined by previous experiences and background knowledge that the spectator brings to the performance.

Ideological codes:

- knowledge of represented reality, of the audience's reality.
- mechanisms of ideological conditioning such as education and the media.

Aesthetic-ideological codes:

- specifically theatrical codes of a period, a type of stage, genre, style of acting.
- codes of narrative.

Codes linking *aesthetics* and *ideology*; these include:

- the spectator's expectations of theatre.
- aspects of social reality the spectator may look for in the play.
- the means whereby the dramaturgical work and staging can be used to find an ideological code that will enable today's audiences to read past plays.
- preferences for certain genres such as tragedy, comedy or the absurd in certain periods. (Pavis 1998: 304–6)

In recent years, semiotic performance analysis has been combined with more empirically oriented audience research in an attempt to overcome the dichotomy between production and reception. This kind of research usually proceeds in two phases. In the first stage, semiotic signs and codes are identified in a production. In the second stage, these results are collated with audience reactions and opinions, which are normally gathered by questionnaires or discussions. The two sets of data are then compared, with a view to ascertaining the 'success' of the production in reaching its audience (Martin and Sauter 1997).

The premise behind this kind of research can, of course, be questioned. In much experimental theatre and performance, there may be no conscious wish to 'communicate', at least not in the semiotic understanding of the term. The forms of experience at stake may be much more aimed at irritating and disorientating; in fact, in preventing easily consumable discourse, at least of the type that can be formulated in terms of questions and responses.

Recent adaptation of reception theory includes the idea of 'ghosting', which refers to the way experience in the theatre is often influenced by previous knowledge or experience. In his seminal study *The Haunted Stage: The Theatre as Memory Machine* (2003), Marvin Carlson has demonstrated to what extent the reception of a production is determined by memory: 'The present experience is always ghosted by previous experiences and associations while these ghosts are simultaneously shifted and modified by the process of recycling and recollection' (Carlson 2003: 2). Carlson asks what memories a spectator brings to a production and how these previous experiences are crucial in the reception process. These memories may refer to previous productions, the actors or, most commonly, the play text in the case of classical works.

In more general terms, the individual spectator's response to a performance – his or her horizon of expectations – is decisively shaped by what Ric Knowles has called 'public discourse', a broad term encompassing the wealth of information a theatre generates about itself and its productions:

> This includes, of course, publicity materials relating to a particular show (posters, programs, advertising, pre-show interviews and features, and so on), as it includes reviews and public discussions of the production, all of which can shape response in quite direct and obvious ways. It also, however, includes the cumulative impact of such materials, together with logos, season brochures, fundraising materials, artistic directors' statements, company histories and retrospectives, programming traditions, lobby displays and amenities, even ticket prices and the quality and type of refreshments available.   (Knowles 2004: 91)

Knowles demonstrates, with examples, that the public discourse surrounding a theatre, which can often be stage-managed by marketing and advertising campaigns, usually transcends a particular production. It works through 'cumulative impact' over time, sometimes years, occasionally even decades in the case of famous theatres such as the Abbey Theatre in Dublin with its link to Irish nationalism, or the Berliner Ensemble's association with Brecht and political theatre.

The research reviewed here documents little more than the first tentative steps towards developing analytical instruments for studying spectator responses to performances. It is perhaps overly optimistic to expect a similar level of complexity and quantity that we have at our disposal for the analysis of the performance as an aesthetic product.

Reception and reader-response theory focuses mainly on what we have called here the cognitive aspect of spectatorship. The spectator in the theatre behaves and reacts in many different ways. These reactions may range from extreme emotional agitation – tears, laughter, revulsion – to utmost boredom ending in slumber and snoring. As early as the 1950s, researchers began to study the psychological and physiological reactions of theatre spectators. Using techniques developed for advertising, spectators were given a *response machine* by means of which they could press a button and give expression to their impressions. In the 1960s, semantic differential analysis, a technique developed to measure psychological attitudes, was also applied to estimate the emotional dimension of theatre. The aim was to gauge the difference between what the producers/artists intended and the way the spectators actually reacted. In semantic differentials, spectators (or consumers) are asked to judge performances (or products) according to categories such as good/bad, funny/not funny, pleasant/unpleasant, etc. on a sliding scale. The collated responses are then plotted on graphs to demonstrate inclinations and preferences. Quantitative data of this type, however, produce results of a limited kind. While such methods are clearly of use when it comes to gauging the effectiveness of advertising slogans or the attractiveness of packaging, its application to aesthetic products such as a theatre performance is clearly restricted. One or more groups of spectators react to one performance or set of performances. Therefore the data collected are of little use outside one specific receptive situation.

The most crucial insight that has emerged from this tradition of research is that there is no such thing as 'the spectator'. The plethora of cognitive and emotional reactions, mental acts and interpretive interventions that come into play when watching a performance are all influenced by any number of differentiating factors. Apart from individual dispositions such as age, level of education and even attention spans, collective experiences determined by gender, class and ethnicity but also locale are also brought to bear on the way spectators make sense of performances. The shift in focus from spectators to audiences, to which we will now turn, is determined largely by the degree of collectivity we are interested in.

Audiences

Empirical audience research asks, following Peter Eversmann, three basic questions: '1) Who goes to the theatre? 2) Why do they go there? And 3) how do they evaluate their visit?' (Eversmann 2004: 134). Questions one and two are clearly very important for the organizations sustaining theatre. It may be the theatre itself trying to better ascertain its audience's needs, or the funding body attempting to gauge whether its subsidies have been well spent. This kind of data can be and is regularly gathered using questionnaires or by studying official statistics that most public and private institutions are required by law to provide. More complex questionnaires can provide clues about audience demographics such as age, gender, level of education, profession, as well as tastes and preferences for particular genres or works, information which can contribute to answering question three.

One of the largest surveys ever conducted on the audience composition of the professional performing arts was carried out in the early 1960s by US economists William Baumol and William Bowen for the Twentieth Century Foundation. Although their study was primarily about the economics of the performing arts and would result indirectly in the foundation of the new discipline of cultural economics, Baumol and Bowen also employed conventional sociological survey methods to gain more accurate knowledge about the socio-economic makeup of audiences. They also surveyed British audiences to gain comparative data. They distributed questionnaires at a variety of performing arts venues across the country. From those returned, they obtained 29,413 usable replies from the US, and 2,295 usable replies were returned from the UK (exclusively London). They summarized their findings as follows: firstly, they remarked on the remarkable consistency of the composition of audiences from art form to art form, from city to city and from one performance to another. Secondly, audiences were drawn from an extremely narrow segment of the American and British population. In the main, a theatre audience consists of persons who are extraordinarily well-educated, whose incomes are very high, who are predominantly in the professions and who are in their late youth or early middle age (Baumol and Bowen 1973: 469). They admitted that even when provided with cheap or even free performances, the audience composition attending highbrow performing arts events (theatre, concerts, opera, ballet) did not change significantly, although some broadening of audience base was detected. Their final conclusion – 'Obviously much remains to be done before the performing arts can truly be said to belong to the people' (Baumol and Bowen 1973: 470) – was an indirect call for increased public subsidy for the performing arts in the USA.

Obviously, more complex factors are at work than just money when understanding the relationship between certain types of theatre and the audiences that attend them. Baumol and Bowen had no explanation other than to suggest that lowering prices might make the performing arts more democratic. The French sociologist Pierre Bourdieu has argued that capital, but of a much different sort, does indeed determine the relationship between individuals and their choice of aesthetic consumption. His most famous book, *Distinction: A Social Critique of the Judgement of Taste* (Bourdieu [1979] 1984), is based on sociological surveys carried out in the 1960s in France. Although not specifically about the theatre, Bourdieu's findings and arguments are evidently important for better understanding the sociology of theatre audiences. His book looks at the whole field of cultural consumption, ranging from food to cars, from popular music to opera. More interesting today than the actual empirical data (which are outdated now) is Bourdieu's explanatory theory for the correlation between cultural consumption (taste) and socio-economic background. Consumption in the arts and culture is determined by a complex dynamic of prestige accumulation that involves economic capital on the one hand and social and cultural capital on the other. Cultural capital refers to acquired competence in a society's high-status culture. Social capital involves the accumulation of contacts and social networks for one's own social advancement. There is a high degree of correlation between the three forms, and they are mutually convertible. The most important of these for Bourdieu (and for theatre studies) is cultural capital. The knowledge and skills it entails must be acquired over time. Every visit to the theatre represents a potential growth in cultural capital. Bourdieu remarks that 'most of the properties of cultural capital can be deduced from the fact that, in its fundamental state, it is linked to the body and presupposes embodiment' (Bourdieu 1986: 244).

In Bourdieu's work, philosophical theories of aesthetics (the subtitle of his book is a direct reference to Kant's foundational work on aesthetics, *The Critique of Judgement*) are grounded in hard empirical facts reflecting a massive disjunction between the socio-economic position in Western society and access to cultural capital. The close link between large amounts of economic capital (wealth) and a big investment in cultural capital (a taste for opera or highbrow theatre, which gain the lion's share of public arts subsidy in Western European countries at least) suggests that massive inequalities are at work, whereby low-income people (whose taste for popular culture receives little or no government subsidy) finance, through their taxes, opera and theatre for the cultural elite.

Sociological surveys such as those of Bourdieu examine audience demographics for particular regions, cities or even theatre buildings. They use methods developed in other contexts such as television audience research or marketing. They are seldom conducted by sociologists on a regular basis because – with the exception of large metropolitan centres such as New York, London or Paris – theatre audiences are small and insignificant in terms of large-scale consumption.[2]

Combining quantitative and qualitative methods

The shortcomings of purely quantitative approaches when it comes to ascertaining *aesthetic* responses to theatre are obvious. Techniques developed to gauge differing responses of consumers to competing bars of soap are only marginally applicable to such a complex event as a theatre production with its manifold stimuli. Therefore some researchers have attempted to combine quantitative with qualitative methods. Qualitative techniques require respondents to actually articulate their impressions, feelings and opinions, either in writing or verbally.

The most sustained attempt to bridge the gap between qualitative and quantitative methods can be found in John Tulloch's study, *Shakespeare and Chekhov in Production and Reception: Theatrical Events and Their Audiences* (2005). Tulloch brings his background in media studies to bear on the study of the two most widely performed dramatists in the Western canon. Tulloch seeks to integrate questions of production and reception by combining aesthetic and sociological perspectives. Most important for this chapter is his application of quantitative methods. Using particular productions of the two authors in the UK and Australia, he analysed audience response with a variety of methods. These include:

- quantitative data surveys, which recorded statistical data of audiences such as age, sex, genre preferences and theatre-going habits.
- focused qualitative surveys, which obtained detailed responses from school pupils attending the performances. They were asked to write answers to particular questions formulated by the researcher.
- long interviews, which were conducted with selected audience members who indicated their willingness to participate.
- case studies, which were written up on selected audience members on the basis of voluntary information and extended interviews. The aim here was to investigate how spectators related the 'in the theatre' experience to everyday reality, their actual social world.
- focus group discussions, which were conducted with homogeneous groups (school pupils, workmates) to obtain a broader range of aesthetic response and reflexivity. For example, at the University of Stockholm, a method called *Theatre Talks* was developed that consisted of guided discussions with spectators who had attended different performances of the same production. Subjective impressions and judgements were collected and correlated to hard data such as age, sex and level of education (Sauter 2000: 174–86).
- follow-up surveys, which were used to gauge the long-term 'effect' of theatre performances in terms of spectator approval, memory, comparison with other subsequent productions, etc. (Tulloch 2005: 274–93).

In general, it is necessary to distinguish between methods that are applied before, during or after a performance. *Theatre Talks*, for example, is a *post-performance* method, as are surveys involving questionnaires, which remain the most widespread technique of audience research. There have been attempts to gauge audience reactions during performances using the aforementioned response machines, and even physiological measuring instruments have been applied. Such experiments, however, remain marginal, and their results have never been discussed seriously within mainstream theatre studies.

The reasons for this marginalization are clear. Until recently, audience research proceeded from a clear dichotomy between production and reception. For methodological reasons, it was little concerned with the production side of the equation. The recent methodological shift towards the broader frame of the 'theatrical event', as demonstrated in Sauter's (Sauter 2000) and Tulloch's (Tulloch 2005) work, points a way forward that integrates, rather than separates out, production and reception.

Some positions promulgated by reception research have achieved general acceptance. Vexed questions such as aesthetic innovation and artistic value, which are particularly intractable in an ephemeral art form such as theatre, have received clear answers from reception research. From the perspective of reception, no performance or production is intrinsically innovative, but is only so in respect to the receptive standpoints of the spectators present. An experimental stage and a Broadway theatre can, with respect to their respective audiences, both be innovative and derivative, although their products are entirely different. Innovation can only be located on a sliding scale within differentiated audience groups.

Further reading

The best introduction to audiences and spectatorship remains Susan Bennett's 1990 study, *Theatre Audiences*, revised in 1997. It is particular good on reception theory and on the necessity to involve questions of cultural specificity. Martin and Sauter devote the first section of their book *Understanding Performance: Perfomance Analysis in Theory and Practice* (1997) to reception research and provide a useful survey of existing research up to that time. Part 3 of Patrice Pavis's *Analyzing Performance: Theater, Dance, and Film* (2003) is devoted also to reception, with a particular emphasis on the spectator's role in decoding performance. It is less useful for questions of audience research. Herbert Blau's massive study, *The Audience* (1990), brings together poststructuralist ideas (see Chap. 5), particular Lacanian psychoanalysis and the concept of the 'gaze', with personal experiences as an experimental director. Difficult to read, Blau's book is full of startling insights amidst some difficult prose. Willmar Sauter's most recent study, *The Theatrical Event: Dynamics of Performance and Perception* (2000), tries to bridge the dichotomy between production and reception, and argues for integrating reception research into performance analysis (see Chap. 8). The most persuasive demonstration of this new approach is Tulloch (2005).

Historical theatre audiences have been the subject of study throughout the second half of the twentieth century. Alfred Harbage's *Shakespeare's Audience* (1941) ushered in a new sociological perspective on Elizabethan theatre, and remains an important point of reference, even though some of the factual detail has been superseded by more recent studies such as Andrew Gurr's *Playgoing in Shakespeare's London* (2004). John Lough's *Paris Theatre Audiences* ([1957] 1972) provides a similar approach to the theatre of seventeenth- and eighteenth-century France.

Chapter 3

Spaces and places

Given the centrality of space in the performance experience, it is perhaps somewhat surprising to find that critics do not have a precise, widely shared vocabulary to enable them to name and talk about the multiple dimensions of the way space functions in performance.

(Gay McAuley 1999)

The Italian-style stage is the space of [a] lie: everything takes place in an interior which is surreptitiously opened, surprised, spied upon, savoured by a spectator hidden in the shadow.

(Roland Barthes 1972)

Roland Barthes's characterization of Western theatre's dominant spatial configuration as deceitful and voyeuristic is both overstated and accurate at the same time. In the context of his discussion of Japanese Bunraku puppet theatre, the European proscenium does indeed seem to hide the spectator from the stage. Yet the 'spectator hidden in the shadow' is, historically speaking, a late development (dating from the late nineteenth century), and is therefore by no means inherent in the Italian-style stage. Barthes's comment does, however, point to a question of central interest to theatre studies, and that is the close relationship between stage forms and spectatorial attitudes. In this respect, this chapter is in part a continuation of the discussion of spectators and audiences begun in Chap. 2. It will, however, concentrate primarily on the physical conditions of performance, and outline ways in which the discipline of theatre studies has studied this problem.

Today, the question of performance space is seen primarily as an interactive relationship between spectators, stage and the wider architectural or spatial environment encompassing both. This is, however, a relatively recent development. Initially, scholars focused on only two aspects: theatre buildings and stage design, both of which were more properly in the domain of art historians. Yet a focus on purely architectural or scenographic aspects of performances, past or present, neglected the crucial aspect of the dynamic character of theatrical space, even when the relationship seems to be stable and unchanging.

It was the German theatre historian and founder of theatre studies in that country, Max Herrmann (see Chap. 6), who stressed that the theatrical art is fundamentally a spatial one and a central question for the new discipline:

> Theatrical art is a spatial art. This should not be understood in the sense that the representation of space could be an end in itself in theatre . . . In the art of theatre we are not dealing with the representation of space but with the execution of human movement in theatrical space. This space is however never or hardly ever identical with the real space that exists on stage . . . The space that theatre creates is rather an artificial space which only comes into being through a substantial transformation of actual space, it is an experience by which the stage space is transformed into a different kind of space.   (Herrmann 1931: 153)

Herrmann makes three inter-related observations and distinctions that have come to be crucial for our understanding of the spatial dynamics of theatre. The first is that theatrical space only comes into being through the act of human movement. Secondly, theatrical space is the result of an aesthetic transformation: the physical space of the stage is never identical with the space on which actors perform. Thirdly, this transformation from one realm (the physical and actual) to the aesthetic or 'artificial' can only be described in experiential terms.

Herrmann examines this 'experiential' aspect from four different perspectives: that of the dramatist, the actor, the audience and the director. While his specific observations may seem today somewhat dated, he must be credited with being (probably) the first theatre scholar to have grasped the fundamentally communicative, interactive and experiential nature of theatrical space.

Herrmann's approach is a phenomenological one (see Chap. 5) in that he is concerned (in this case) with abstract and suprahistorical categories rather than specific meanings. Although today it is a commonplace to assert that spatial relations are crucial for the success or failure of a performance, we still find considerable terminological confusion when talking about the spatial factor of theatre, as Gay McAuley (1999) has pointed out in her major study of space in performance. Nevertheless, we can, despite oscillating terms, distinguish the following spatial categories:

- Theatrical space refers to the architectural conditions of theatre, usually a building, and encompasses performance and spectator space.
- Scenic space (or stage space) designates space where the actors perform, and includes the set design.

- Place or space of performance is a wider category that includes the wider civic or other environment in which the theatrical event is located.
- Dramatic space refers to the spatial coordinates fixed in and evoked by the theatrical text (drama, libretto, choreography, etc.).

The audience's reaction to the theatrical event is determined by all four factors to varying degrees. In the rest of this chapter, these categories will be examined in more detail, with a heavier emphasis on the first three, as dramatic space is not strictly speaking an area of research specific to theatre studies, as it also belongs to the sphere of textual criticism.

Theatrical space

The term 'theatrical space' is in itself a site of terminological contestation because the word 'theatre' implies, as we have seen (both etymologically and historically) a building or, at least, fixed area. The notion of architectural fixture is, however, by no means a *conditio sine qua non* for theatre. For this reason, Marvin Carlson has suggested that it is more accurate to speak of ludic space. Carlson defines the latter in very broad terms – 'a permanently or temporarily created *ludic* space, a ground for the encounter of spectator and performer' (Carlson 1989: 6) – thus enabling him to include flexible forms, such as street theatre, that do not depend on fixed architectural structures. Above and beyond its functionality as a building or as a temporarily demarcated performance space, theatrical space can be understood as a place of encounter that generates meanings and experiences that are an integral part of the performance itself.

For theatre studies, the category of theatrical space is a central field of research because it focuses most clearly the interactive relationship between actors and spectators. Following a suggestion by Marvin Carlson (see Fig. 2), it is possible to distinguish five basic spatial structures in theatre that regulate the relationship between performers and spectators.

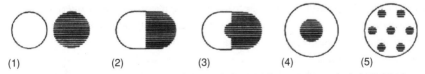

Fig. 2. Forms of theatrical space (after Carlson 1987: 67). (1) divided (cinema); (2) confrontation (proscenium); (3) apron stage; (4) arena; (5) environmental. The black areas represent the stage and the white areas the spectator space.

Of these five forms, *environmental theatre*, with its flexible performer–spectator relations, is both one of the most ancient and the most recent. The term was coined by Richard Schechner in his book of the same name, and refers to a flexible spatial arrangement by which spectators can surround the stage/playing area(s) or vice versa. Schechner's 'reform stage', a counter-model to the conventional proscenium arch, can be extended to include any form of theatrical interaction outside fixed architectural structures. It describes any type of theatrical performance where the spectators can move freely and choose their 'point of view' (see Plate 4). Within these fluid spatial borders, spectators and performers create, as it were, performance and viewing spaces around themselves. Even if spectators and performers are only feet apart (as we often experience in street theatre), they still inhabit quite distinct spaces. The performer is still very much an 'alien' presence, because he/she inhabits a different space, whatever the physical distance from the spectators. Performers demarcate with their own intrinsic rules a world into which the spectators seldom enter.

Theatre history teaches us, however, that the flexibility provided by environmental theatre was seldom regarded by authorities or performers as a particularly desirable state of affairs. We find instead a general tendency to restrict and regulate the spectatorial gaze and the spatial coordinates of the actor–spectator relationship. The reasons for this are manifold: they include aesthetic, religious, political and economic considerations, which will be outlined in the following comments on the other spatial models.

Next to environmental stages, *arena theatre* is the form that permits the largest degree of interaction between stage and auditorium, although here too the basic divide between the two spheres remains. The performance space is entirely surrounded by the audience. As this 'comprehensive' view of the stage permits only the most rudimentary degree of scenographic design, it has never established itself on a large scale in Euro-American theatre. It is found more frequently in temporary, improvised forms such as street theatre.

Historically more significant are those theatrical spaces that make use of the *thrust* or *apron* stage in all its variants. This 'extension' to the normal proscenium stage enables the performance space to be prolonged into the auditorium while at the same time retaining the scenographic possibilities of the separate stage. The apron stage is an ancient and modern form. Both the Greek and Elizabethan stages are examples. In Europe, the apron stage gradually disappeared as the baroque perspective stage with its illusionistic scenery gained dominance, but it made a comeback after 1900 in the course of the anti-naturalistic reform movement. Some reformers saw in it an architectural and metaphorical 'reunification' of spectators and performers after

Plate 4. Théâtre du Soleil, *1789* (1970). An example of environmental theatre. Spectators surround five different performance spaces.

Plate 5. View of the *hanamichi*, the 'flower way' of the *Kabuki* stage at the Kanamaru-za Theatre on the island of Shikoku.

centuries of division enforced by the proscenium theatres with their orchestra pits.

A special kind of thrust stage can be found in Japanese *Kabuki*, with its famous 'flower way' (*hanamichi*) (see Plate 5). The *hanamichi* runs through the whole auditorium and thus enables the performers to act amongst the spectators. This extension of the main stage into the auditorium has undergone changes since its introduction in the eighteenth century, yet its basic principle has been retained. From a European perspective it represented a flexible alternative to the proscenium stage.

In comparison to the other forms, the *proscenium* stage symbolises a clear division between the performer and the spectator. What may seem an unremarkable architectural 'fact' has at different times in theatre history been discussed in highly polemical terms. The lines of arguments have been both aesthetic and ideological. Aesthetic opposition to or support for the proscenium stage is founded on the fact that the performer achieves perhaps the highest degree of integration into the mimetic-fictional world of the stage. This implies a corresponding demand that the spectator also immerse him or herself in this fictional scenic world. Opposition arose around the end of the nineteenth century as the hitherto self-evident mimetic function of theatrical and other art forms was called into question. Calls for an anti-naturalistic or anti-realistic theatre were usually framed by demands that the proscenium stage be abolished in favour of other spatial arrangements ranging from apron stages to arena stages. Ideological opposition arose as well. Ideas of politicizing theatre, whether from the left or right, went hand in hand with critiques of the proscenium stage, which was regarded as the epitome of bourgeois art. Most theories of political theatre demanded a 'unification' of spectators and actors or even a complete dissolution of the categories.

The models presented here must be understood in a *structural* sense. That is, they can occur at any time and are not indicative of a particular historical chronology. If we view theatrical space from a historical perspective, we can see that these models are by no means mutually exclusive: on the contrary, we often find a happy coexistence of different spatial forms in one and the same theatrical culture. A further structural feature of theatrical spaces that oppose spectator and performer (proscenium and apron stages) is the creation of what could be called *intermediary* or *transitional spaces*. These spaces allow for transitions of both spectators and performers from the realms of the everyday to the (usually) fictional and performative. In these intermediary spaces, performers make up and prepare themselves mentally and physically for their appearances. Spectators may deposit their coats, read the programme or, in the case of opera, digest the last minute recasting of singers. The creation of such spaces proved to

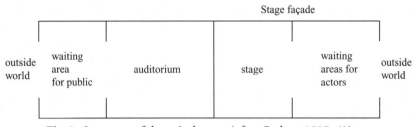

Fig. 3. Structure of theatrical space (after Carlson 1987: 68).

be necessary for cultural and aesthetic reasons: aesthetically, in order to better assist the concentration necessary for the execution and reception of what is a highly complex undertaking: culturally, in order to accommodate evermore complex and important social functions of theatre.

The 'stage façade' marked in Fig. 3 is a structural element that designates a flat plane located behind the stage space and separating it from the performers' rest area. In its simplest form, it can be simply a curtain (Sanskrit theatre, *Commedia dell'arte*, fairbooths). In Roman theatre and its epigonal Renaissance adaptations, it was a fixed architectural element in the form of a decorated arch (e.g. the *scenae frons* in Roman theatre or the seven doors of the Teatro Olimpico in Vicenza).

Today, theatrical space is regarded as a highly flexible entity. New theatres try to take account of the multi-faceted nature of performer–spectator relationships. This may be in the form of different stages in the same building. A famous example of this is the Royal National Theatre in London, which opened in 1973. It has three different stages to accommodate different kinds of performance texts: a large apron stage (the Olivier), a smaller proscenium theatre (the Lyttelton) and a small multi-functional 'black box' (the Cottesloe). Many larger municipal or state-funded theatres now support several different spaces to take account of different performance requirements.

Stage space

In comparison to theatrical space, which regulates spectator–performer relationships, stage or scenic space refers to the narrower realm where the performer acts and thereby transforms his or her surroundings. Theoretically speaking, we can divide this space into two categories: the *kinetic* space (i.e. of movement) of the performer and the *visual* space of the spectator. While the visual space (that which the spectator sees) usually encompasses the movement space (the space physically used by the performer), this does not work the other way round. What may appear as a unified space from the point of the spectator's perception is, in fact (especially when viewed historically), a complex inter-relationship that has not always been seen as a unity. In extreme cases such as the scenographic theatre of G.N. Servandoni (1695–1766), which consisted primarily of spectacular scene changes and did without performers altogether, the stage space can become exclusively a visual one.

Theatre studies has traditionally investigated the visual space, usually the area of scene design. Here, theatre studies intersects with art history, especially when the set or scene designer is a famous artist. The danger here is that the emphasis will be on questions of artistic style and less on the inter-relationship with the performative dimension of the design. Older terms for scene design such as 'scene painting' or 'décor' accentuate a purely decorative/ornamental view of stage space. Today, scholars are increasingly using the term 'scenography' instead of set design because it refers to the dynamic combination of visual image, lighting and space, including technical questions (Howard 2002).

Western theatre employs two main forms of stage space:

(1) The dominant form is the *successional* stage, where all action takes place on one and the same space; changes of time and place are usually indicated by exits and entrances of the actors and/or changes in the visual space (scene changes).

(2) The *simultaneous* stage refers to a plurality of spaces coterminous with one another and which usually represent concrete places. The stage action does not usually take place at the same time, but this is also possible. Historically speaking, this form is associated with the late Middle Ages and the production of large-scale Passion Plays, but it is occasionally revived as in Ariane Mnouchkine's production of *1789* (see Plate 4).

The 'rediscovery' of the successional principle in the Renaissance was a result, as already mentioned, of renewed interest in the theatre of classical antiquity. It reflects – and was indeed determined by – the move from representing simultaneous actions in paintings to representing one scene regulated by the rules of perspective. The reasons for this shift to the successional principle are manifold: they have as much to do with new thinking about history and science as they do with purely aesthetic questions. The successional stage of the Renaissance corresponds to a growing desire for empirically verifiable copies of historical or contemporary reality – even if the subject presented is Greek mythology.

A further innovation of the Italian Renaissance was the introduction of perspective scenery in the early sixteenth century. The development of the perspective stage resulted in a far-reaching shift in perception on the part of both artists and spectators, in the sense that the visual space of the stage became increasingly divided and separate from the kinetic space of the performer. The visual space was increasingly subjected to the aesthetic demands of painting, with the proscenium arch taking on the role of picture frame. Architects and scene painters were confronted with the dilemma of harmonizing the static visual space with the physical presence of the performer. The most famous dilemma, and one that plagued scene designers until the end of the nineteenth century, was that the rules of perspective require that the backstage space slope upwards in order to achieve an illusion of depth. Placing life-size performers in front of the backstage area produced distorted proportions, with human beings towering over buildings. Generally speaking, this resulted in a restriction of kinetic space to the area in front of, rather than beside, the painted backdrops. One 'solution' to the problem (and one which was used until the end of the nineteenth century) was to position children dressed as adults in the back reaches of the stage.

The twentieth century saw the gradual disappearance of perspective scenery, which was replaced by the three-dimensional stage with its unlimited potential for movement and design. The abolition of perspective scenery ended the long division between kinetic and visual space. The stage now became accessible as a performance space without visual restrictions. The most important theoretician of this shift was the Swiss designer Adolphe Appia (1862–1928), who demanded the introduction of a three-dimensional 'practicable' stage utilizing moveable elements such as steps and platforms. The latter are both kinetic and visual spaces, especially useful as surfaces for lighting, and became for Appia the central element of stage design.

The 1960s and 1970s saw a trend towards overcoming the restrictions of the physical space of the open stage. Productions sometimes dispensed with decoration altogether and revealed the naked walls of the theatre. Sometimes the back doors of the stage were even opened to reveal the outside world. This tactic was designed to make spectators reflect on the relationship between life and art.

This process of spatial extension seems to have become even more acute in the age of multi-media theatre. The possibilities of integrating *live* radio, television or even internet links into stage action suggest that the question of stage space will become an important area of experimentation in the coming years. If stage is linked in real time with the outside world via other media, then the whole notion of stage space in the terms discussed here becomes a contested one. The stage space is no longer, then, a division between visual and kinetic space with the aim of creating a third fictional space. Stage space becomes a thematic and philosophical problem in its own right.

The ideology of dramatic space

Although we will not be dealing with the spatial semantics of dramatic texts in this book, it is still important to think about the conventions regulating the use of space, especially in the realistic tradition still prevalent on the mainstream Anglo-American stage. Dramatic space can be divided into two broad subcategories: *mimetic* and *diegetic* space. Mimetic space refers to space depicted on stage and visible to the spectator, while diegetic space is only described or referred to by characters in the play. Mimetic space can also include space evoked by acoustic signs such as off-stage noises, but is mainly connected with scenography and the visual design of a stage space. It corresponds to the differentiation suggested by Hanna Scolnicov of 'perceived space' (dramatic) and 'conceived space' (diegetic) (Scolnicov 1987: 15).

If we look at these conventions from non-European perspectives, as most postcolonial dramatists do, then they appear highly problematic. Thus, even an apparently neutral spatial notion such as a living room as a place of encounter is a highly problematic phenomenon, as the Indian dramatist and director Girish Karnad has argued. The living room is the quintessential space of Western realistic drama, and, as such, it was adopted by Indian dramatists working in the realistic mode as the setting for their plays:

> From Ibsen to Albee, the living room has symbolized all that is valuable to the Western bourgeoisie. It is one's refuge from the sociopolitical forces raging in the world outside, as well as the battleground where values essential to one's individuality are fought out and defended. But nothing of consequence ever happens or is supposed to happen in an Indian living room! It is the no-mans-land, the empty, almost defensive front the family presents to the world outside.   (Karnad 1995: 10)

In a traditional Indian house, caste and social status determine which parts of a house are accessible:

> [It] is in the interior of the house, in the kitchen, in the room where the gods are kept, or in the backyard, where family problems are tackled, or allowed to fester, and where the women can have a say . . . It may also be said that the refusal to go beyond the living room exactly mirrored the reluctance of these Westernized, upper-caste writers to go to the heart of the issues they were presenting.   (Karnad 1995: 10)

The fact that Indian dramatists continued to set their social–critical plays in living rooms, despite the evident discrepancy in cultural spatial conventions, is, for Karnad, symptomatic of a tendency amongst colonial and postcolonial dramatists to use imported aesthetic tools without adapting them sufficiently to local conditions.

The place of theatre

The generation of meaning in the theatre is not just restricted to factors within the enclosed space of the building (if a building is indeed where it takes place). Of equal importance is the positioning of theatre space in the wider cultural, usually urban, environment. This means that the place of performance is defined to a large extent by the field of relations created by the urban or rural environment. This placement in a system of mostly urban signs has a decisive influence on the receptive codes of the audience, i.e. expectations spectators have of the theatre they visit. It determines which spectators visit which theatres. The history of spatio-cultural interaction between spectators and spaces would be a history of how theatrical spaces change under different cultural conditions, owing to factors such as location, size and shape of the theatre space.

Research on the place of theatre in this sense is a relatively recent development in theatre studies, and is largely a product of semiotics. The most thorough study to date on the place of theatre is by Marvin Carlson in his book, *Places of Performance: The Semiotics of Theatre Architecture* (1989). Here he investigates the question: how do theatres mean? Carlson examines a number of important theatre buildings from the Renaissance to the present in respect to the way they are integrated into the semiotic system of the urban environment. Carlson describes the inter-relationship between space, work and performance as a semiotic process: 'places of performances generate social and cultural meanings of their own which in turn help to structure the meaning of the entire theatre experience' (Carlson 1989: 2). According to this definition, even specially constructed theatre buildings generate a whole spectrum of connotative meanings in addition to their functional level of signification. These connotative semantic dimensions depend, in turn, on other cultural codes, for a theatre building is part of the cognitive cartography of a town or city. Thus, a place of performance is determined by its integration into the wider referential system of the urban environment. This position in the urban system influences, in turn, the construction of receptive codes, with the result that any discussion of theatrical or performance space must take cognizance of questions regarding audience and theatrical reception.

Before looking at the specifics of theatre buildings and cities, it is necessary to take a step back and ask a larger question regarding the inter-relationship between culture and space in general. Firstly, we should note that the concept of 'space' in its abstract sense is a relatively recent one. Before the eighteenth century, no architectural treatise ever used the word 'space' in the general sense we do today. Yet the assignation of special meaning to particular spaces is one of the basic conditions of cultural definition. Space is, as the German philosopher Ernst Cassirer put it, one of the fundamental 'symbolic forms'. As with all symbols, the meanings assigned to spaces are dependent on the cultures that use them. Each culture has its own way of organizing and semanticizing space. Cassirer illustrates his thesis by reference to what he calls 'mythic or sacred space'. Cassirer argues that the consecration of space begins by separating off a certain section from everyday space as a whole and defining it as religious or sacred. The notion of religious sacrality, which implies also spatial delimitation, is contained in the etymology of the word 'temple'. It goes back to the term 'templum' (Greek $\tau \acute{\varepsilon} \mu \nu o \varsigma$) and the root $\tau \varepsilon \mu$, meaning to 'cut' (Cassirer 1955: 100).

Theatre scholars have adapted Cassirer's concept to describe how theatrical space has been demarcated from the space of everyday culture. Viewed in evolutionary terms, it could be argued that the place of performance developed from a sacred to an aesthetic one. In ancient Greek theatre, the theatre is part of the *templum*, not separate from it. In early medieval liturgical drama performed within the space of the church, theatre and *templum* are also spatially indistinguishable.

The examples of Greek and liturgical theatre illustrate two further fundamental distinctions that have to be made in respect of the semantic dimension of the place of theatre. We must distinguish between (1) theatres that are purpose-built as theatres, and (2) those spaces that were created for another practical function but which are temporarily or permanently used as theatres. The question of function leads either 'inside' to considerations of theatre space as defined above, or 'outside' to questions of how the building is located in the wider cultural environment. For example, the particular form of the Elizabethan stage may originally have had less to do with the type of plays staged there than with the necessity to transform it into a bear-baiting pit in case the theatre performances did not provide enough profit (Dillon 2006: 36). This hypothesis draws attention to the fact that Elizabethan theatre had to compete in a cultural system where it was perceived less as high art than as one form of popular entertainment among others. The existence or absence of specialized theatre buildings do give an indication of the status of the medium within a culture.

Compared to Elizabethan theatres, the theatre buildings of the Italian Renaissance were, in the early stages, temporary constructions erected within the confines of palaces. They were not even visible to the normal citizen, let alone accessible. Extant examples in Northern Italy are the Teatro all'Antica in Sabbionetta and the Teatro Olimpico in Vicenza. Both are 'concealed' within the confines of their respective buildings: the former in the Ducal palace; the latter within the walls of the local academy. Both are today museums, but in former times they have served in a variety of functions ranging from storehouses to cinemas.

The question of theatrical cartography gains in importance with the growth of cities. Scholars have begun to investigate the question of location and clustering. The Elizabethan public theatres were located outside the city boundaries of London to remove them from municipal jurisdiction. With the growth of commercial theatre in the eighteenth and especially nineteenth centuries, particular sections of the larger cities were reserved for theatrical entertainment, often those in close proximity to red-light districts. The most famous examples of such clustering are London's West End and New York's Broadway. A major theatre city such as Berlin, which was divided for forty years, reflects different processes of clustering as both parts of the city created their own theatre districts.

The choice of venue can and does have a decisive influence on the theatrical experience, both positively and negatively. This insight is the result of a historical development that begins at the end of the nineteenth century with the call for theatre festivals at places of cultural and/or political significance. Generally speaking, theatre festivals are site-specific and often draw some of their legitimacy from a particular place, often away from the madding crowd of the larger theatre centres. In some cases, the place is somewhat remote and has the added function of a pilgrimage (Oberammergau, Bayreuth) or it is endowed with a special artistic tradition (Salzburg, Glyndebourne). The Salzburg festival, founded by Max Reinhardt and Hugo von Hofmannsthal in 1920, is perhaps the most rewarding example for an investigation of the inter-relationship between place and performance, as it has a famous tradition of changing non-theatrical spaces into theatrical ones (cathedral fronts, churches, riding stables).

Site-specific performances

Perhaps the most important development in recent times has been the move out of specialized theatre buildings and into spaces not originally designed for theatrical performance but usually defined for some other cultural function. These many experiments have been grouped under the rubric 'site-specific' theatre. These are performances that take place outside pre-existing and pre-defined theatrical spaces. Site-specific performances utilize natural features or historical spaces and buildings to provide a spatially determined semantic frame for the actual performance. They use the properties and meanings found at a given site, be it a landscape, a city, a building or a room. This form of the-atre emphasizes particular images, stories and events that reveal the complex relationship between ourselves and our physical environment. Needless to say, the defining aspect of site-specificity is its rootedness in a particular place and hence the impossibility of transferring such performances to other locales. That such performances, do in fact, get transported has meant that the cat-egory itself has become too broad to accommodate the various experimental forms emerging under its conceptual umbrella. Indeed, a new subcategory has emerged, that of site-*generic* performance. These are performances that require a specific *category* of space but are not tied to one place (Wilkie 2002).

Today, it is generally accepted (and not just among theatre scholars) that theatre can take place anywhere. It is the task of the theatre scholar to investigate, with the different methodologies at his or her disposal, the complex interactions that take place on the levels of theatrical, scenic and cultural space. Theatre is very much a spatial experience, and its investigation is a central task of students, artists and scholars alike.

Further reading

The best discussion of theatre space from a systematic and mainly semiotic point of view is Gay McAuley's *Space in Performance: Making Meaning in the Theatre* (1999). It provides the most extensive discussion to date of the various terminological difficulties and confusions involved in analysing the many spatial dimensions at work in theatre. Marvin Carlson's *Places of Performance* (1989) has been very influential with its combination of semiotics and historical case studies of particular theatre buildings. David Wiles's *A Short History of Western Performance Space* (2003) is an excellent combination of historical survey and theoretical reflection. Nick Kaye's *Site-specific Art: Performance, Place and Documentation* (2000) provides a good combination of theoretical discussion, documentation and case studies of a rapidly developing trend in contemporary performance. A fascinating combination of theoretically informed relection on site-specific practice and case studies can be found in *Theatre/Archaeology: Disciplinary Dialogues* by Mike Pearson and Michael Shanks (2001). Pearson, co-founder and director of the innovative Welsh-based performance group Brith Gof (1981–2004), collaborated with archaeologist and archaeological theorist Michael Shanks to investigate the inter-relationships between the past, both collective and personal, and how performance can provide a way of accessing these relationships. Historical treatments of theatre buildings in Europe include Allardyce Nicoll's *The Development of the Theatre: A Study of Theatrical Art from the Beginnings to the Present Day* (1966) and Richard and Helen Leacroft, *Theatre and Playhouse: An Illustrated Survey of Theatre Building from Ancient Greece to the Present Day* (1984). Scenography and theatre architecture are closely linked.

Pamela Howard's *What is Scenography?* (2002) provides a sometimes provocative discussion of both historical and systematic aspects of the practice by a leading scene designer. This is a book both for budding scenographers and for scholars of the subject. Christopher Baugh's *Theatre Performance and Technology: The Development of Scenography in the Twentieth Century* (2005) is an important study of the impact of technology on twentieth-century scenography, and extends into general questions of space and performance. Highly recommended is the collection of essays by Arnold Aronson (2005), a leading US scholar of scenography. Oddey and White's (2006) collection of essays extends the discussion of scenography into digital technology and experimental performance.

Subjects and methods

Chapter 4

Theories of theatre 1: historical paradigms

What is theatre theory? What makes a particular statement or argument about theatre 'theoretical' in comparison to other forms of discourse? There is, as so often, no easy answer. It has often been pointed out that in terms of their etymology, 'theatre' and 'theory' are in fact closely related. Both have their roots in the Greek word *theôría* ($\theta\varepsilon\omega\rho\acute{\iota}\alpha$), which has two quite different meanings: it can mean observation, examination, viewing or beholding and, more concretely, being a spectator at a festival or theatrical performance. In other words, the Greek term established a semantic field that linked both abstract theoretical reflection and direct theatrical observation.

The term 'theatre theory' could be defined, according to Marvin Carlson, as 'statements of general principles regarding the methods, aims, functions, and characteristics of this particular art form' (Carlson 1984:10). Such statements are seldom comprehensive, as Carlson explains, but rather perforce selective, i.e. they treat particular facets of the theatre and are often penned by authors representing highly divergent fields such as philosophy, theology, rhetoric, painting, poetry and so on. In addition, such theoretical statements pursue quite different goals and strategies in terms of 'what theatre is, has been, or should be' (Carlson 1984: 10). Theatre theory can therefore comprise three temporal dimensions: the past, present or future. Each dimension also implies a different function and field of application. Theories that describe and systematize present theatre usually belong to the realm of aesthetics in its widest sense, and often discuss theatre in relation to other art forms. Theoretical treatments of historical theatre forms often serve to instrumentalize particular periods with a view to making them serve as models to critique the present. Theatre theories that project into the future are usually programmatic in nature, and seek to envisage new forms and functions for the theatre. Since the Renaissance, European dramatic theory has continually reread Aristotle's *Poetics* as a past authority, reinterpreted it as a critique of contemporary practices and reformulated it as model for future playwriting.

As we have seen in previous chapters, theatre is a very complex medium. If we take the dictionary definition of 'theory' as meaning 'general principles independent of the particular things to be explained' (*Concise Oxford Dictionary* 1990: 1266), then we will be required to provide at least two perspectives. Theatre theory includes the history of theoretical reflection on the medium, as well as contemporary attempts to expound such principles, which usually take current theatre practices as their point of departure. Ideally, theatre theory as an academic subdiscipline should aim to achieve a double perspective, negotiating between past discussions and models and their relevance for contemporary debates. This chapter and the next provide such a double perspective. In this chapter, we will briefly discuss the three main theoretical debates. In the next chapter, we will focus on the theoretical discussions produced within the discipline of theatre studies itself.

The previous chapters have already demonstrated, however, that 'theory' cannot really be separated off as a separate branch of study, but should provide the basis for all the different subdisciplines of theatre studies discussed in this book. The debates surrounding acting theory, for example, have been discussed in Chap. 1 and theories of viewing in Chap. 2; historiography will be outlined in Chap. 6 and so on. The following pages try to identify broader theoretical questions that cut across the various subdisciplines.

Western theatre theory is usually seen to begin with Aristotle's *Poetics* (ca. 330 BC, cited from Aristotle 1965). This is actually only partially accurate because the *Poetics* is largely a treatise on literature, in particular drama, and contains very few remarks about theatre as a medium or art form. The visual aspects of theatre are dealt with laconically under the category *opsis*, usually translated as 'spectacle'. In Chap. 6 of the *Poetics* Aristotle concedes that *opsis* is an essential part of tragedy, along with diction and song. But at the end of the chapter, he relativizes the statement somewhat by terming *opsis* an 'attraction' that 'has the least to do with the playwright's craft or the art of poetry'. There follows one of the most controversial statements – from the point of view of theatre studies at least – in the whole treatise: 'For the power of tragedy is independent both of performance and of actors, and besides, the production of spectacular effects is more the province of the property-man than of the playwright' (Aristotle 1965: 41). With this judgement, Aristotle establishes a hard dichotomy between the literary-textual and theatrical-visual aspects of drama, with the latter being consigned to the province of props and stage accessories. His somewhat iconophobic stance means that the *Poetics* is only partially applicable as a theatre theory in a narrower sense. Nevertheless, the text still provides a number of concepts that, in the course of history, have generated intense debate. Three terms or themes in particular have been vigorously debated:

(1) 'mimesis'
(2) 'poiesis'
(3) 'catharsis'.

Of the three, 'mimesis' (imitation or more broadly representation) is the most important. Even in antiquity it was a complex and somewhat ambiguous word. The term 'poiesis' can be understood to refer to the textual or dramaturgical aspect of theatre and is primarily the domain of literary and dramatic theory. 'Catharsis' refers to the long tradition of debate about the effects of theatre and drama. Although Aristotle defines the term in a narrow sense, it has become synonymous with the whole area of the usually detrimental influence that theatre can exert. The area of acting theory finds no mention in the *Poetics* (in classical times it was regarded as part of rhetoric). It is dealt with in this book under acting (see Chap. 1).

Mimesis

'Mimesis' is a central concept in Greek thinking, and is applied to all the arts, not just to drama and theatre. The term is probably derived from the word *mimos* (actor) and is therefore closely connected to theatrical performance. All things represented on stage are regarded as imitations of reality, a relation the Greeks termed 'mimetic'. This mode of imitation extends to all things: the story being enacted as well as the actions of the performers who represent characters by means of movement and speech. Beyond this fundamental level of definition, the understanding and, above all, evaluation of the concept diverge considerably.

One can distinguish between a Platonic and an Aristotelian interpretation of mimesis. In Books III and X of his dialogue *The Republic*, Plato begins the systematic discussion of mimesis with reference to the arts. For Plato, mimesis is primarily an ontological and epistemological problem and only in a second step an aesthetic one. Plato famously defines our perception of reality as being mediated by stages: we do not actually perceive things in themselves directly, but only imperfect partial versions of things. Most artistic products, therefore, are imitations of representations and are therefore highly unreliable: 'the artist's representation stands at third remove from reality' (Plato 1955: 374). Not only that, but Plato suspects that mimetic representations are positively dangerous and have a tendency to spread in almost epidemic proportions, so should therefore be placed under theoretical and political quarantine.

Plato uses the concept of 'mimesis' to attack the arts, above all the per-forming arts, and accuses them of untruthfulness and distorting reality. With

Plato begins the philosophical discussion about the ontological status of people, things and actions represented on stage. They attain through mimesis a particular status that we now term 'fictional' or 'as if'. While the fictional status of the represented story is mostly unproblematic, the same is not true for the status of people, objects and spaces, which are actually present on stage. Plato launches the debate on theatre as a place of deception and deceit, and provides the key arguments for the long tradition known as the 'anti-theatrical prejudice' (see p. 73). These arguments posit that mimetic representation on stage might incite spectators to emulate the same actions in real life: 'it feeds them [desires and feelings] when they ought to be starved, and makes them control us when we ought, in the interests of our own welfare and happiness, to control them' (Plato 1955: 384). Even today, these arguments resurface in connection with media and computer games, where excessive exposure to violent games or films is considered to be potentially harmful for young people. These discussions are essentially Platonic in orientation.

It is Plato's former student, Aristotle, who formulates the first influential counter-argument to the former's interpretation of mimesis. Aristotle argues that the relationship between model and imitation is less problematic epistemologically and in terms of possible effects. When Aristotle speaks of poetry, he refers to epic, lyric and dithyrambic verse as well as to tragedy and comedy. He also draws many comparisons with music and the visual arts. The bulk of the *Poetics* is devoted to language as the main sphere of mimesis in drama – one of the reasons why the treatise is mainly of interest to literary scholars rather than theatre studies. For Aristotle, mimesis in literature encompasses three areas: the media, the objects and the manner of imitation. The media of imitation are rhythm, language and music; the objects are 'men in action' (Aristotle 1965: 33); the manner is either dramatic (mimetic) or narrative (epic). The categories are further explained in Chaps. 6 and 12 of the *Poetics*, when Aristotle deals with tragedy. The following diagram provides an overview of the different applications of the term 'mimesis' in reference to tragedy.

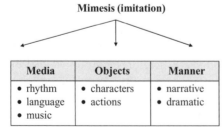

Media	Objects	Manner
• rhythm • language • music	• characters • actions	• narrative • dramatic

The main reason for his affirmative use of the mimesis concept can be found in Aristotle's belief that mankind has an innate mimetic instinct: 'The instinct for imitation is inherent in man from his earliest days; he differs from other animals in that he is the most imitative of creatures and he learns his earliest lessons from imitation' (Aristotle 1965: 35). Artistic imitation is by definition natural, and cannot therefore be harmful. From this anthropological disposition, art gradually developed its various forms.

If mimesis is an innate human drive, then it is clear that its applications far exceed just theatre or even the arts as a whole. For literature, Aristotle rejects the idea of mimesis being simply a direct copy of reality, and emphasizes that the artist can employ a degree of creative freedom, even idealization, in the sense of improving on the model (*Poetics*, Chap. 15). Mimesis and the artistic creative process are closely linked or even synonymous, a conjunction that finds further justification in Aristotle's natural philosophy, where he argues that nature is itself a continual process of striving to find more perfect forms.

The relation between nature and mimesis is one of the most controversial and most frequently reinterpreted precepts of the *Poetics*, and one that every age redefines in its own fashion. Equally controversial is the concept of 'probability', a requirement that mimetic art must obey, according to Aristotle: 'it is not the poet's function to describe what has actually happened, but the kinds of thing that might happen, that is, that could happen because they are, in the circumstances, either probable or necessary' (Aristotle 1965: 43). From this requirement, Aristotle derives his claim that poetry has a 'philosophical' orientation, a preference for the general over the particular, the universal rather than the factual.

The pejorative and the affirmative interpretations of mimesis that we find in Plato and Aristotle still provide the discursive framework for theatre theory. Rather than being seen as hostile and mutually exclusive perspectives, today the two sides of mimesis should perhaps be seen as inextricably interconnected and, in fact, dependent on each other.

Poiesis

European theatre theory has been dominated quantitatively, and possibly qualitatively, by *poetological* debates, i.e. the rules determining the ways texts for the stage should be composed. Since this refers in the main to the form and content of dramatic texts, it has been argued that theatre theory in the narrower sense does not begin until the twentieth century. While it is certainly true that theories of staging do not arise before the end of the nineteenth century, we shall see that it is reductive to define theatre theory too narrowly as either text- or staging-related. However, there is no doubt that from a historical perspective, theatre theory has focused on the drama and has been concerned with redefining parameters outlined by Aristotle.

Both Aristotle and Plato agree that texts can be presented in two modes: *mimetically* or *diegetically*. Plato defines diegesis as a narrated rather than enacted action. It is accordingly the mode used by story-tellers, and serves the recitation of myths (and Homer) and is therefore tolerated by Plato. Mimetic (re)presentation, on the other hand, as used in the theatre, requires the transformation of language by an actor, and is opposed by Plato for the reasons given above. For Aristotle, all poetry is mimetic, so he distinguishes between diegesis and drama as two modes of representing an action. Even the Greeks recognized that the distinction is far from exact. In epic poetry, there are passages where the narration shifts to direct speech, and in drama there may be narrative passages recited directly to the audience. Indeed, a pure drama consisting only of dialogue appears, from a historical and contemporary perspective, to be only one option for stage performance. Today, the term 'diegesis' is a central concept in narratology, and is now widely used in art and film studies as well as in theatre and literary theory to refer to the story being told in a performance, film or painting.

The main emphasis of Aristotle's *Poetics* is on the analysis of dramatic action or *mythos*, the imitation and construction of a story taken from Greek mythology and which is often translated as 'plot'. In Chap. 14 of the *Poetics*, he says: 'the plot should be so ordered that even without seeing it performed anyone merely hearing what is afoot will shudder with fear and pity' (Aristotle 1965: 49). The means or media of dramatic representation Aristotle divides into two categories, which later became known as the *qualitative* and the *quantitative* parts of tragedy. The qualitative parts refer to the general means of representation employed by theatre, the quantitative parts to the internal structure of a Greek tragedy:

Means of dramatic representation

Qualitative	Quantitative
• action (*mythos*)	• prologue
• characters	• parodos or stasimon
• thought	• episode
• diction	• exodos
• music	
• spectacle (*opsis*)	

It is very clear from the quantitative parts that the Aristotle was describing the dramatic practice of his time, and it was clearly designed on the basis of rules derived inductively from an existing body of plays. The later interpretation and transformation of the *Poetics* from the Renaissance onwards proceeds from the opposing principle. The so-called *neo-Aristotelian* poetological writings, which appear from the middle of the sixteenth century in great numbers, set down guidelines for the production of dramatic texts on the basis of Aristotle's 'rules'. Although they differ in points of detail and interpretation, they agree that a tragedy should contain the following elements:

- primacy of a unified action
- characters capable of reflection
- verse.

All emphasize the genres of tragedy and comedy with a clear hierarchical preference for tragedy.

Aristotle's treatise deals with the primacy of action in most detail. An ideal dramatic action must be unified in the sense that no episode or part may be removed without causing damage to the development of the action. With Aristotle, we find the beginnings of the metaphor of 'construction': a play is like a building from which no section may be removed without the whole edifice collapsing. This is also the origin of the famous Aristotelian unities: action, time and place. Aristotle himself is only specific about action; the unity of time is only referred to in passing as not exceeding twenty-four hours, whereas the unity of place finds no mention at all and is a later 'conclusion' drawn by Renaissance commentators.

All theories of drama developed on the basis of Aristotle adopt his criteria. One could say that they discuss, in different ways, how one should best construct stories in which characters interact over time and space. Aristotle's requirements for dramatic characters – they should be capable of reflection – provided the basis for numerous disquisitions in the context of changing social environments. In terms of the history of dramatic theory, we can observe a fundamental change in the eighteenth century from the primacy of action to a primacy of character. As theorists tried to reconcile dramatic theory with a diverse body of dramatic work – the 'ruleless' legacy of Elizabethan drama on the one hand with the neoclassical homogeneity of French playwriting on the other – it became clear that effective drama was no longer guaranteed by slavish adherence to formal norms, but should instead be sought in questions of characterization and identification. A high degree of commensurability between the language and behaviour of characters on stage and that of the spectators became the new norm.

In the twentieth century, Aristotelian dramatic theory was challenged from two main perspectives. The first came from Bertolt Brecht's theory of epic theatre, which he termed 'anti-Aristotelian' (Brecht 1964). Brecht contrasts the exclusively dialogue-based drama predicated on illusion and identification with an epic drama, which includes narrator figures, songs and acknowledgement of the audience. The second challenge is even more radical because it questions the diegetic (i.e. story-telling) function of theatre. Antonin Artaud's call for a redefinition of theatrical language in his manifesto *The Theatre of Cruelty* (1938, cited from Artaud 1970) relegates the diegetic level to a subordinate position in comparison to other functions, although it is not dispensed with altogether. Here, we are at the very borderline of the dramatic. As Hans-Thies Lehmann demonstrates in his study *Postdramatic Theatre* (2006), the very notion of the postdramatic is dependent on acknowledging in some way the Aristotelian tradition that is being challenged and superseded.

Catharsis

The concept of 'catharsis' forms the basis of the hotly debated question, first raised by the Greeks, as to whether theatrical performances can have a direct effect on the spectator. It is used in this section in a broader sense than we find in Aristotle's *Poetics*, where he defines the cathartic effect of tragedy as producing *phobos* and *eleos* (translated variously as fear and pity or terror and commiseration) in the spectators, and thereby ridding them of these emotions. There has been much conjecture about the precise meaning of catharsis in this context. Aristotle seems to be using the term in its medical sense of purgation of something harmful. The word also had a religious connotation close to the notion of expiation or ritual cleansing. However we translate it, it is clear that for Aristotle, witnessing a tragedy had a positive psycho-dynamic effect on the spectator who was effectively purged of potentially dangerous emotions. As with his interpretation of mimesis, Aristotle directly opposes his teacher Plato on this point. Aristotle introduces the fundamentally positive term 'catharsis' into the discussion on mimetic representation to indicate how the arousing of potentially harmful emotions can find a positive outlet.

The different translations of *phobos* and *eleos* point to an important shift in theorizing about the effects of theatre. Aristotle's claim that catharsis functioned to rid the spectator of emotions is gradually redefined over time to mean moral purification or even edification. Although Aristotle's concept of 'theatre', or rather 'tragedy', certainly contains moral implications in as much as the represented action should be of a certain grandeur and import, there is no specific mention that catharsis should be regarded in terms of moral edification. This changes in the Roman period, with Horace's famous dictum of *aut prodesse aut delectare*. In his extremely influential treatise *Ars Poetica* (ca. 18 BC), Horace claimed that 'poets aim at giving either profit or delight, or at combining the giving of pleasure with some useful precepts for life' (Horace 1965: 22). The combination of pleasure and usefulness becomes, during the Renaissance and well into the eighteenth century, a defining idea and indeed justification of a potentially dangerous art form. In the middle of the eighteenth century, the German theorist and playwright Gotthold Lessing translated *phobos* and *eleos* as 'fear' (instead of terror) and 'pity' (instead of 'commiseration') in his *Hamburg Dramaturgy* (1962). This retranslation underlined the Enlightenment argument that the emotions represented on stage and aroused in the spectators could be morally beneficial in as much as they produced 'pity', a central Christian precept. This translation remained current until well into the twentieth century, when classical scholars returned to the term's original Greek meaning and emphasized the medicinal-purgative connotations of catharsis.

The redefinition of catharsis in moral rather than physical terms was motivated certainly by the necessity to justify theatre against its opponents. As we have seen, the argument against the imitative arts in general, and the harmful effects of theatre in particular, begins with Plato. His objections are adopted by early Christian writers and adapted to the new religious doctrine to create a powerful counter discourse to theatre known as the *anti-theatrical prejudice* (Barish 1981). Early opponents of theatre such as Tertullian and St Augustine stress the incompatibility of Christian doctrines such as gentleness with the violent emotions engendered by theatrical spectacle. Their basic arguments are adopted and radicalized by Protestant theologians in the Reformation. Between 1550 and 1700, we find a large number of anti-theatrical treatises, which, for all their extremism, occasionally arrive at theoretical positions of considerable interest. In Jeremy Collier's anti-theatrical treatise, *A Short View of the Immorality and Profaneness of the English Stage* ([1698] 1972), we find thoughts on the differentiation between fiction and reality and the relationship between actors and their roles (see box on p. 74). The anti-theatrical prejudice constitutes a theoretical discourse in its own right and encompasses most areas of theatre theory, from dramatic theory to mimesis and catharsis, as well as acting theory.

The dangers of the stage

And which is still more extraordinary: the Prologues, and Epilogues are sometimes scandalous to the last degree . . . Now here properly speaking the Actors quit the Stage, and remove from Fiction into Life. Here they converse with the *Boxes*, and *Pit*, and address directly to the audience. These Preliminaries and concluding Parts, are designed to justify the Conduct of the Play, and bespeak the Favour of the Company. Upon such Occasions one would imagine if ever, the Ladies should be used with Respect, and the Measures of Decency observ'd. But here we have Lewdness without Shame or Example: Here the Poet exceeds himself . . .

People love to see their *Passions* painted no less than their *Persons*: And like *Narcissus* are apt to dote upon their own Image. This bent of self Admiration recommends the Business of *Amours*, and engages the inclination. And which is more, these Love-representations oftentimes call up the Spirits, and set them to work. The *Play* is acted over again in the *Scene* of Fancy, and the first Imitation becomes a Model. *Love* has generally a *Party Within*; and when the Wax is prepared, the impression is easily made. Thus the Disease of the *Stage* grows Catching: It throws its own *Amours* among the Company, and forms these Passions when it does not find them. (Collier [1698] 1972: 13, 281)

The effects of theatre on the audience, both detrimental and beneficial, dominate theatre theory in the first half of the eighteenth century, when it is forced to justify itself against the attacks of the anti-theatrical faction. Both friend and foe of the theatre stem from the bourgeoisie for whom theatre becomes an increasingly important medium in its struggle against the aristocracy. For all its potential dangers, the most important legitimating argument in favour of theatre is its ability to provide – still in the Horatian tradition – moral instruction as well as entertainment. In the dedication to his immensely influential bourgeois tragedy, *The London Merchant* (1731), George Lillo defined the end of tragedy as 'the exciting of the passions, in order to the correcting such of them as are criminal' (Lillo 1974: 215). Indeed, the passions become the central theme of theatre theory for the rest of the century.

The power of cathartic response needed to be redefined to make it more compatible with an age of sentimental comedy and emotional sensibility. As noted above, an influential reinterpretation was formulated by Lessing who translated *phobos* and *eleos* as 'fear' and 'pity' and defined the latter as the primary passion to be aroused in tragedy. Catharsis should function to transform 'passions into virtuous capabilities'. Lessing sought to domesticate the play of emotions excited by serious theatre, and make them compatible with an age obsessed by reason and the possible perfectibility of human relations. Not all Enlightenment thinkers were so optimistic, however. In his famous attack on theatre, the *Letter to D'Alembert on the Theatre* (1758), Jean-Jacques Rousseau expressed doubt that emotional excitation caused by theatrical performance could be controlled at all: 'The only means to purify emotions is reason, but I have said that reason has no effect on the stage whatsoever' (Rousseau 1968: 20).

The reinterpretation and domestication of cathartic response into a moral attitude transforms the debate into a question of aesthetics in which identification becomes the ruling precept. Almost all eighteenth-century theorists insist on a high degree of commensurability between the characters represented on stage and the spectators sitting in the audience. This is both a question of social class and empathetic identification. Nowhere in Aristotle do we find the term 'identification' or its equivalent. For the Greeks, the emotional response to tragic action was, as we have seen, much more visceral. In the eighteenth century, however, new theories of psychology began to be formulated that reinterpreted catharsis as a process of identification with the character's suffering. There are many different formulations of this idea, but most are based on the idea of sympathy and sensibility. In his influential *Elements of Criticism* (1762), Henry Home, Lord Kames elevates sympathy to a pre-eminent position in aesthetic theory: 'Sympathy invites a communication of joys and sorrows, hopes and fears: such exercise, soothing and satisfactory in itself, is necessarily productive of mutual good-will and affection' (Home 1762: 13).

In the seventy-fifth contribution to his *Hamburg Dramaturgy*, Lessing applied such ideas in his famous reinterpretation of catharsis as 'pity directed at ourselves':

> It is the fear for ourselves, which derives from our similarity with the suffering person; it is the fear that misfortune that we see befall others could also befall us; it is the fear that we could become the object of pity. In a word: this fear is pity directed at ourselves.   (Lessing 1962: No. 75)

Lessing's redefinition of cathartic response corresponds to what today is generally termed 'sympathetic identification' or simply 'identification'. This model of spectator response remained unchallenged until the twentieth century. Even today, it is still assumed in many forms of realistic theatre to be the primary form of emotional and cognitive reaction to events depicted on stage.

The domestication of catharsis as identification in bourgeois realistic theatre remained dominant until the early twentieth century, when it came under attack. The challenges came from two almost opposing camps. On the one hand, the rise of political theatre forms and more complex forms of modernist art that eschewed realistic representation meant that cathartic identification was no longer considered apt or complex enough to explain responses to these new developments. The German playwright and theatre theorist Bertolt

Brecht formulated the most influential anti-identificatory theatre theory with his concept of 'epic theatre', which he termed at an earlier stage of development 'anti-Aristotelian' theatre. In place of emotionally driven empathetic identification, Brecht required a distanced critical attitude. Its achievement was only possible if the major elements of theatre – dramaturgy, acting, staging – were refashioned to enable the new spectator response. Brecht visualized the differences between cathartic (dramatic) and critical (epic) theatre by means of a comparison, shown in Table 1.

Table 1. Brecht's comparison of cathartic (dramatic) and critical (epic) theatre

Dramatic theatre	Epic theatre
plot	narrative
implicates the spectator in a stage situation	turns the spectator into an observer but
wears down his capacity for action	arouses his capacity for action
provides him with sensations	forces him to take decisions
the spectator is involved in something	he is made to face something
suggestion	argument
the spectator is in the thick of it, shares the experience	the spectator stands outside, studies
the human being is taken for granted	the human being is the object of the enquiry
feeling	reason

Source: Brecht 1964: 37

The second major challenge was less a rejection of catharsis than its radicalization. At the same time as Brecht was developing his theory of epic theatre, the French surrealist poet, actor and theorist Antonin Artaud proposed a return to the original meaning of catharsis. His main object of attack was psychological literary theatre, and his disparate visions of an alternative theatre include a conception of theatre 'collectively made to drain abscesses' (Artaud 1970: 22). Artaud never formulated a coherent theory of cathartic theatre in the Brechtian sense, but formulated instead radical poetic images of a theatre-to-come that influenced a whole generation of theatre makers such as Peter Brook, Jerzy Grotowski and Julian Beck (The Living Theatre). From his writings it is never clear whether he sees catharsis on an individual or collective level, but the original idea of catharsis as purgation is certainly a recurrent theme in his writings.

Further reading

The best chronological account of theatre theory remains Marvin Carlson's *Theories of the Theatre: A Historical and Critical Survey from the Greeks to the Present* (1984, 2nd and expanded edn, 1993). Beginning with the Greeks, Carlson summarizes a wide range of canonical texts in several languages, including contemporary poststructuralist writings. His discussion includes both dramatic criticism as well as theatre theory in the narrower sense. For those students wishing to engage directly with the texts, a useful anthology of dramatic and theatre theory is Bernard F. Dukore's *Dramatic Theory and Criticism: Greeks to Grotowski* (1974). A less comprehensive but also less Eurocentric anthology is Dan Gerould's *Theatre/Theory/Theatre: The Major Critical Texts from Aristotle and Zeami to Soyinka and Havel* (2003). Gerould has opted for fewer but longer excerpts, which enable a more thorough study of the texts. All these texts reference the three themes of mimesis, poiesis and catharsis. Each field also has its own specialized literature. For a discussion of the Greek notion of mimesis, see S. Halliwell's introduction and commentary to the *Poetics* (1998). Because it impinges on so many aspects of aesthetics, the literature on mimesis is overwhelming, and much of it does not engage primarily with theatre. An excellent overview of the concept is provided by Gunter Gebauer and Christoph Wulf in their study, *Mimesis: Culture, Art, Society* (1995). For a critical reading of mimesis as the foundation of Western realist theatre, see Elin Diamond's feminist study, *Unmaking Mimesis: Essays on Feminism and Theatre* (1997). The concept of 'poiesis' has been extensively studied in literary criticism, particularly in treatments of neo-Aristotelian dramatic theory. Both Carlson (1984) and Dukore (1974) cover this material. The Cambridge University Press series, *Sources of Dramatic Theory* (4 Vols., 1991 ongoing), edited by Michael J. Sidnell, collects and introduces a range of texts from the Greeks to the present that are otherwise difficult to access. Treatments of catharsis overlap frequently with theories of spectatorship and also with applied theatre (see Chap. 11). The concept itself is dealt with either in the context of commentary on Aristotle (see Halliwell 1998), or within the framework of drama and theatre therapy (see Blatner 2000).

Chapter 5

Theories of theatre 2: systematic and critical approaches

The previous chapter looked at fundamental questions of theatre theory as defined by Greek philosophy and Western traditions of poetological reflection. With the rise of theatre studies as an independent discipline in the 1960s and 1970s, there emerged a need to theorize the subject over and beyond the traditional themes. There are a number of reasons for this. Firstly, the emergence of the director as an independent theatre artist during the twentieth century made it clear that the staging itself was a complex artwork *sui generis* that could not be analyzed using the available tools of literary criticism. Secondly, far from being a purely historical discipline, theatre studies began to redefine itself also as one concerned with understanding contemporary artistic practice. Thirdly, all branches of the humanities began to be challenged in these decades by what later became known as the theory revolution. A succession of 'paradigms' critiqued existing historical or close-reading models of scholarship, some of which will be discussed in this chapter.

Semiotics

Theatre semiotics concerns itself with the study of how meaning is produced on the stage by means of signs. It is a subdiscipline of the general theory of semiotics that developed in the twentieth century in the wake of Ferdinand de Saussure's (1857–1913) theory of language. Following Saussure's insights into the structures of language, semiotics was rapidly applied to other areas of cultural expression. As a multidiscipline, semiotics investigates all forms of human (and animal) use of signs.

What is a sign? According to Saussure, and earlier philosophers as well, every word is a sign; a green light at the traffic lights is a sign; and the sight of smoke is also a sign – a sign of fire. However, these three examples belong to different categories of sign, and they are only signs because someone interprets them as such. A sign is in fact made up of two or three components. Saussure divides the linguistic sign into two parts (a dyadic model) whereas the American philosopher Charles Sanders Peirce (1839–1914) uses a three-part (triadic) system. Theatre semiotics uses a combination of both systems, depending on the object of study.

According to Saussure, a linguistic sign consists of two parts: a material component (the actual sound of a word), which he termed the 'signifier', and a semantic part (the meaning evoked in a listener), the 'signified'. The actual physical object or idea to which the completed sign refers is termed the 'referent', so, in fact, the Saussurean linguistic sign is implicitly triadic as well. Peirce's theory of signs is not explicitly linguistic but can be applied to all areas of human life. From Peirce stems the famous definition of a sign: 'A sign is something that stands for something else to someone in some respect' (Peirce 1985: 5). Peirce gives these three components technical terms: the 'something' is the 'representamen'; the 'something else' is the 'object', and the comprehension of the sign process ('to someone in some respect') Peirce terms the 'interpretant'. This sign model is often represented in the form of a triangle (Fig. 4).

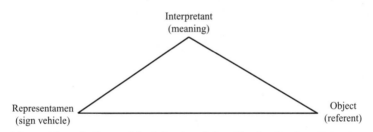

Fig. 4. The triadic model of the sign (after Charles Sanders Peirce).

Although these technical terms are little used in present-day theatre semiotics, the triadic process is widely accepted. In 1998, a pioneer of theatre semiotics, Patrice Pavis, stated that the Peircean model remained marginalized in theatre studies because of its complexity. In its totality, Peirce's sign theory is indeed extremely complex and therefore almost unmanageable for analytic purposes (Pavis 1998: 165).

Despite the somewhat hesitant acceptance of the Peircean model in its entirety, parts of it have found their way into theatre semiotic discourse. The most important of these is the 'object' part of the semiotic triad. The object can, according to Peirce, be further divided into three types of signs, which he terms 'icon', 'index' and 'symbol', and defines as follows:

- Iconic signs are based on similarity between sign and object; for example, the picture of a dog on a 'beware of the dog' sign.

- Indexical signs are those based on a spatial or temporal connection between sign and object; for example smoke as a sign of fire or a fingerprint as a sign of a person.
- Symbolic signs are those whose meanings have been established by conventions and custom; all words are symbols in the Peircean sense, as are the red and green lights at an intersection.

This distinction is an important one for semiotic analysis because it enables us to better understand different kinds of sign use in a particular production or a specific historical period or cultural manifestation of theatre. All forms of theatre use all three, because human beings communicate all the time with all three. More specifically, we can observe that iconic signs resemble broadly the concept of 'mimesis' because they are predicated on a relationship of recognizable similarity.

Indexical signs can be found in the dramatic text in as much as it uses personal pronouns and references to time and place such as 'there' or 'then', as well as in the gestures of the actors. Theatre makes extensive use of symbols in the Peircean sense. Apart from language itself, we find symbols in all forms of stylized theatre, which create symbolic signs continually: theatrical signs are by definition infinitely flexible and polyfunctional, as we shall see below.

Mobility and polyfunctionality

Every theatrical sign can be replaced by another sign or class of signs: for example, space by language, an object by a person or vice versa. This flexible quality testifies to the mobility and polyfunctionality of theatrical signs. Mobility means that signs on stage are by no means tied to their counterparts in the lived-in world. The Shakespearean stage almost certainly eschewed the concrete representation of place by pictorial representation, and made do with verbal description; pantomime represents spaces and objects by gesture. The polyfunctionality of theatrical signs refers to the fact that particular signs can actually change their function during a performance. A table can be a table but it can also be a mountain or a tunnel. One and the same actor can play different roles or, in the case of monodrama, perform all the roles in a play without causing confusion on the part of the audience. In general, one can say that realistic theatre (the type still largely encountered on the West End and Broadway) tends to limit the semiotic potentiality of mobility and polyfunctionality, whereas non-realistic theatrical styles (for example most classical Asian forms) rely heavily on them. Such distinctions are, however, always heuristic ones, and one must be careful not to reify them in absolute terms.

Codes and sign systems

Semiotic terminology, also in theatre semiotics, has been largely influenced by linguistics, the field where structuralist semiotics (Saussure) began. Theatre semiotic theory of the 1970s and 1980s embarked on translating and adapting concepts developed to describe and explain language for the theatre. As we shall see, this was ultimately a somewhat problematic process because it involved what could be called terminological metaphoricization. This creation of new metaphors under the guise of appearing scientific is one of the reasons semiotic theory was (and continues to be) so strongly resisted in some quarters of theatre studies.

The first and probably most widely used of these metaphors is the notion of code. In semiotics, a code is usually understood to be a kind of system or set of rules that controls the use of signs so that they can be understood. Individual signs will make little sense if they are not regulated by a code. To understand a theatrical performance, we need, therefore, to be familiar with the code or codes being employed. Because of its medial complexity, it is clear that one cannot speak of a theatrical code in the singular, but only of many different codes that come together. Although the notion of code would suggest that it precedes and is more general than a particular work, some scholars have argued that individual productions in fact generate their own code, which the audience has to decipher in order to make sense of the production as a whole. Patrice Pavis differentiates between specific, non-specific and mixed codes (Pavis 1998: 53–4).

Specific codes would include, for example, the workings of realist theatre: actors embodying roles, the convention of the fourth wall, painted scenery, etc. Another example would be Japanese *Nô* theatre with its use of masks, the appearance of spirit figures and a specific movement style. Non-specific codes are those that exist outside the closed space of the theatrical performance, such as linguistic, psychological or ideological codes. They are part of every spectator's semiotic competence and are invariably brought to bear on the performance. Mixed codes are those that provide a relay between the first two types in performance. Theatrical performance is, in fact, dependent on the interplay of the two types. In some respects, it could be argued that the regularity implied by the notion of code contradicts the uniqueness and unrepeatability constituent of performance. One could say that in our contemporary understanding of innovation-driven theatre, we are less interested in the perfect realization than in the adaptations and alterations to the expected theatrical code(s).

Inventories and typologies

Is it possible to systematize theatrical signs in a structured way so that we can identify overarching categories? Building on the work of the Prague School, the Polish semiotician Tadeusz Kowzan was the first to attempt a systematization of theatrical signs (Kowzan 1968). His model was adapted and refined by later scholars (Elam 1980; Fischer-Lichte 1992), but not substantially changed. Table 2 is based on Kowzan but contains some slight modifications.

Table 2. Theatrical sign systems (after Kowzan 1968)

	Actor-related	Space-related
Visual	• facial signs • gestural signs • proxemic signs • makeup • hair • costume	• props • stage design • lighting
Auditive	• language • sound effects • music	• sound effects • music • language

According to Kowzan, theatrical signs are either actor- or space-related. That is, they either emanate from the actor's body (and more precisely his/her voice), or they are generated by the stage itself: the setting, the lighting effects and the visual and auditive special effects. Whereas Kowzan regards space-related signs as belonging to the visual component of theatre, as shown in Table 2 they are also part of the auditory channel because space is often represented by linguistic means or by sound effects. Theatrical signs also have a temporal quality and temporal distinctions.

Theatre semiotics can be considered the first major general theory of theatre that attempted to encompass all aspects of the medium, and not just one or two. While there have been innumerable attempts to theorize drama, theatre semiotics – at least in the 1970s and later – was centrally interested in accounting for the interplay of the many different signs at work in the performance. Its descriptive power is considerable, and semiotic terminology has certainly changed the way theatre studies speaks about performance. In its optimistic excesses, theatre semiotics tended towards over-systematicization and to the creation of a metaphorical vocabulary that was continually making a transfer from linguistic terms to non-verbal phenomena. Already in the 1960s, a leading French semiologist, Roland Barthes, designated the theatre 'a semiotically privileged object since its system is apparently original (polyphonic) compared to that of language (which is linear)' (Barthes 1972: 261). This would suggest that the insights and theories derived from linguistics cannot be simply applied one-to-one to theatre. Theatre is, semiotically speaking, a special case. It is not surprising, then, that semiotic theory was confronted by critiques from different quarters that have also had a productive and invigorating influence on theatre theory.

Poststructuralism and psychoanalysis

Poststructuralism emerged in French philosophy in the 1960s at a time when the very movement it critiques – structuralism – was establishing itself as a dominant school of thought throughout the humanities and social sciences. 'Poststructuralism' is a somewhat vague term covering a varied array of thinkers and theories who are unified, however, in their critique of structuralism as it had been developed in linguistics (Ferdinand de Saussure and A. J. Greimas), cultural and literary analysis (Roland Barthes) and social anthropology (Claude Lévi-Strauss). On the one hand, poststructuralism retains a close connection with structuralism, as it often develops its own theories in dialogue with and critique of the former. On the other hand, it branches off in many different directions and is diametrically opposed to structuralism in the way it argues and develops ideas. If structuralism attempts to create an almost science-like denotative 'objective' language, poststructuralism delights in metaphor, paradox and sometimes even wilful obfuscation (which can make it often extremely difficult to read).

In the field of theatre theory, the first impulses come from the French philosophers Jacques Derrida (1930–2004) and Jean-François Lyotard (1924–1998). Derrida's contribution to theatre theory is based chiefly on two essays dealing with Antonin Artaud, published in 1966 and collected in the volume *Writing and Difference* ([1968] 1978). The most cited of these is 'The Theatre of Cruelty and the Closure of Representation' in which Derrida interprets Artaud's famous attacks on Western psychological drama not only in terms of a manifesto for a theatre of the future but also as a fundamental critique of representation itself. He is more interested in the paradox inherent in Artaud's conception of theatre that he terms the 'closure of representation'. Derrida argues that Artaud's repeated calls for a new type of theatre of immediate and visceral experience reflect an ultimately fruitless search for a theatre of 'pure presence'. The search is pointless because theatre is predicated on repetition and, hence, re-presentation: the achievement of pure presence would mean the end of theatre. Derrida's argument is ultimately a philosophical one, but its relevance to theatre theory is evident because it demarcates an aesthetic borderline that much contemporary performance art and postdramatic theatre has explored: the move from representation to presentation, from mere repetition of a role to the presence of the human body as a phenomenological experience.

Lyotard's ideas on theatre theory are formulated in direct opposition to semiotics. In a famous essay entitled 'La dent, la paume' ('The Tooth, the Palm') (1973), he challenged the relevance of the semiotic model of the sign as a useful means for analyzing theatrical performances.[1] Like Derrida, Lyotard takes Artaud as his point of departure to critique Western psychological theatre:

> Silencing the body through the theatre of the playwright, a form of theatre dear to middle-class Europe of the 19th century, is nihilistic; but making it speak in a vocabulary and a syntax of mime, songs, dances, as does the Noh, is another way of annihilating it: a body 'entirely' transparent, skin and flesh of the bone that is the spirit, intact from any pulsional movement, event, opacity.   (Cited in Pavis 1981: 80)

Lyotard regards Artaud's interest in Asian theatre as a compromise on the way to a genuinely 'pulsational', 'libidinal' theatre because it replaces the dominant language of psychological theatre with the 'hieroglyphs' of mime and dance. Lyotard posits instead an 'energetic theatre' *ex negativo* by stating what it is not, and argues for a 'generalized desemiotics' based on the notion of the event, the singular moment of presence. Instead of a semiotic system predicated on the idea of substitution by representation, Lyotard imagines a theatre of energy streams and libidinal displacements. Ultimately, it is not entirely clear whether Lyotard's ideas are intended as a way of looking at theatre or as a manifesto for a theatre to come.

Lyotard's interest in 'libidinal displacements' makes explicit reference to a key concept of psychoanalysis, a tradition of thought that occupies a central place in poststructuralism, thanks to the influence of the French psychoanalytic theorist Jacques Lacan (1901–81). His contribution to psychoanalysis was to combine Freudian concepts with Saussure's semiotic terminology in order to construct a model of the human unconscious that is structured like language. Lacan's thought is extremely complex, and his writing frustratingly opaque, but he has elaborated concepts or terms that have found their way into theatre theory.

Although Lacan expressed little or no interest in the theatre (he did write on literature and art), his ideas generated keen interest in many disciplines, including theatre and performance studies. The most famous Lacanian concept is the 'mirror stage', which in English translation has a fortuitous theatrical connotation that the French original ('le stade du miroir') lacks. According to Lacan, the decisive stage in early child development is when the young child recognizes itself in a mirror for the first time. Before this moment, the child lived in a prelinguistic, libidinal state. The self-perception in the mirror coincides with language acquisition (six to eight months). The theatrical resonance of the mirror stage did not remain unnoticed. The mirror as a theatrical metaphor is at least as old as Shakespeare (see Hamlet's speech to the players in act 3 scene 1), and has been invoked repeatedly as a way of conceptualizing the way the stage *reflects* the world. It is at the heart of most mimetic theories that explore the relationship between the world and its representation on stage, and between the representations and the perceptions of the spectators. As far as the latter are concerned (the stage–spectator relationship), Lacan's psychoanalytic theory can provide an interesting explanation for understanding the power of the stage. If, as Lacan claims, desire is driven by a continual perception of lack, the subjects represented on stage could provide a whole set of possible gendered identifications for the desiring ego of the spectator.

Lacan's ideas were intensively discussed within feminism and gender theory. It is not possible to draw clear lines of distinction between poststructuralism, psychoanalysis and the gender theory emerging from it. One should also be careful not to conflate feminism and gender theory, although they are clearly inter-related. Theories that developed in the wake of subversive feminist theatre and performance art were mainly concerned with deconstructing and reversing what was deemed a normative male gaze (Reinelt and Roach 1992: 386). This psychoanalytically inflected theory originated in cinema studies to describe the dynamics of the gaze in Hollywood cinema (Mulvey [1975] 1986), but has been applied to theatrical performance as well (Case 1988; Diamond 1997).

Phenomenology

Strictly and chronologically speaking, phenomenological theatre theory should not come after poststructuralism, because it is based on philosophical thinking developed around the end of the nineteenth century by Edmund Husserl, and developed throughout the twentieth century. Phenomenological and poststructuralist theatre theories share, however, a common critique of semiotics.

Both display an interest in those aspects of theatre and performance that seem to elude semiotic classification as signs. In its early form, phenomenology was interested in describing the 'essence' of experience as perceived by the consciousness. It does this by looking at phenomena from different perspectives and by stripping away non-essential characteristics or traits. What phenomenology does, philosophically, is to place particular emphasis on the perceiving subject or consciousness. The act of perception itself can receive as much attention as the object being perceived and described. Where poststructuralism diverges radically from early phenomenology is in its radical rejection of and deconstruction of essentialism, i.e. the idea that it is possible to grasp an essence of anything.

Phenomenology applied to theatre re-emerges in the 1980s as a corrective to theatre semiotics, which had by then begun to dominate theatre theory. Bert O. States's short book, *Great Reckonings in Little Rooms: On the Phenomenology of Theatre* (1985), signalled a re-evaluation of phenomenology for the theatre. His point of departure is a critique of the mimesis-based principle of referentiality in theatre. This principle is predicated on the idea that (theatrical) art, because it is always imitation, must by definition refer to something absent, something beyond itself. In this observation, he follows similar arguments articulated in poststructuralist critiques of the Western artistic tradition: 'Theatre becomes a passageway for a cargo of meanings being carried back to society (after artistic refinement) via the language of signs' (States 1985: 6). States takes his lead from the French philosopher Maurice Merleau-Ponty, who remains a seminal influence on modern phenomenological thinking. Perception, in the theatre and elsewhere, cannot be divided up into analytic categories. It is a holistic act that bears little resemblance to the typologies and sign categories developed by semiotics.

To illustrate his phenomenological method, States identifies a category of phenomena in the theatre that appears to resist semiotization in the sense of being signs of signs. Clocks, children and animals are, according to States, things that contain a high degree of *en soi* (Merleau-Ponty's term for the intrinsic quality of things). They are what they are, and seem to resist being made into signs standing for something else. Concepts such as 'atmosphere' also defy semiotic analysis. They can only be described phenomenologically, not semiotically. States does not, however, reject semiotics outright. On the contrary, he acknowledges the important work done in theatre semiotics and proposes instead a 'binocular' vision. It combines a semiotic perspective, used in order to describe the semantic aspects of a production, with a phenomenological gaze, which would tend to focus on the direct experiential aspects of the performance.

This combination of perspectives is essential if one wants to begin to understand much of contemporary postdramatic theatre, but also older performance art. Performances that seem to employ things on stage for their material qualities, and not to generate meanings or to stand in for something else, are working in a phenomenological mode.

Cultural materialism

Today, the term 'cultural materialism' in theatre studies is mainly associated with provocative reinterpretations of Shakespearean texts, both in historical and contemporary contexts, and with the writings of the critic Raymond Williams (Williams 1980). To understand this approach from a theoretical point of view, it is necessary to look briefly at the origins of the term 'materialism'.

The cultural materialist approach to art is primarily influenced by Marxist philosophy, which identifies economic material factors as the determining forces shaping society and hence also artistic production and reception. The roots of Marxist thinking in turn lie in eighteenth-century materialist philosophy, which argues that spiritual and intellectual phenomena have concrete physical, material causes. The materialist approach to art proceeds from the idea that art and culture form a kind of structure on top of the material, economic foundation of society. If the economic and political struggles taking place influence all human interaction, then this must be true for artistic expression as well. At its simplest (and most reductive), a Marxist view of art proposes a direct, vertically conceived relationship between economic structures (base) and artistic activity (superstructures). The big question remains: how does this relationship express itself? What is the link between impressionist painting or anti-naturalistic theatre and late-nineteenth-century capitalism? Because early materialist theory could only offer very partial answers to such questions, it concentrated its attention, in the second half of the twentieth century, increasingly on the realm of ideology.

A key figure in this area was Antonio Gramsci (1891–1937), the Italian Marxist thinker active in the 1920s and 1930s. Gramsci argued that in order to attain hegemony, i.e. political control in capitalist societies, the capitalist system is actively dependent on the sphere of culture (i.e. art, books, theatre) in order to subtly reinforce the ideology of capitalism. Gramsci's theory of hegemony led to both a reassessment of culture within Marxist thought – far from being a somewhat irrelevant attribute of the superstructure, it could be seen as crucial to the class struggle – and to the development of a much more complex approach to the way culture affects ideology.

A central sphere of interest for Marxist and cultural materialist theory is the question of commodification. Capitalism can make anything into goods to be bought and sold; even social relations are reduced to an exchange relation in a market place of supply and demand. Fredric Jameson, one of the most influential and sophisticated contemporary neo-Marxist theorists, explains the difference between modernism and postmodernism as, among other things, a difference in attitude to the commodity. Whereas modernist art attempted to critique and transcend the commodification of art, postmodernism more or less embraced or at least acquiesced to the dynamics of commodification, as Warhol's *Campbell's Soup Cans* so clearly demonstrates. The apparent victory of commodification over all spheres of life marks postmodernity's reliance on the 'cultural logic of late capitalism' (Jameson 1991).

Any theatre that needs to assert itself in the market place, from Elizabethan theatre onwards, is imbricated in capitalist modes of production and negotiation with the 'market'. A cultural materialist approach to a text or production, especially if it is of a classical author, will follow, according to Barry (2002), three main strategies:

(1)   The literary text will be analysed in such a way as to enable us to recover its lost histories; that is, the context of political and economic power relations from which it emerged. In the case of Elizabethan theatre, this will invariably include the monarchy, the emerging capitalist system and England's dominance as a maritime power.

(2)   Readings will foreground those elements in the work's present transmission and contextualizing that, for ideological reasons, caused those histories to be lost in the first place (e.g. the 'heritage' industry's packaging of Shakespeare in terms of history-as-pageant, national bard, cultural icon, and so on).

(3)   Readings use any combination of methodological approaches to the text that will enable hidden oppositional, subversive or even revolutionary positions to emerge, in order to fracture the previous dominance of conservative social, political and religious assumptions, in Shakespeare criticism in particular.

Although developed in the context of Shakespearean studies, cultural materialist approaches to theatre can be applied to many other contemporary theatrical contexts as well. They may concentrate on the large-scale global theatre production scene of Andrew Lloyd Webber and Disney (the so-called 'McTheatre') but may also investigate the inter-relationships between smaller-scale theatre and cultural festivals, and the political and economic alliances (sponsorship) they forge in order to function. Whatever their object of investigation, cultural materialists tend to be highly suspicious of approaches to performances that are only interested in 'artistic' questions.

Theatricality and performance theory

All the theories surveyed above define their object in terms of texts enacted on stages before an audience prepared to suspend its disbelief and enter into the fiction of role-playing. This model is also applicable to certain non-European theatre forms – such as Japanese *Nô, Kabuki,* Chinese opera or Indian *Kathakali* – that have long been included in the purview of theatre studies. In the theories to be discussed in this section, we will be looking at an extension of the concept of 'theatre' to include forms of structured behaviour such as rituals, festivals or ceremonies. One could say that any kind of 'staged reality' is related in some way to theatre and performance, and is therefore a subject of theatre theory. The oxymoron 'staged reality' is intentional because central areas of activity such as politics or news communication are making increasing use of staging techniques we would normally associate with putting on a play. By extending the notion of theatre to encompass such phenomena, theatre studies is brought into dialogue with other disciplines such as anthropology, cultural studies and media studies.

'Theatricality' is a term that was first used in the early nineteenth century in its current nominalized form, but in its adjectival form it is much older (Davis and Postlewait 2003: 3). In the eighteenth century, to term something 'theatrical' could signify one of at least three things:

(1) It could mean having the concentration, dramatic excitement and visual spectacle of a theatrical performance; this usage was even extended to places and landscapes.
(2) It could emphasize the moral category of spectatorship in social life as outlined by the philosopher Adam Smith with his category of the 'impartial spectator'.
(3) To deem something theatrical in this period – and this still holds true today, although with varying degrees of emphasis in different cultures and languages – was to equate it with second-handness, deceit, and duplicity.

All three definitions make clear that theatricality is primarily a 'mode of perception' (Burns 1972). This means that things and actions, peoples and places are not in themselves theatrical – they possess no inherent theatricality – but rather are rendered as such by a combination of aesthetic conventions and discursive practices. They in turn determine around which phenomena we place the 'frame' of theatrical apprehension. Thus, theatricality can be understood as both a *discursive* and *performative* practice by means of which theatre (as an institution and aesthetic form) intersects with wider cultural contexts.

Recent discussions have documented the astonishing semantic breadth of the term, which has prompted scholars to question whether it can be considered a concept in the narrower sense at all. As Tracy Davis and Thomas Postlewait note: 'the domain of theatricality cannot be located within any single definition, period, or practice'. This does not mean, however, that it is 'meaningless'. On the contrary, the editors point to theatricality's 'protean flexibility that lends richness to both historical study and theoretical analysis' (Davis and Postlewait 2003: 3–4). When examined more closely, it will become clear that this 'protean' quality, the fact that the set of elements identifying theatricality changes over time, is in keeping with the changing nature of the theatrical medium itself. Just as the theatres of the eighteenth and twentieth centuries differ in many respects, so too is the theatricality of the eighteenth century not necessarily commensurate with that of the twentieth. Theatricality is an interdisciplinary cultural, rather than a narrowly aesthetic, perspective on a wide range of phenomena. The increasing, almost inflationary, use of the term in current discourse suggests that human intercourse, especially under the influence of the mass-media, is being permeated by modes of perception we would in the past have normally restricted to performances in the theatre. It is especially observable in the realm of politics, where all political activity seems to be stage-managed for television cameras.

The flipside of the theoretical discussion on theatricality is its putative opposite: *authenticity*. If theatricality appears to cast ontological doubt on people or situations, then by definition we would seem to assume that a condition of authenticity must be the ideal state to be returned to. This term too has engendered much controversy for the very same reasons. Can things or people be authentic? If so, what are the distinguishing characteristics? Authenticity has not played a significant role in traditional theatre theory for very obvious reasons: if theatrical performance is always based on signs of signs, on representation and imitation, its very *raison d'être* would seem to stand in direct contradiction to such a notion. This is changing, however, particularly in the area of performance art and its successor, postdramatic theatre. Here we find a growing tendency to integrate objects and persons who seem to retain the aura of the authentic (children, animals, mentally disabled people), or intergrate authenticity spatially (a move outside the theatre to, semiotically speaking, 'uncontaminated' sites (see Chap. 3)). In earlier performance art, some artists used self-inflicted wounds as a sign of 'reality'. There are also genres of theatre, such as tourist performance, that require an authentic 'ethnic' body to be taken seriously (Balme 2007). On closer inspection, it would seem that theatricality and authenticity, far from being opposites, are actually laminated together and should be regarded as variations of the same cultural symptom: an increasing awareness of the constructedness and mediatedness of so much experience.

Closely related to theatricality, but much wider in scope, is *performance theory*. The concept of 'performance' lies at the heart of the new discipline performance studies, which, although not the subject of this book (as explained in the introduction), is so closely intertwined with theatre studies that it cannot always be neatly separated out. In its broadest sense, performance is a norm of all human activity. The main difficulty is to discern what is not performance and hence demarcate a circumscribed set of activities to investigate them – the precondition for any discipline. Part of the problem lies in the remarkable semantic flexibility of the word itself in the English language. Other European languages require at least three quite separate terms to encompass even the central meanings potentially available to the English word in its various forms as a verb, noun or adjective.

The programmatic foundation for performance theory was outlined in 1966 by Richard Schechner in his essay 'Approaches to Theory/Criticism' (reproduced in Schechner 2003). Schechner proposed a concept of performance transcending text-based drama and embracing the formal relations between play, games, sports, theatre and ritual. In the following years, Schechner demonstrated in numerous publications the interdisciplinary potential of such a concept. The definition of performance within the broader parameters of the social sciences implied a departure from the aesthetic and historical paradigms that had until then dominated theatre studies. In this understanding, dramatic theatre is just one possible manifestation of performance.

The move towards performance and performance theory can be seen as a clear critique of the semiotic paradigm outlined above. The performance scholar Dwight Conquergood diagnosed in the late 1980s a fundamental shift in the humanities and social sciences from 'viewing the world as text to the world as performance (Conquergood 1991: 190). Viewing the world as text is a direct reference to the above-mentioned tendency of semiotics to regard all phenomena within a textual paradigm with a whole complex set of consequences. Texts are legible, replete with meaning and basically immutable. Viewing the world as a performance, on the other hand, implies a shift of emphasis away from referentiality, immutability and legibility to ephemerality and spectatorship. The paradigm shift, following Conquergood, can be rendered as a set of oppositions:

World as text	World as performance
production	reception
products	processes
fixed meanings	dynamic changes
emphasis on space	emphasis on time
scholar as decoder of meaning	scholar as observer of processes

In the early phase of its development, performance theory had close affinities with cultural anthropology and sociology. Seminal texts and concepts include the notion of 'cultural performances', first advanced by Milton Singer in his study of modernization in India (Singer 1959). These could include weddings, funerals, festivals and ceremonies. Another influential anthropologist was Victor Turner, whose concept of 'social drama' and studies of ritual further strengthened ties between cultural anthropology and performance theory. Another important theorist of performance was the sociologist Erving Goffman, who repeatedly used theatrical metaphors to describe social behaviour.

A second branch of theoretical enquiry has emerged from what could be broadly termed 'performance art'. New genres of performance – such as happenings, Fluxus and, later, the work of feminist performance artists – created aesthetic phenomena that were initially inexplicable in terms of theatre theoretical terminology. Michael Kirby provided perhaps the first serious attempt to theorize the development in his anthology *Happenings: An Illustrated Anthology* (1965). Kirby defines 'happenings' as a type of performance that dispenses with a matrix of time, place or character, in contrast to traditional theatre that requires such a matrix in order to distinguish its fictional world from that of the lived-in world (Kirby 1965: 17). Happenings work with time, place and human beings, but their relationship to one another is of a different order; they become 'materials' of the performance, not substitutions for something else. In this field of artistic activity, performance is almost equated with action – simply 'doing something' rather than re-enactment.

By reducing the human aspect of performance to its very basic component, performance artists such as John Cage and Alan Kaprow were experimenting with concepts being developed in philosophy at exactly the same time. Performance in the sense of 'to do' or 'carry out' is a fundamental concept of speech act theory, which has also been integrated into performance theory, although its origins lie in the philosophy of language. In a groundbreaking series of lectures collected in the book *How to Do Things with Words* (1962), the British philosopher John L. Austin (1911–60) argued that language does not just make true or false statements about the world (so-called 'constatives'), but there are types of utterances that can affect or change it. To utter the words 'I do' during a wedding ceremony actually changes the relationship and legal status of the two people involved. Even the words 'I promise' or 'I swear' carry with them social effects that can have long-lasting consequences. These types of statements Austin called 'performative utterances'. He later expanded the constative/performative dualism into a tripartite model whereby he replaced the term 'performative' with 'illocutionary'. Illocutionary utterances or speech acts encompass all situations that imply an action when saying them. This is a much broader category than the original performatives because it includes a whole range of speech forms such as orders, implorations, exhortations, requests, etc. A special feature of performatives (to stay with the original term), and one of the reasons they are of interest to theatre and performance theory, is that they usually only come into existence when actually spoken, often in the first person. Performatives such as promises, oaths, christenings, sentencings, ship-launchings, etc. have to be seen and heard to be done: like theatre, they need an audience of at least one to function. There are, of course, exceptions to this – one can make a promise in writing – but the general rule pertains.

Speech-act theory has been adapted by theatre and performance studies in a number of contexts. Conventional dramatic dialogue has been analysed in terms of speech act theory because it would seem to offer a particular type of language, which is almost exclusively illocutionary (Elam 1980). The ideal of dramatic dialogue in which every utterance in some way affects the action would, in theory at least, give credence to such an assessment. More importantly, though, the shift from thinking about language in terms of what it does to and in the world, rather than simply referring to it, has focused attention much more sharply on speech in performance rather than language as conserved in a play.

The concepts 'performative' and 'performativity' have now permeated throughout the humanities, and are not just restricted to theatre and performance studies. An extremely influential intervention has been in the area of gender studies, and in particular the work of Judith Butler. Although philosophical in orientation, Judith Butler's books *Gender Trouble: Feminism and the Subversion of Identity* (1990), *Bodies that Matter: On the Discursive Limits of 'Sex'* (1993) and *Excitable Speech: A Politics of the Performative* (1997) develop a concept of the performative derived from speech-act theory that has been particularly influential within theatre and performance studies. Butler adapts the notion of performativity to rethink the whole sex/gender distinction. Opposing the idea that gender is a natural biological given, she argues that it is constituted by performative acts: we 'do' gender rather than 'are' a gender. Performativity implies repetition, and the performativity of gender is a largely invisible process of learned, repeated behaviours that force the individual into the cultural mould of what Butler terms 'compulsory heterosexuality'. She asks: 'In what senses, then, is gender an act? As in other ritual social dramas, the action of gender requires a performance that is repeated' (Butler 1990: 140). The important and radical implication of this statement is that if gender identity is performative rather than simply expressive of a predetermined 'essence', then it can be changed.

Butler's writings have occasioned much controversy, particularly in feminist circles where her ideas of 'performed' genders collided with more essentialist notions of female/male sexuality and gender. In theatre and performance studies, her ideas have been applied to a large body of performance work, particularly by women artists such as Karen Finley, who thematize directly the 'performativity' of gender.

Recent performance theory has moved in other directions as well. The semantic richness of the word stem 'perform' can be demonstrated by simply typing the word 'performance' into Google. The results will include references not only to the theatre and entertainment but probably also to automotive and software engineering, job performance and big business. In an innovative book entitled *Perform or Else: From Discipline to Performance* (2001), performance scholar Jon McKenzie traces three paradigmatic shifts in the concept of 'performance': cultural, organizational and technological performance. McKenzie's point of departure is the economic-technological use of the term encapsulated by his title. If, following Foucault (see Chap. 6), discipline was the paramount paradigm of the eighteenth and nineteenth centuries, then performance has become its successor in the twentieth and twenty-first centuries as an 'onto-historical formation of power and knowledge' (McKenzie 2001:18). McKenzie contends that performance is the new 'mode of power' that underlies both our educational and economic systems. This stimulating aspect of the theory lies in the interconnections that McKenzie documents between the apparently disparate realism of theatre and management studies.

Further reading

A good general introduction to the questions covered in this chapter is Mark Fortier's *Theory/Theatre: An Introduction* (2002). Fortier is able to discuss in much more detail most of the concepts touched on in this chapter. Also recommended is Marvin Carlson's *Theories of the Theatre: A Historical and Critical Survey from the Greeks to the Present* (1984). The field of theatre semiotics has been well covered and can be accessed through a number of publications. Elam (1980; 2nd edn 2002) was the first introduction in English, and the first three chapters provide an excellent overview and in-depth discussion of key semiotic concepts and their application to theatre and drama. The chapters on dramatic logic and dramatic discourse are much more technical – even inaccessible – and appear now somewhat dated. An important update to the semiotics of drama and theatre is provided by Aston and Savona (1991), which avoids some of the obfuscation of Elam's text and extends semiotics into performance analysis. A key reference work for anyone dealing with semiotics is Patrice Pavis's *Dictionary of Theatre: Terms, Concepts, and Analysis* (1998), which provides lucid explanations of many of the difficult concepts and extended references. The various strands of post-semiotic theory, including cultural materialism, are well covered in Janelle Reinelt and Joseph Roach's collection of essays, *Critical Theory and Performance* (1992), especially in the editors' introductions to the different sections. The multi-faceted areas of performance theory can be explored in Carlson (1996), Schechner (2006), Bial (2007) and Loxley (2007).

Chapter 6

Theatre historiography

Until well into the 1960s, the terms 'theatre studies' and 'theatre history' were largely synonymous, because the first and major concern of the new subject was the theatrical past. Although today theatre history is by no means the exclusive field of teaching and research, historical study remains an important area of work for scholar and student alike. In this chapter, we shall explore the most important methods and research paradigms employed by theatre historians. We shall begin by identifying the principal sources employed by historians and then move on to discuss the different types of information they provide. In the second part of the chapter, we shall address the question of periodization, i.e. the way we can divide up theatre history into epochs and periods. The third and final part of the chapter will introduce and discuss recent theoretical approaches to theatre history, which in their most extreme positions question the very idea of theatre history itself. This focus on questions of theory and methodology means that we will not be looking at specific periods of theatre history (the Greeks, the Elizabethan period, etc.) but rather at the problems involved in the writing of it, which is technically called historiography.

What then does the theatre historian deal with? The answers to this question are as divergent as the approaches that can be followed. It is certainly not the task of the theatre historian to provide a seamless narrative of theatre productions in a given period. The approach will rather be determined by the way the historian views theatre itself in a particular period. Any form of historical research is informed by a set of (often not entirely conscious) preconceptions. One of these would be the definition of the object of study as, say, *aesthetic* in nature rather than *cultural* or *social*. (We have already pointed out that this distinction is an artificial one but it serves for the moment a heuristic, i.e. practical, function: see p. 2.) From this interest in aesthetic questions would probably follow that the historian might focus on past performances and productions, i.e. the theatrical 'work of art'.

It was the German scholar Max Herrmann (1865–1942), the founder of modern European theatre studies, who declared that the reconstruction of past performances should be the main object of scientific study. In his major work, *The History of German Theatre in the Middle Ages and the Renaissance* (1914), Herrmann described the goal of the theatre historian to be 'essentially the restitution of lost achievements until they appear before us with the vividness of a palpable image' (1914: 7).[1] This is indeed a bold programme, and means that the historian has to first obtain enough evidence and documentation to enable such a reconstruction. Herrmann's approaches were essentially philological and art historical in nature, drawing on the two dominant disciplines of his time.

Herrmann's goal leads us to the central question of all theatre studies, and not just theatre history: how can ephemeral phenomena of the past be captured and rendered suitable for aesthetic study of the kind envisaged by Herrmann? What documents can theatre historians draw on and how should they be studied?

Sources and reconstruction

It was, again, Max Herrmann who first provided a theoretical and systematic approach to theatre history within the framework of a method he termed 'reconstruction'. Although it is today a contested term, Herrmann meant that the theatre historian could, with sufficient source material at his or her disposal, visualize past theatre buildings and productions in enough detail that a physical reconstruction of a lost building, stage form or even of productions in historical style could be carried out. Apart from the academic gain of such an exercise, Herrmann imagined that such research could have immediate consequences for practical theatre. In *The History of German Theatre in the Middle Ages and the Renaissance*, he wrote:

> We set ourselves the task of making a theatrical performance of the past live again in such detail that, if the financial means were made available, one could indeed present it to a modern audience without fear of provoking offence. (Herrman 1914: 13)

The problematic and controversial nature of such an approach provoked criticism in Herrmann's own lifetime, and has continued ever since. Herrmann became embroiled in a dispute with another theatre historian over the reconstruction of the early Renaissance Mastersinger stage in Nuremberg's Church of St Martha. Although this controversy appears, with hindsight, to be fairly pointless and tangential to the concerns of modern theatre historians, the methods Herrmann developed and, above all, his systematization and critical approach to source material set standards for theatre-historiographical methodology.

Basing his work on Herrmann's initial categories, the German theatre scholar Dietrich Steinbeck has attempted a further systematization of sources (see Table 3). On one level, Steinbeck differentiates sources into two groups, which he terms 'direct' and 'indirect'. The former are directly involved with the production of theatre. These sources may include the theatre building or performance space; the stage and its machinery; costumes and masks. Indirect sources are those that report on a production such as reviews, letters, diary entries, etc. The second distinction he makes concerns the language of mediation. Language is meant here in a metaphorical sense. Steinbeck differentiates between

Table 3. Sources for theatre history

Direct	Indirect
objective	**meta-commentary**
theatre buildings	scenarios
performance space	reports of performances
stage	descriptions of actors in performance
stage machinery	minutes
parts of the set	yearbooks
costumes	almanachs
props	theatre reviews
masks	theatre periodicals
prompt books	letters
individual roles ('parts')	diaries and memoirs
director's copies	biographies
stage manager's copies	anecdotes
model sets	theatre novels
technical drawings	pamphlets
contracts, deeds, account books	theoretical writings
playbills	posters and playbills
	representations in visual art (theatre iconography)
meta-commentary	interviews
stage photos	
films and video recordings	**objective**
ground plans	scripts and dramas
costume and stage designs	music (piano and full scores)
	notated choreographies

'objective language' and 'meta-language'. Objective language is that employed with a minimal degree of reflection. A contract or a deed of ownership documents relatively directly certain facts pertaining to legal and economic questions. Sources containing meta-commentary are always one level removed from the object of description and thus contain a higher degree of reflective commentary.

The distinction between objective language and meta-language is an important one on a theoretical level because it throws light on the epistemological status of sources used, i.e. the kinds and status of knowledge they provide. It draws the theatre historian ineluctably into questions of reliability, the past 'as it really was' and similar contested issues. These are questions that concern all historical research, of course, and are not particular to theatre. Because of the ephemeral nature of the theatrical experience, however, they are particularly acute.

The importance and difficulty of such distinctions can be illustrated by looking at a playbill. Playbills are a particularly valuable and complex source for theatre historians. They were produced in huge numbers throughout the eighteenth and nineteenth centuries, where they provided the double function of theatre poster and programme. According to the taxonomy in Table 3, they belong primarily to the category of direct objective sources because they were, on one level at least, an integral part of the production process, in the sense that they usually give 'unmediated' information about the details of a performance: time, place, names of performers, synopsis, etc. In this sense, they provide a wealth of empirical data. A playbill demonstrates that a typical theatrical evening in the first half of the nineteenth century consisted of four or five different items and performative genres: a tragedy, a song, an interlude (a short play), a highland fling and a farce. Playbills document that theatre had not yet separated out into different institutions for different genres. Playbills, as our example from the New Theatre Royal in Glasgow in 1840 (Plate 6) indicates, usually included meta-commentary in the form of self-laudatory critical responses: 'received with shouts of laughter and applause'. Apart from performance-related data, playbills were often used by theatre managers for a variety of communicative functions ranging from self-promotion to audience regulation. In this case, the playbill announces in detail the reopening of the theatre and includes a form of promotional advertising for the local tradesmen involved in the building. The playbill also advertises for doormen; it contains information of a regulatory nature ('children in arms are not admitted and no smoking allowed in the galleries'); and in the 'Notice to the Frequenters of the Boxes', it describes an innovation to provide better circulation of air. Playbills invariably include information on pricing and, in this case, we learn that it was common practice to be admitted later at a reduced price.

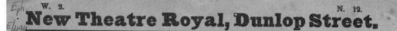

New Theatre Royal, Dunlop Street.

Continued Success! Crowded Houses—and roars of laughter and applause!!!

The PUBLIC is respectfully informed that this THEATRE, being COMPLETED, has now

Opened for the Season.

In announcing the Completion of this important and hazardous undertaking, the Proprietor wishes as much as possible to abstain from the too hacknied custom of "puffing," or lavishing on his exertions that praise which the magnitude of this speculation might warrant, the Public alone will judge of the efforts which have been made for their Accommodation, it may not, however, be too much to say, that this Edifice has been erected with a splendour and magnificence (regardless of cost), and will bear comparison, it is presumed, with any thing of a Theatrical nature in this country. The Manager has, on many occasions, found his exertions responded to by the Citizens of Glasgow, and has not thought it too much, at least, a third time, to peril his capital and "hazard the die," in the service of that Public who have so frequently honoured his exertions with patronage and support.

THE BUILDING,

From Designs by Mr. W Spence, Architect, is Erected by Mr. W. Brown. The JOINER WORK, by Archibald Edmiston, Esq. The PLUMBER DEPARTMENT, by Mr. Archd. Ferguson. The SLATER WORK, by Mr. S. Wilson. The PILLARS and other CASTINGS, from the Foundry of Mr. W. Gray. The PLASTER and ORNAMENTAL STUCCO WORK, by Mr. J. Caird. The GAS FITTINGS, by Messrs. Andrew Liddell & Co. The CHANDELIERS, by Mr. Alexander Browne. The ROYAL ARMS, over the Stage, and ORNAMENTAL CARVING, by Mr. Murray. The STAINED GLASS WINDOW, in Front of the Building, by Mr W. Cairney. The DECORATIVE PAINTING, by Messrs. Michael Bogle & Co. The whole of the Scenery, by Mr. Dudgeon, of that Firm. The IMITATION MARBLE, PILASTERS, and COLUMNS, by Monsieur Victor Bourgeot, Decorative Painter from Paris. The MACHINERY of the STAGE, upon the improved Principles of the Theatres Royal, Drury Lane, Covent Garden, and Liverpool, by Mr. W. Harvey, and numerous Assistants. The whole under the entire direction of Mr. ALEXANDER.

THE COMPANY,

So far as the superintendence of this important undertaking would permit, has been selected with the utmost care, from the principal Theatres in the United Kingdom, but as this is a portion of the undertaking negociated for at a distance, the Manager does not warrant with the same freedom as that contracted for on the spot, and which has been submitted to his judgment, he can only say, that in point of numbers it is Efficient, and complete in many Departments, and whatever is found dissatisfactory will be changed or improved, according to trial and the opinion of the true unprejudiced patrons of the Drama in this City.

This Evening, Saturday, March 28, 1840,

Will be presented, the favourite Tragedy of,

Jane Shore :

Or, The Unfortunate Favourite.

Lord Hastings, Mr. CHARLES PITT—Duke of Glo'ster, Mr. ALEXANDER—Dumont, Mr. J. W. BENSON—Belmour, Mr. HOLMES.
Sir William Catesby, Mr. CLIFTON—Sir Richard Ratcliffe, Mr. BECKETT—Lord Derby, Mr. CHAPMAN—Lord Lovaos, Mr. BELFOUR.
Earl of Pembroke, Mr. COVENEY—Porter, Mr. J. NEWTON—Officer, Mr. ARMSTRONG.
Jane Shore, Mrs. FISHER—Alicia, Mrs. J. NEWTON.

END OF THE PLAY,
A FAVOURITE SONG, BY MISS J. COVENEY.

After which, for the third time this season, the very popular Interlude, in one Act, entitled

STATE SECRETS:

OR, THE TAILOR OF TAMWORTH.

Received on Tuesday evening, with shouts of laughter and applause.
Gregory Thimblewell, the Tailor of Tamworth, Mr. ALEXANDER.
Master Hugh Neville, (an officer serving in the army of the Parliament, commanded by General, Fairfax,) Mr. HOLMES.
Calverton Hal, a Cavalier belonging to the army of Prince Rupert, Mr. BELLAIR.
Humphrey Hedgehog, a wealthy Miller, and Landlord of the Black Bull Inn, Tamworth, Mr. J. NEWTON.
Robert, Son of Gregory Thimblewell, Mr. BECKETT—Soldiers, Peasants, &c.
Maude Thimblewell, (the Tailor's Wife), Mrs. CLIFTON—Lettie, Daughter of Hedgehog, Mrs. J. NEWTON.

IN THE COURSE OF THE EVENING,
THE HIGHLAND FLING, BY MISS H. COVENEY.

To conclude with, for the second time this season, the laughable Farce of,

ENGLISH,
Irish, and Scotch.

Received last night with loud laughter and applause.
Patrick O'Shocknessy, Mr. J. DALY—Donald, Mr. ALEXANDER—Timothy Clod, Mr. J. NEWTON—Captain Charleton, Mr. J. W. BENSON.
Charles Fairfield, Mr. HOLMES—Old Drovoly, Mr. FISHER—Young Drovoly, Mr. BECKETT.
Dick, Mr. CHAPMAN—John, Mr. BELFOUR—Gardner, Mr. COVENEY—Servant, Mr. ARMSTRONG.
Maria Wilburton, Mrs. J. NEWTON—Louisa, Drovoly, with a Song, Miss J. COVENEY—Peggy, Mrs. ARMSTRONG.

On MONDAY, Massinger's admired Play of A New Way to Pay Old Debts, after which Mr and Mrs White. To Conclude with, False and True; Or, The Irishman in Naples.

☞ In preparation, a New Farce entitled THE HAPPY MAN, which will shortly be produced, with various other Novelties.

WANTED,

Two active, steady, respectable Persons, as CHECKERS at the Doors. Apply to the Manager.

Tickets and Places for the Boxes may be had of Mr Muir, at the Box Office of the Theatre, from 11 till 3 o'clock.
Pass-out Checks not Transferable—Children in arms not Admitted to any part of the Theatre—and no Smoking allowed in the Galleries on any account.

PRICES:—

FIRST PRICE.—Lower Boxes, 4s. 0d.—Upper Do., 3s. 6d.—Pitt, 2s. 6d.—First Gallery, 1s. 6d.—Second Do., 1s. 0d.
SECOND DO.—Lower Boxes, 2s. 6d.—Upper Do., 2s. 0d.—Pitt, 1s. 6d.—First Gallery, 1s. 0d.—Second Do., 6s. 6d.
SECOND PRICE AT A QUARTER BEFORE NINE O'CLOCK.

☞ NOTICE TO THE FREQUENTERS OF THE BOXES.

This part of the Theatre has been constructed on a novel and it is hoped improved principle, the backs have sliding panels, which on a night when the Theatre is crowded the Manager has reserved to himself the power of opening, for the purpose of allowing the heated air to escape, and of giving accommodation to any persons wishing to occupy the lobbies. This inclination is considered necessary in order that no complaint may be made against such privilege, at the same time it is respectfully submitted to public approval and hoped will be found an improvement rather than an inconvenience to any person frequenting that part of the Theatre.

☞ The following Certificate from the Lord DEAN OF GUILD, is respectfully submitted to the Public:—
Having again considered this Petition, with the Report of Mr. Robert Taylor, Mason and Builder, and John Scott, Wright and Builder, Find it established by the said Report, that the NEW THEATRE, in Dunlop Street, lately erected by the Petitioner, has been Constructed in a Sufficient Manner; and that it may be Opened for the Reception of the Public, with complete Safety to the Lieges, and particularly to the persons frequenting the same; and declare and decern accordingly.

(Signed)   JAS. BROWNE, D. G.

P. Mackenzie & Co., Printers.

On a more abstract level, we can see playbills as a crucial medium regulating the relations between theatre and the public sphere or, in other words, between the inside and the outside, between art and its social context. They provide ocular proof of the complex functions the institution of theatre fulfilled in towns and cities. Theatres were one of the few genuine public spheres (outside of churches, inns and racetracks) where large numbers of people could congregate on a regular basis.

As the example of the playbill demonstrates, the problems posed by sources are not just questions of interpretation but also of epistemology. This means we have to distinguish, or least be aware of, the type of knowledge provided and created by them. Because a performance is always irretrievably lost the moment it has finished, any attempt to study or 'recreate' it, even if the source material is abundant, implies that we can only have access to it via conceptual constructs that we ourselves create. A phenomenologist would differentiate between an *intentional schema* created by the artists involved (directors, designers, actors, etc.) and a *presumed form* resulting from the concretizations of the spectators. These distinctions derive from phenomenology (see Chap. 5). One could also speak of levels of production and reception. Irrespective of how we term these levels or perspectives, theatre historical research should attempt to come to grips with them. If there is any one question on which theatre scholars agree, it is that one should see theatre as the connection between aesthetic production on the one hand and spectatorial concretization on the other.

Even if the notion of complete reconstruction on the level envisaged by Herrmann remained utopian, it nevertheless had far-reaching consequences. It spurred intensive research into the theatrical past, and increased greatly the amount of source material available to historians. We can certainly say that today we have a 'palpable image' of Greek, medieval and Elizabethan theatres in their architectural forms and in their epochal characteristics. Our knowledge of specific performances is, however, practically non-existent. At best one might be able to reconstruct an ideal type.

Over the past decades, reconstruction has fallen into disfavour. At its most simplistic, it did little more than collect documents and material. This became known as the 'positivist' method (see below). Although reconstructionism has a bad press among many theatre historians, it is alive and well in various forms of theatre practice and theatre research. The most famous example is

---

Plate 6. Nineteenth-century playbill for the New Theatre Royal, Dunlop Street, Glasgow. The playbill is for performances that took place at the New Theatre Royal, Dunlop Street, Glasgow, on the evening of Saturday 28 March 1840.

without doubt the rebuilding of Shakespeare's Globe Theatre on the South Bank in London. The architects and scholars involved in this ten-year project expended considerable time and money 'reconstructing' the theatre in Elizabethan terms. Not only that, but the building is supposed to provide the necessary requirements for authentic period productions, again a dream of Max Herrmann not achieved in his lifetime.

Reconstructionist projects are also under way using computer-based techniques. The Theatron Project is devoted to providing advanced multi-media teaching and research material documenting the history of European theatre. This project makes use of a virtual reality interface to access a great many 3D architectural models of major European historic theatres linked to supporting textual and graphic databases (see www.theatron.org – last accessed 17 February 2008).

The Virtual Vaudeville Project, based at the University of Georgia, is currently working on reconstruction using a combination of motion capture, computer-gaming technology and traditional documentation to create an environment that allows users to enter a virtual theatre to watch a simulated late-nineteenth-century vaudeville performance: 'The objective is to reproduce a feeling of "liveness" in this environment: the sensation of being surrounded by human activity onstage, in the audience and backstage, and the ability to choose where to look at any given time (onstage or off), and to move within the environment.'[2] Using motion capture technology, the movements of real performers are grafted onto computer figures to simulate natural movement. The computer game software also enables users to navigate in a 3D environment and observe the stage action from a variety of perspectives (see Plate 7).

Projects such as Theatron and Virtual Vaudeville combine archaeological and high-tech perspectives to reinvestigate the theatrical past. The term 'theatre archaeology' can also have much more contemporary resonances, as we saw in Chap. 3. The work of Mike Pearson and Brit Gof (Pearson and Shanks 2001), but also of other groups with a commitment to exploring historical connections with living communities (see Chap. 11), indicate that the connection between theatre and history is much more complex than just a question of reproducing past production practices – however interesting these may be.

Theatre iconography

Theatre iconography is a subdiscipline of theatre historical research with a focus on visual, as opposed to written or oral, sources. Broadly speaking, one can say that theatre iconography is concerned with theatre as a theme

Plate 7. Virtual Vaudeville Project, University of Georgia.
Reconstruction of The Union Square Theatre, New York, 1895–6.

or subject of the visual arts. However, the visual material of interest to the
theatre historian is extremely varied, and intersects only in certain cases with
the interest of the art historian. In practice, theatre historians are interested in
particular kinds of figurative visual sources, such as Greek vase-painting, illustrated medieval manuscripts, woodcuts, engravings, paintings, lithographs,
caricature and photography.

Theater iconographical research can be divided into the following phases:

(1) Discovery and identification of visual sources as a means to reconstruct
    the 'reality' of past theatre practices. These sources serve to 'document' in a
    purely illustrative fashion theatre-history books, and are seldom subjected
    to rigorous examination in terms of their reliability and contextualization.
    It is assumed that pictures more or less 'speak for themselves'.
(2) Systematic propagation of theatre iconography as an autonomous field of
    collection and archival activity. In the late 1950s, there were the first calls
    for picture collections based on scholarly criteria. However, only in recent
    years have such demands been genuinely met, with the aid of computer
    technology. The Dionysos Project at the University of Florence has now
    made available on DVD-ROM an archive of over 20,000 images.
(3) Critical reflection on the referential status of theatrical images. To what
    extent can such images be regarded as 'evidence' or as 'eyewitness'
    accounts of theatre practices? This has led to a theoretical re-examination
    of fundamental questions regarding visual conventions, the media of
    images and their relation to other sources.

A subdiscipline under the name theatre iconography, which combined the second and third phases, did not emerge until the late 1980s. It includes researchers whose areas of interest – for example the *Commedia dell'arte* or eighteenth-century acting – are heavily dependent on the interpretation of visual sources. Some are also researchers who are primarily interested in the theoretical and methodological problems of iconographical research. The field can be regarded as the combination and productive interchange between these two perspectives: focused historical investigation balanced by theoretical reflection on the status of the visual documents.

Theatre iconography or iconology?

There are various ways of studying historical pictures. The art historian Erwin Panofsky differentiated three levels of pictorial analysis: pre-iconographical, iconographical and iconological. The first two levels attempt to establish relatively incontrovertible facts regarding, say, historical persons depicted or the use of an allegorical motif. Iconological analysis is, in Panofsky's words, devoted to interpreting images in relation to their historical context to elucidate their 'actual meaning'. The Polish semiotician Tadeusz Kowzan has adapted the terms to theatrical pictures to propose essentially a differentiation between documentation and interpretation:

> Iconography would be the term for designating 1) an ensemble of documents representing this or that phenomenon, 2) their description and classification. The term iconology would be reserved for an interpretative and comparative study, for research into the relationship between the iconographic object and its historic context, between the icon and its referent.   (Kowzan 1985: 68)

Although Kowzan does not develop his distinction further and gives no examples, it is clear that he sees scope for an entirely new field of research, which goes beyond problems of documentation, identification and ascription of pictorial documents, to a putative historical reality. What is implicit rather then explicit in his essay is that theatrical *iconology* could become a field of study in its own right, an area of hermeneutic research *sui generis*, and not just an aid for theatre or art historians. This distinction has been further developed in the essay 'Interpreting the Pictorial Record: Theatre Iconography and the Referential Dilemma' (Balme 1997).

Theatre-iconographical research has developed around those epochs where there is an abundance of source material, or where there is a dearth of written documents so that the visual sources gain in value or are indeed indispensable. The latter case pertains to Greek vase-painting. Thousands of painted vases have been uncovered in Greece and the former Greek settlement areas such as Southern Italy. The images provide a great deal of information about ancient Greek culture, including theatre. The collection and cataloguing of these images has long been a field within classical studies and archaeology, and in recent years specialist studies on the theatrical images have appeared (Taplin 1993 and 2007).

The vast number of images created around the activities of the *Commedia dell'arte* troupes have made the visual record a central feature of *Commedia* research as a whole. Because of the large number of these images and their often complex genesis, we find contributions from both theatre and art historians. The *Commedia dell'arte* also provides a link to the importance of theatrical subjects for artists such as Callot, Watteau and Longhi, who often represented Italian actors in their pictures. This has also meant that art historians have contributed to theatre-iconographical research, albeit indirectly (see Katritzky 2006).

Acting and actors in the eighteenth century form another central focus in theatre-iconographical research. From the mid eighteenth century onwards, individual actors were discovered as an interesting subject by painters such as Hogarth, Reynolds and Gainsborough. These popular paintings were frequently copied and rendered in other cheaper visual media such as engravings and even porcelain, and were thus made accessible to a wider public. At the same time, we find an intense theoretical discussion on the status of acting, and some research has focused on the interplay between visual discourses on the one hand and theoretical discourses on the other (West 1991).

The presentation of the actor via images continues and expands with the invention of photography in the nineteenth century. Theatre photography as an area of theatre-iconographic research has as its focus the second half of the nineteenth century, when the medium went through a number of technological changes. Although photography can potentially record any aspect of the theatre, most research has concentrated on the interplay between the new medium and acting. Like painting or caricature, photography is regulated by highly specific codes and conventions, which are closely connected with other pictorial media (such as painting) and with acting practices. In the early period of theatre photography, roughly the time 1860 to 1910, when photographs were produced almost exclusively in studios, there emerged a productive financial and artistic co-operation between actors and photographers.

The photographs of this period testify to a media revolution of considerable significance. A crucial innovation concerned the size and availability of photographs. Large portrait photographs were replaced by the so-called *carte-de-visite* format. These small images, which measured approximately 2.25 by 3.5 inches, could be produced, and above all reproduced, very cheaply. The replacement of the older daguerreotypes, which only existed in one version, by the mass production of *cartes-de-visite* and later by the postcard created a whole new economy of mass distribution. This increased circulation of images resulted in turn in a complete rearrangement of perceptive practices. The aesthetics of the glass-plate daguerreotype, which still retained the aura of uniqueness, corresponded to the conventions of portrait painting. The mass-produced *cartes-de-visite*, on the other hand, tapped into, or indeed created, an unexploited expressive dimension that appealed directly to the emotions. Photographs were now no longer expensive acquisitions for the decoration of middle- and upper-middle-class drawing rooms. They became articles of consumption. Persons depicted in various poses on late-nineteenth-century photographs (whether members of the family or eroticized performers) established a new, much more intimate relationship with the owner of the pictures.

Actors and actresses had a considerable involvement in these wider social changes. They quickly discovered the publicity and staging potential of the new medium, and used their corporeal know-how to great effect. Above all, they influenced the practices of portrait photography. The photographic studio became a kind of miniature stage, with painted backdrops and the usual theatrical accessories where actors could demonstrate their abilities in self-advertisement. It is no doubt this element of staging that connects past and present theatre photography. Photographs were produced as postcards and sold as souvenirs. Like the stage itself, the theatre photograph is always an image of an image, because it never represents a piece of found, authentic reality, but something that has already been shaped and staged.

Periodization

Theatre historiography encompasses more than just critiquing source material and reconstructionism. Of equal importance is the question of periodization; that is, how we divide theatre history into discrete epochs and geographical spaces. Because theatre studies arose relatively 'late', it turned initially to more established disciplines – mainly literary and art history – for its models of structuring the past. Neither proved, however, to be entirely suitable for transferral to the theatre.

An approach that focuses on productions of specific works, particularly of famous dramatists, throughout history arrives at a conundrum: literary reputation and theatrical practice do not always coincide. Therefore the periods defined by historians of literature do not necessarily have the same relevance to historians of theatre. Perhaps the most striking example of this disjunction is Romanticism. Doubtless a central period of European literature, its application to drama, let alone to questions of staging or acting, produces a different set of coordinates for each area of theatrical activity, as well as a different set of stylistic characteristics. This problem is exacerbated even more when one leaves the mainstream stages and attempts to include popular forms such as pantomime, vaudeville or music hall.

The oldest and most widespread approach to periodization divides up theatre history along geocultural lines, but here too there are different possibilities. They range from expansive histories of European or Asian theatre to the more common national histories of French, German, Italian theatre, etc. and include more detailed regional, or even city-focused, studies. When the latter are capital cities (e.g. a history of theatre in Paris), then the claim is usually of a national scale, as capital cities are often regarded as metonyms of the whole nation.

Large-scale studies – those of international or continental sweep – follow, in principle, the same patterns and norms of periodization. On closer inspection, however, these appear to be somewhat arbitrary and subject to the problems discussed above. They follow criteria designed in other disciplines, or simply switch from literary, art historical or theatre-specific coordinates as they see fit. Table 4 is a compilation of period designations as found in accessible and widely read theatre histories.[3]

Although these studies are by no means uniform in their specific valuations and emphases, they basically do share the same approach to periodization, which, from the Middle Ages onwards, is structured around individual nation states, particularly Italy, France, England and Germany on the one hand, and cultural and aesthetic movements (Renaissance, Baroque, Classicism) on the other. After beginnings in classical antiquity with individual chapters for Greece and Rome, the history of European theatre is divided into national developments during the Middle Ages, and this division is retained throughout. These are usually merged with period classifications deriving from other disciplines such as Humanism, Renaissance, Baroque, Enlightenment, etc.

Although this division seems, at first glance, quite familiar and not particularly problematic, closer inspection reveals that it is actually based on eclectic criteria. The theatre historian Thomas Postlewait has identified twenty-two separate criteria by which theatre periods are determined (Postlewait 1988: 305–6). Many of these can be found in Table 4. Examples are:

(1) *political empires or dynasties*: Egyptian, Roman
(2) *monarchies*: Elizabethan, Restoration
(3) *intellectual and artistic change*: Middle Ages, Renaissance, Enlightenment

Table 4. Periodization in European theatre historiography

Time	Period	Theatre forms and dramatic genres (selection	Place
to 500 BC	pre-theatrical forms	mystery cults; dances; rituals; ceremonies	Mediterranean; Egypt; Africa
500–350 BC	classical antiquity	attic tragedy and comedy; satyr plays; *mimus*	Greece; Asia Minor
300 BC–500 AD	classical antiquity	atellane; Roman comedy and tragedy; pantomime	Roman Empire
1000–1550	Middle Ages	tropes; liturgical drama; saints plays; miracle plays; mystery plays; interludes; *Corpus Christi* plays; morality plays; passion plays; *sacra rappresentazione; joculatores*	Europe
1490–1600	Renaissance and Humanism	Humanist theatre; *trionfi; intermezzi; commedia erudita;* tragedy; pastoral plays; *Commedia dell'arte; Rederijker*	Italy; Germany; Netherlands
1550–1642	Elizabethan and Jacobean	major dramatic genres; court masques	England
1580–1700	*Siglo de oro* and Baroque	auto sacramental; *entremeses;* cloak and dagger plays; *comedia; zarzuela*	Spain
1600–1700	Baroque and Classicism	*Commedia dell'arte;* opera; Jesuit theatre; *tragédie classique;* comedy; farce; *ballet de cour; opera seria*	France; Italy; Germany

Period	Movement	Forms/genres	Regions
1700–1780	Enlightenment	restoration comedy; *comédie larmoyante; genre sérieux*; bourgeois tragedy; Storm and Stress; Singspiel; reform opera; *ballet d'action*	Europe
1780–1850	Neo-Classicism; Romanticism	neo-classical drama (Germany); romantic ballet; melodrama; Grand Opéra; *Musikdrama*	Europe; North America
1850–1900	Realism; Historicism; Naturalism	*pièce bien faite*; vaudeville; Meininger; free theatres	Europe; Russia; Americas
1890–1915	Modernism	symbolism; art nouveau	Europe; Russia
1919–1939	Avantgarde	futurism; expressionism; constructivism; surrealism; Bauhaus; political; agit-prop	Europe; Russia; North America
1940–1968	post-war theatre	absurd drama; happenings; political popular theatre	Europe; North America
1968–present	contemporary	postmodern; intercultural; postcolonial; postdramatic	Africa; North America; Caribbean; Europe

 (4) *normative attributes*: neo-classical
 (5) *nation states*: English, German, French
 (6) *pan-national*: Scandinavian, Slavic, African
 (7) *philosophical schools*: Humanist
 (8) *chronological*: 1470–1590, eighteenth-century, post-war
 (9) *literary movements*: Romanticism, Naturalism, Modernism
(10) *famous persons*: Shakespearean
(11) *art history*: Baroque.

The multitude of criteria used is not just due to the fact that information has been compiled from different books. The period designations listed here (and some others besides) are common to the studies consulted. In fact, the situation is more complicated even still because the table only lists major dramatic forms and styles. Not included are the criteria of stage design, theatre architecture and technology or institutional forms, which give quite different divisions and points of change.

Seen positively, this categorical confusion could be adduced to the complexity of the phenomenon, theatre's inherent multi-medial constitution that combines literature (drama) and the fine arts (set design, architecture), anthropology (traditions of acting) with social and political change (theatre as an institution). It is probably not even sensible to try and unify all these disparate factors and their different chronologies of change under homogeneous periodic categories.

It may be of some solace to know that the problems presented here are by no means unique to theatre history, but are discussed with equal, if not more, vehemence in disciplines such as history, literature and art history. Historical periods are today regarded by many scholars as necessary cognitive constructs rather than as immutable and clear-cut lines of demarcation. Some of the new approaches to theatre historiography discussed in the next section proceed from an explicit or implicit critique of periodization.

Is there a way of out of this dilemma? One can simply ignore it, as some traditional theatre historians seem to, who continue to structure their material along the same mixture of national or pan-national criteria. Although there is certainly no easy solution, it is essential that theatre historians take cognizance of the problem and consciously position their work in reaction to it. A good example of this critical self-positioning can be found in the textbook, *Theatre Histories: An Introduction* (Zarrilli *et al.* 2006). Not only does this volume group together Western and non-Western developments – rather than separate them out – but the authors provide a new approach to periodization by structuring theatre history around 'modes of human communication':

One of the identifying characteristics of human awareness and consciousness is the development of the ability to reflect upon and communicate who we are. Theatre and performance are complex, culturally embedded, historically specific kinds of communal reflection and communication. Because major new developments in modes of human communication led to profound changes in the ways people thought about, related to, and organized their worlds, each of the four parts of this book are organized to mark such transformations and relate them to theatre and performance.   (Zarrilli *et al.* 2006: xxviii–xxix)

The four parts focus on orality, the emergence of print culture, modern media culture and the age of global communication. Constructing periods according to modes of communication is certainly a new solution to the old problem of periodization. It is probably the best way to cope with the complexity of the medium of theatre in its diverse cultural and aesthetic manifestations through time. Notwithstanding such approaches, the novice student of theatre studies will still have to deal with the canonized categories and divisions of theatre history – but hopefully with a sharpened awareness of their constructedness.

Contemporary approaches

The critique of periodization is one of the many discussions that arose in the 1970s and 1980s, when a new generation of theatre scholars began to question many of the premises they themselves had been trained under. The overarching paradigm they began to question is known as *positivism*. Philosophically speaking, positivism is based on the premise that scientific disciplines should only concern themselves with phenomena that can be deemed empirically verifiable and are thus intersubjectively communicable. In terms of methodology, positivism proceeds from hypotheses that can be verified or falsified on the basis of trial and error. Although familiar as the basis of the natural sciences, in the nineteenth century this method was also applied to the 'soft sciences' such as history and the study of literature. Because of its rigorous attitude to ascertaining the 'truth' of past events, positivism came to be synonymous with an almost obsessive interest in gathering and ascertaining the reliability of source material, rather than with interpreting it in social or aesthetic contexts. At its best, positivist research provides the basis of any historical branch of the humanities; at its worst, it does little more than gather and order putative facts.

The positivist consensus of many disciplines in the social sciences and humanities came under attack in the 1960s. The critique was led in the main by scholars with a materialist or Marxist orientation. Their major argument was that knowledge was by no means 'value-free' as positivist scholars would like to believe. On the contrary, knowledge is determined by specific 'interests' that influence how scholars define their objects of enquiry and organize the whole process of research. The epithet 'materialist' meant, in the context of historical research, a stronger focus on social and economic factors as opposed to more abstract 'ideas' or aesthetico-stylistic trends.

After some delay, the positivist debate eventually reached theatre historiography. The major influences on theatre historians came, as usual, from other disciplines. Important scholars and theories included the historian Hayden White, Michel Foucault's theory of discourse and Stephen Greenblatt's New Historicism or 'cultural poetics'. Of these, Hayden White's theory of 'metahistory' has had the most profound effect on historiographical debates in the narrower sense (to Foucault and New Historicism we shall return below). In a series of publications, most notably *Metahistory: The Historical Imagination in Nineteenth-century Europe* (1973) and *Tropics of Discourse* (1978), White claims that historical science, far from arranging incontrovertible 'facts' in a natural order, employs the same techniques of narration as literature. Historians employ techniques of emplotment arranged in genres such as comedy, tragedy and satire, and resort to tropes familiar to literature such as metaphor, metonymy and synecdoche. A student of structuralism, White argues that language determines the historiographical as much as it does the 'poetic act' (White 1973: x).

An early response to the challenges posed by White and others came from the American theatre historian Bruce McConachie in his essay 'Towards a Post-positivist Theatre History' (1985). McConachie develops his critique of traditional positivistic theatre history from phenomenology (see Chap. 5) and hermeneutics (in the main the writings of the French structuralist Paul Ricoeur). Put succinctly, McConachie argues that it is not possible for theatre historians to assume an objective point of view. As an example, he cites the famous production of John M. Synge's *The Playboy of the Western World*, which, when premiered at Dublin's Abbey Theatre in 1907, led to riots because of its excessive realism:

> Was the Abbey Theatre production of Synge's *The Playboy of the Western World* done realistically? The historian would need to add, 'From whose point of view?' Seen through the eyes of the Dublin working men and patriots who rioted in 1907, the play was not 'realistic' at all, if by realistic we mean, in part, a faithful rendering of everyday reality. From Synge's, Lady Gregory's and Yeats's angle of vision, on the other hand, the

production more or less reflected the reality of Irish peasant life . . . But why 'take sides' at all? Seen through a postpositivist lens, there were several kinds of performances of *Playboy* at the Abbey in 1907 because there were several kinds of audiences.   (McConachie 1985: 481)

The epithet 'postpositivist' does not specify a particular methodology, but rather a general discontent with established ways of narrating and representing theatre history. If there is a common denominator to the different theoretical approaches that began to emerge in the 1980s, then it is an increased concern with the factor 'audience'. McConachie's example illustrates that an understanding of theatrical performances is incomplete without taking cognizance of the meanings audiences (as a collective) and spectators (as individuals and groups) attribute to them.

The 'postpositivist' critique articulated by McConachie and others (and we find similar arguments articulated in France, Italy and Germany) led to a comprehensive methodological pluralization within theatre historical studies. In place of ideologically 'neutral' chronologies we find a plurality of 'histories': the theatre of class groups, from the perspective of gender and/or ethnicity. Not only do we find the unitary concept 'theatre' being questioned and defined through the perspective of different interest groups, but the supposedly objective position of the theatre historian comes under scrutiny as well. The logical corollary of such pluralist approaches is that the theatre historian is also asked to locate him/herself in relation to the object of investigation. Far from being an objective observer, the scholar is implicated explicitly and implicitly in the research, and asked to articulate this position. The process of self-reflection as part of research (and it extends beyond the field of historical research) has been termed 'positionality' (Dolan 2001: 65).

In the remaining pages of this chapter, it is only possible to sketch briefly some of the important influences that have made themselves felt within recent theatre-historiographical debates. The field is always changing, and once discrete approaches seem to be forming forever-new alliances. The following is intended as a record of past achievements that still influence, in some way, contemporary endeavours of theatre historians.

The work of the French historian and philosopher Michel Foucault has had a decisive influence on theatre historians since the 1980s. The key concepts here are 'discourse' or 'discourse analysis' and 'power'. Foucault's theory of 'power' undertakes a fundamental revaluation of the concept itself. In contrast to a Marxist understanding, which sees power in pejorative terms as an instrument of repression in the hands of the ruling classes, Foucault argues that power is a productive force regulating all levels of social relations. He makes this argument most clearly in his study *Discipline and Punish: The Birth of the Prison* (1979), where he calls for an end to the negative application of the word 'power'. Power does not just negate, he argues, it also produces and manifests itself more thoroughly, albeit covertly, in everyday social and cultural practices than in centralized state institutions.

The method Foucault developed to examine the hidden dynamics of power is called 'discourse analysis'. Discourses are highly complex networks of rules governing language. In Foucault's terminology, a discourse determines knowledge for a given society and period by governing what can be said and written and in what forms it can be articulated. Knowledge is thus a product of the discourses rather than the other way round. The concepts of 'discourse' and 'power' are highly abstract, and function independently of individual subjects.

Foucault repeatedly drew attention to the fact that power can be studied in the way changing discourses construct our understanding of the body differently – the body is one of the main locations of power in the Foucauldian sense. The body has been one of the main *loci* where theatre history (and theatre studies more generally) have made use of his theories. An obvious place of encounter has been the actor and the 'art' of acting. In his study *The Player's Passion* (1985), Joseph Roach makes explicit use of Foucault's concepts, and analyses the rise of theories of acting in the eighteenth century. Roach places these theories in the context of philosophical and scientific discourses on the body, which shifted from the old Galenic notion of 'humours' to newer concepts elaborated by Descartes and others. This approach enables Roach to illuminate the 'old' discussion about the actor and emotion (see Chap. 1) from a variety of new perspectives.

Foucault's ideas have also had a decisive influence on feminist and gender theory, although the feminist discussion is much wider and pre-dates the reception of Foucault. Concepts such as 'hidden history' or 'her-story' were formulated to demonstrate that women's contributions to theatre history have been repressed and consciously or unconsciously 'written over' to obscure their presence. In an initial stage, this approach concentrated on the contribution of women dramatists, actresses and theatre managers to write an alternative history to the one formulated in the positivist studies.

A seminal study in this re-evaluation is Sue-Ellen Case's *Feminism and Theatre* (1988). Case argues that theatre and its history have been dominated by a triple-male perspective. In Greek theatre, for example, male writers produced texts acted by men for (predominantly) male spectators. Thereby, a male perspective attains the status of 'universality' and is imposed on female spectators as their own. Of particular interest is the convention of male actors playing women (which we find in Greek, Elizabethan and some Asian

forms). Case argues that research has hitherto neglected the possible homo-
erotic implications of such conventions in the context of predominantly male
audiences.

A second major impulse for theatre historiography came from cultural and
historical anthropology. Since the early 1970s, a number of scholars have been
working to establish a field of research that applies ethnographical perspectives and methodologies to historical phenomena. Traditionally, the cultural
anthropologist has always studied contemporary societies *in situ*, an approach
that privileged the present and made it difficult to accommodate the problem
of historical change. At the same time, historians began to see the possibilities
offered by the 'microperspective' developed by ethnography. Leaders in this
field have been Carlo Ginzburg (Italy), Emmanuel Le Roy Ladurie (France),
Natalie Zemon Davis (USA) and Greg Dening (Australia) to name only some.
Important contributions from the anthropological side of the fence have come
from Clifford Geertz and Marshall Sahlins.

Two central questions arose here. The first was methodological and theoretical. Essentially, it was the problem of how the basically structural-synchronic
approach of anthropologists could be reconciled with the chronological-
diachronic perspective of historians. The American anthropologist Marshall
Sahlins focused the debate around the key terms 'event' and 'structure'. How
do events (the domain of the historian) influence structure (the domain of
the social scientists) and vice versa? This extremely complex problem led to
the second question of territorial divisions. The anthropologist Clifford Geertz
described the territorial realignments brought about by the cross-fertilization
between the two disciplines as 'a change in the ecology of learning that has
driven historians and anthropologists, like so many migrant geese, into one
another's territories: a collapse of the natural dispersion of feeding grounds
that left France to the one and Samoa to the other' (Geertz 1990: 324). What
Geertz implies here is that France has a history and Samoa does not (or at least
has only a very recent one); and that Samoan culture is characterized by 'time-
less social structures', whereas French history is only of interest in as far as it is
manifested in significant, i.e. political, 'events'. It became evident to perceptive
observers on both sides of the feeding grounds that such a dichotomous view
was untenable.

To effect productive interdisciplinary exchange, it was necessary to bridge
some missing links. These bridges came from a variety of sources. One was
Victor Turner's theory of social drama. Although developed on the basis of
fieldwork among a Central African tribe, it was eagerly adopted by historians
and projected back onto Europe's tribal past – ancient Greece for instance –
where historians had been gradually realizing that the structures and cultural
patterns obtaining there may have had just as much in common with Central

Africa and pre-contact Samoa as with Louis XIV. Another bridge was provided by the so-called interpretive turn in anthropology, represented by the work of Clifford Geertz himself who began to adopt and adapt theories of hermeneutics and textual analysis for the analysis of social phenomena. His method of thick description was eagerly adopted by historians as a means to obtain a microperspective on particular historical events.

Theatre history has responded to this 'anthropological turn' in a number of ways and under influence from different disciplines. Perhaps the most far-reaching has been 'New Historicism', a term coined by the literary historian and Renaissance scholar Stephen Greenblatt. Taking his lead from Foucault's notion of discourse on the one hand, and Clifford Geertz's 'interpretive anthropology' on the other, Greenblatt has argued for a radical reconsideration of the relationship between Shakespearean drama and the cultural 'background' from which it arose. For Greenblatt, a Shakespearean tragedy and a treatise on exorcism are part and parcel of the same cultural system in which texts circulate and interpenetrate one another. New Historicists subject 'objective' documents to complex readings that are normally reserved for literary texts, and thus upset established hierarchies. They also, in Greenblatt's case at least, move effortlessly between the past and present, in an attempt to elucidate the complex inter-relationship between the historian and his/her object of study.

The influence of New Historicism on theatre history has been considerable, and not only because Greenblatt's own field of research, Shakespearean drama and theatre, coincides with a key period of theatre history. The complex readings engendered by this approach have provided valuable stimuli to theatre historians working in different periods, although the major focus of new historical research continues to be on the early modern period. Important studies outside the English Renaissance include such diverse topics as Joseph Roach's *Cities of the Dead: Circum-Atlantic Performance* (1996), which moves between London and New Orleans and the eighteenth and the twentieth centuries in its analysis of performance, cultural memory and the slave trade; and Stephen T. Brown's study of the rise of *Nō* theatre in medieval Japan, *Theatricalities of Power: The Cultural Politics of Noh* (2001). These two examples must suffice as proof of the breadth of application that these very different studies demonstrate.

Summary and outlook

Discussions of theatre historiography have over the past ten to fifteen years tended to reiterate the 'crisis' of theatre historiography. Although this continuous lament is beginning to wear thin it is for no other reason than that the flow of theatre historical studies is increasing in quality as well as quantity. If we take the word 'crisis' to mean a state of instability, then it can be seen in a more positive light. The impact of 'critical theory' on the humanities over the past thirty years has been far-reaching and palpable in all but the most inaccessible niches of historical research. Students of theatre history will be confronted by a range of approaches in the works they read. They will need to find their own 'middle ground' between an understandable need for 'solid historical facts' and the necessity to question this very foundation with the help of new theories and methodologies.

Further reading

The best discussion of theatre historiography still remains Postlewait and McConachie (eds.), *Interpreting the Theatrical Past: Essays in the Historiography of Performance* (1989). Apart from the editors' theoretical remarks, the volume contains a number of essays that illustrate different approaches ranging from reconstruction to feminism. Vince's contribution to this volume provides a useful historical overview of the discipline. A more concise discussion of some of these questions can be found in the section on historiography in Reinelt and Roach, *Critical Theory and Performance* (1992), 293–8. Brockett and Hildy's *History of the Theatre* (2007) contains in its later editions useful exercises at the end of each chapter under the rubric 'Looking at Theatre History'. These include reflexive discussions of sources and different scholarly viewpoints on issues. A feminist view of theatre history was introduced by Sue-Ellen Case in her book *Feminism and Theatre* (1988), which sparked off a great many specific studies of women in theatre in different periods and countries, such as Davis (1991), Aston (1995) and Canning (1996). For an application of new critical methodologies to British history, see Bratton (2003). An important recent work is Zarrilli *et al.*, *Theatre Histories* (2006), a multiple-authored approach to theatre and performance history that includes cross-cultural perspectives from different continents and time periods.

Chapter 7

Text and performance

To state that performance analysis is at the centre of theatre studies is a claim that would have met twenty years ago with a degree of sceptical reserve. Until the mid 1980s, theatre studies had consisted either of theatre history or dramatic analysis, with an emphasis on questions of staging. The idea that the performance itself could be analysed and studied was certainly recognized as desirable but was generally regarded as an impossible task. How could one analyse something that is essentially ephemeral, that disappears the moment it has been enacted? Does not analysis presuppose the existence of observable elements that can be scrutinized at length and ideally be checked and verified by other scholars? The analysis and interpretation of texts and pictures in literary studies and art history respectively, or of films or television programmes in media studies, have recourse to more or less stable artefacts. Performance analysis, it would seem, does not.

This apparent impasse was resolved by a combination of technological and theoretical advances. The technological aspect is linked to the development of cheap and accessible video technology, which made available to scholars an increasing number of recordings of performances for detailed study. While performance analysis today is not necessarily dependent on video recording (it can be done without), in most cases it is used because it allows study of movement, sound and image, albeit filtered through the perspective of one or more cameras (to this problem we shall return below).

The second development (which roughly parallels the first one) was the introduction of semiotics to theatre studies in the 1970s and its spread in the 1980s and 1990s. As a theory, semiotics emphasizes, by definition, the synchronic and the structural. It looks at phenomena (including theatrical performances) in terms of the signs and codes used and the way they generate meaning. For all its theoretical shortcomings (see Chap. 5), semiotics provided a vocabulary and approach that seemed to 'work' for performance analysis. In particular, the aspects of *staging* – the contribution of director, designer and actor to interpreting a work – could be described relatively accurately in the language of signs. The colour of a costume, even the shape of furniture or the hint of a gesture – all these things were signs on stage generating meaning for the spectators. It became the task of performance analysis to read and interpret these signs. That this can be an exceptionally complex task will be quickly recognized as soon as one begins to analyse even a short scene on stage.

In the following chapters, the task of performance analysis will be approached in a series of steps. In this chapter, we shall examine the complex relationship between text and performance. The European theatrical tradition has, in most cases, utilized a production process that proceeds from a written drama, libretto or even choreography *preceding* the performance. In other words, texts are transformed into signs of a different material basis: voice, movement, fabric, paint, video and so on. Written texts are encoded into other sign systems, and it is the task of the scholar to decode these signs back into written language. This path from page-to-stage-to-page is complicated in itself. Performance analysis investigating this relationship is essentially hermeneutic: it interprets *transformations* between page and stage. Today, however, there are an increasing number of productions that do not translate a pre-written drama or libretto into a stage production. The whole area of performance art, and much experimental theatre, work without written texts. Although such productions may produce a text, often they are not available for study; the text may only exist metaphorically in the sense that it is written into the corporeal memory of the performers. This is also true of many performance forms outside the European tradition.

Because of the continuing dominance of text-based theatre, the first part of this chapter will be devoted to outlining a theatre studies-based approach to analysing the dramatic or theatrical text. In Chap. 8, the most important models for analysing the actual performance – and not just its relationship to the text – will be introduced. In Chaps. 9 and 10, it will be shown how these models can be applied to music and dance theatre.

Status of the text

What makes a text theatrical? Can we identify particular characteristics – such as, for example, the use of dialogue, the presence of stage directions (which give information about the appearance and movement of characters) or details of the stage set – that would seem to designate a text as being designed for stage performance? The excerpts on p. 121 from the opening scenes of three well-known 'dramas' give an idea of the huge differences between conventions governing the written basis of a theatrical performance. The First Folio edition of *Hamlet* (the first official but posthumously printed version of the play) contains hardly any stage directions whatsoever. The only information provided concerns the acts and scenes and the exits and entrances of characters. It is even unclear where and when the play takes place and who the speaking characters are. Where we are faced with a dearth of information in Elizabethan drama, late-nineteenth-century realism goes to the other extreme. Henrik Ibsen became famous for providing detailed descriptions of the rooms inhabited by his characters, including details of the pictures on the wall and the position of the furniture. We find also details of characters' appearance, dress and movement, even before they have spoken a word. Heiner Müller's *Hamletmachine* dispenses in the beginning with stage directions, characterization and even a list of *dramatis personae*. What is left is a text that is only recognizable as 'dramatic' on the basis of the first-person speaking voice: 'I was Hamlet'. While *Hamlet* and *A Doll's House* are immediately recognizable as dramas, for Müller's *Hamletmachine*, the very term is problematic.

If we are to approach these texts from the point of view of performance analysis, then our interest in them will probably be different to that of the literary critic. We will try and investigate, in some way, the text's relationship to the performance, rather than examining whatever intrinsic qualities the text may have for the reader. This distinction is often a difficult one to draw, but throughout its history the discipline of theatre studies has insisted on this distinction, if only to differentiate itself from the wider field of literary criticism or history. The distinction is, however, problematic, because, as we shall see in this book, theatre studies itself is a highly differentiated field with many different scholarly perspectives.

While the text is definitely not the performance, it can be studied with the performance in mind. The question is: what performance? For the theatre historian, the theatrical text may offer evidence to assist in studying historical performance conditions. As early as 1914, the German founder of theatre studies Max Herrmann stated unequivocally that the theatre historian has little or no interest in the aesthetic qualities of a dramatic text.

> The drama as literary creation is only of interest to theatre historians in as much as the dramatist took account of stage conditions when writing his play, and in as much as the drama provides us with an unintentional imprint of past theatrical conditions; we regard it furthermore as part of the theatrical repertoire and as an object of study with regard to the way later artists adapt it to new theatrical conditions. The specific literary qualities do not concern us; the most inartistic play may in certain circumstances be more important for our perspective than the world's greatest dramatic masterpiece.   (Herrmann 1914: 4)

William Shakespeare: *Hamlet*, First Folio edn (1623)	Henrik Ibsen: *A Doll's House* (1879) (The Project Gutenberg eBook)	Heiner Müller: *Hamletmachine* (1977) (tr. Christopher B. Balme)
Actus Primus. Scoena Prima. *Enter Barnardo and Francisco two Centinels* *Barnardo.* Who's there? *Fran.* Nay answer me: Stand & vnfold Your selfe. *Bar.* Long liue the King. *Fran.* Barnardo? *Bar.* He. *Fran.* You come most carefully vpon your houre. *Bar.* 'Tis now strook twelue, get thee to bed Francisco. *Fran.* For this releefe much thankes: 'Tis bitter cold, and I am sicke at heart. *Barn.* Haue you had a quiet Guard? *Fran.* Not a Mouse stirring. *Barn.* Well, goodnight. If you do meet Horatio and Marcellus, the Riuals of my Watch, bid them make hast. *Enter Horatio and Marcellus.* *Fran.* I think I heare them. Stand: who's there?	ACT I *[SCENE.– A room furnished comfortably and tastefully, but not extravagantly. At the back, a door to the right leads to the entrance-hall, another to the left leads to Helmer's study. Between the doors stands a piano. In the middle of the left-hand wall is a door, and beyond it a window. Near the window are a round table, arm-chairs and a small sofa. In the right-hand wall, at the farther end, another door; and on the same side, nearer the footlights, a stove, two easy chairs and a rocking-chair; between the stove and the door, a small table. Engravings on the walls; a cabinet with china and other small objects; a small book-case with well-bound books. The floors are carpeted, and a fire burns in the stove. It is winter. A bell rings in the hall; shortly afterwards the door is heard to open. Enter NORA, humming a tune and in high spirits. She is in outdoor dress and carries a number of parcels; these she lays on the table to the right. She leaves the outer door open after her, and through it is seen a PORTER who is carrying a Christmas Tree and a basket, which he gives to the MAID who has opened the door.]* *Nora.* Hide the Christmas Tree carefully, Helen. Be sure the children do not see it until this evening, when it is dressed.	1 FAMILY ALBUM I was Hamlet. I stood on the coast and spoke with the waves BLABLA, behind me the ruins of Europe. The bells sounded for the state funeral, murderer and widow a couple, behind the coffin of the Great Carcass goose-step the councillors, wailing in badly paid mourning WHO IS THE CORPSE IN THE HEARSE FOR WHOM IS THE WAILING AND LAMENTING THE CORPSE IS A GREAT GIVER OF ALMS the people form a guard of honour, the product of his statesmanship HE WAS A MAN TOOK EVERYTHING ONLY FROM EVERYBODY. I stopped the procession, prised open the coffin with a sword and broke the blade, but with the blunt stub I succeeded and divided up the dead progenitor FLESH AND FLESH IN HAPPY UNION amongst the wretched bystanders. The mourning turned to jubilation, the jubilation to loud feasting, on the empty coffin the murderer mounted the widow

It is clear that in this early stage of the discipline's history, Herrmann is trying to establish a clear division of labour between theatre and literary studies. If we break his comment down into categories, then we can see that Herrmann regards the theatrical text from two main perspectives:

(1) drama as a historical document: an imprint of past conditions and repertoire
(2) adaptation of texts to new theatrical conditions.

While it is the second point that is of specific interest in this chapter, the first has also been applied to performance analysis, albeit in a normative fashion in the sense that the putative historical context can be used against a production that may seem to be taking too many 'liberties'.

The explicit repudiation of literary or aesthetic qualities is understandable for the theatre historian, perhaps, but cannot be so easily transferred to the field of performance analysis, which is still principally guided by aesthetic questions and perspectives. Furthermore, when we consider that many of the methods and theories developed and discussed in literary studies can also be fruitfully applied to performance analysis, then it becomes clear that Herrmann's rigid demarcation cannot hold. Nevertheless, it is still impressively prescient. Sixty years later, the theatre and drama scholar John L. Styan notes, without reference to Herrmann: 'the true student of drama will find a bad play to be as exciting as a good one . . . the doldrums of dramatic history are as worthy of his interest as the great periods of so-called flowering' (Styan 1975: 6).

One of the first systematic attempts to apply a performance-related approach to the reading of dramatic texts was Raymond Williams's influential book, *Drama in Performance* ([1954] 1972), where one of the founders of cultural studies asks the very simple but fundamental question: 'what, historically, is the relation between a dramatic text and a dramatic performance?' (Williams [1954] 1972: 2) As his book shows, the answer is by no means easy to provide. Finally, he concludes that 'there is no constant relation between text and performance in drama' (Williams [1954] 1972: 175), but the elucidation of the relation can be regarded as an important scholarly undertaking.

Williams's approach is most productive when used as a form of historical research. The most consistent application of the technique of reading plays as historical documents of staging practices, the 'stagecraft' approach as it is usually called, has been in the field of Shakespeare studies. This kind of reading regards the dramatic text as a reservoir of indications providing implicit or explicit information on the playing conditions of the Elizabethan stage. A simple and well-known example of this kind of reading regards the often poetic, descriptive passages of Shakespearean drama as verbal scenery, which compensated for the lack of actual scenery on the supposedly empty Elizabethan stage. If we look briefly at the opening scene of *Hamlet* (see table on p. 121), we can detect a great deal of theatrically relevant information. Because there are no stage directions, we discover from the first exchange between Barnardo and Francisco, who evidently cannot see each other, that the scene takes place in the dead of night. That the situation is the changing of the guard at midnight is communicated in the next dialogue. We also learn that it is chilly and that Francisco is suffering from the cold. The dialogue also regulates the exits and entrances. The names of the characters about to enter are announced before they enter the stage – 'If you do meet Horatio and Marcellus ... bid them make hast' – so that stage directions are in fact superfluous. Francisco's reaction underlines once more the darkness on stage – the performance would have taken place in the afternoon – because the new characters are standing on the stage and are thus visible to the audience.

Because Shakespearean dramas contain a plethora of such stage-related indications (if they are read in this way) a whole generation of scholars in the 1960s and 1970s advocated that plays by definition contain something approaching an intrinsic performance. Some scholars even move beyond strictly historical questions and regard such performance-related readings as a kind of blueprint for performance. A leading advocate, John Russell Brown, asks:

> Why are Shakespeare's plays so actable? How do they draw and hold their audiences? How can we gain an impression of performance from reading a text? How should plays be staged in our theatres to present the fullness of Shakespeare's imagination?   (Brown 1966: 1)

While this approach has thrown much light on the relationship between the texts and possible historical staging conditions and conventions, its application to performance analysis is limited. To apply it to contemporary productions of Shakespeare would be to assume a normative and 'correct' way of reading the text against which individual productions and performances should be adjudicated. It may be that directors and actors do indeed take such cues from the text; but they may also choose to ignore them. It is not the task of performance analysis to engage in this kind of historical 'back-reading' – testing the performance against an assumed correct reading of the text. It must rather seek to uncover the codes and strategies employed by the production team in their particular interpretation.

Main and secondary text

When investigating the relationship between drama and theatre, an important distinction must be made between the main text and the stage directions or '*Nebentext*' (secondary text), a term introduced by the Polish philosopher Roman Ingarden. The main text (*Haupttext*) is composed of the words spoken by the 'represented persons', the secondary text provides information from the author to direct and regulate the performance. For Ingarden, theatrical language, as he calls it, is 'a borderline case of the literary work of art to the extent that, besides language, another medium of representation exists within it – namely, the visual aspects, afforded and concretized by the players and by the "décor," in which represented things and persons, as well as their actions are depicted' (Ingarden 1973: 377). The 'stage play' is thus not autonomous but only fully comprehensible as an aesthetic phenomenon in regard to its function in performance.

Ingarden's terminology has been criticized for its reliance on a concept of dramatic text that is historically bounded; as we have seen, there are many dramatic texts that do not contain an explicit secondary text in Ingarden's sense. In its place, the term '*didaskalia*' has been proposed, which refers not only to stage directions but also to the names of the characters – in short, to everything in the written text that is not definitely spoken by the characters.[1] Both '*didaskalia*' and the distinction between main and secondary text have entered the academic language of theatre studies and are widely used.

The problematic nature of such distinctions can be seen when comparing our three examples on p. 121. The relationship between main and secondary text, or spoken text and *didaskalia*, is highly dependent on historical conventions of playwriting and printing. The example of *Hamlet* shows that, with the exception of the characters' names, *didaskalia* are dispensed with altogether. This is because in the Elizabethan – or in the case of the First Folio edition, Jacobean– period, plays were a hybrid textual genre. Written originally as playtexts in the precise sense of the word (texts to be played by actors), they were seldom destined for publication and the conventions of a reading public. The First Folio edition was in fact intended for a reading public; the first quarto of *Hamlet* contains even fewer *didaskalia*. This began to change and, over time, the playtext adapted itself more and more to the reader until, by the late nineteenth century, main and secondary text had achieved almost a position of balance. The dramatic text emulates increasingly the conventions of prose, providing, as it were, a mental theatre for the armchair theatregoer. When plays of this period, such as the Ibsen example, begin to describe precise details of the characters' physiognomy and moods, this is not because they wish to prescribe and regulate what actors should look like, but rather they are adapting to new reading conventions and erasing the former sharp distinctions between the epic and the dramatic.

From drama to theatrical text

The aspects of the text–performance relationship treated so far refer to texts, which, because of specific textual markers or characteristics (e.g. division into main and secondary text), can clearly be identified as dramas. Today, as we have seen, such identification is no longer so easy. While students will no doubt have to deal with recognizable dramatic texts (from the Greeks to Stoppard, so to speak), an increasing number of texts are being written that are not 'dramas' in any verifiable sense. Samuel Beckett's later texts such as *Not I* or *Ohio Impromptu* – although they are collected within the volume *Dramatic Works* – begin to test the boundaries of the genre, while a work such as Sarah Kane's *4.48 Psychosis* shares very little in common with the generic elements of *A Doll's House*. The concept of drama is being seriously challenged by a growing number of performances so that an alternative term is needed to encompass an operatic score, a dance choreography, a *Commedia dell'arte* scenario or a 'scoreboard' such as that used by Robert Wilson as a point of departure for his productions. In order to accommodate those performance-related texts that may not evince any of the usual stylistic elements of the dramatic form, the term 'theatrical text' has been coined, which is used increasingly in theatre studies to refer to the textual basis of a performance. This terminological shift has proven necessary for both theoretical and practical reasons, as the above examples show. The term 'drama' we can restrict to a historical and generically definable form, which certainly continues to be produced but is by no means synonymous with theatre, as it used to be. In this sense, theatre studies scholars regard text-based dramatic theatre as just one option among several, even though it may still be the most prevalent one in Western theatre. A theatrical text encompasses any kind of textual blueprint that is intended for or attains performance.

Although the terminological shift from 'drama' to 'theatrical text' is a direct result of semiotic theory, the introduction of such a wide term has also proved necessary in order to keep abreast with developments in contemporary theatre practice. As the example of Samuel Beckett indicates, writing for the theatre is subject to historical change. An increasing number of authors are no longer concerned with observing a set of criteria regulating what makes 'a good play'. Instead, we find texts apparently written for the stage that dispense not only with an old-fashioned term such as 'plot', but also with recognizable characters and even dialogue. Such theatrical texts belong to the movement known as 'postdramatic theatre'.

Coined by the German theatre studies scholar Hans-Thies Lehmann in his book *Postdramatic Theatre* (2006), the concept refers to tendencies and experiments defining theatre outside the paradigm of the dramatic text. Also known (somewhat imprecisely) as postmodern theatre, it questions fundamentally the very tenets of the dramatic theatre. Postdramatic performances usually eschew clear coordinates of narrative and character, and therefore require considerable exegetical effort on the part of the spectator. Lehmann argues that the dramatic form is teleological (i.e. goal-directed) in its conception, and thus it operates with a single perceptual frame. Postdramatic theatre, on the other hand, uses multiple frames, which often create confusion for the reader/spectator. Lehmann understands the concept as a historical development emerging from experimental theatre after 1970 (with some precursors beforehand). Most of the examples he gives refer to productions or directors and not to writers. Postdramatic theatre may be created from a set of images, a selection of objects or physical exercises; it may or may not result in a text before or after the fact. Nevertheless, there are some writers whose texts can clearly be defined as postdramatic. Seminal for this development are the late works of Heiner Müller, and most famous perhaps is his text *Hamletmachine* (1977), which has been staged all over the world. Although the move to postdramatic writing has proceeded at a different pace in different parts of the world, its implications for writing for the stage are the same, and are fundamental.

If the move to postdramatic theatre after the 1970s is a response to a perceived crisis of dramatic theatre – which is, above all, a crisis of how the dramatic form is perceived by theatre artists, critics and academics – then this is also a crisis of or challenge to how we analyse the texts. If we still apply to postdramatic texts criteria that they consciously do not seek to meet or even challenge, this throws up a set of new problems. As long as we examine contemporary texts with analytical instruments developed for a different aesthetic system (if we continue to look for character, plot, identification, etc.) without first trying to understand the communicative and aesthetic codes that these new texts seek to activate, we will miss a large part of the aesthetic and innovative potential of such texts.

If we look briefly at the opening lines of Müller's *Hamletmachine* (see table on p. 121), we can see that it seems to ignore all the elements of 'stagecraft' evident in the original *Hamlet*. Where Shakespeare's text conveys immediate information about time, place, mood, atmosphere and, if we were to read on, creates tension of expectation (will the ghost appear again tonight?), Müller's text does none of this. Not only are there no stage directions, but the spoken text provides none of the clues indicating time and place – the building blocks of narrative – that audiences or readers require to orientate themselves. The opening line – 'I was Hamlet' – even seems to contradict a basic law of dramatic theory that emphasizes the 'here' and 'now' of dramatic speech. While there is a speaking character (Hamlet), he immediately negates his own immediate presence, so we must ask: what is the identity of the speaking subject we see on stage? What we are confronted with is not a text specifying details of stage action, but a web of intertextual references. Some of the lines relate to the Shakespearean text (Hamlet, the murderer and widow being a couple); others conjure up images of the Nazis and World War II or the Eastern bloc countries (the goose-stepping councillors, the ruins of Europe); while the capitalized sections are quotations from other texts. As the text progresses, it gains in complexity, both in terms of internal and external reference, while the stage directions resemble apocalyptic visions rather than blueprints for action.

Play, production, performance

Before proceeding further to investigate the problems associated with analysing the transposition of a theatrical text into performance, it is necessary to clarify key concepts. When a text is enacted on stage, the spectator is confronted with three different entities or, semiotically speaking, sign systems.

(1) The play or theatrical text constitutes a structure of linguistic signs regulating the story and the characters. If it is a well-known one, there will be considerable expectations on the part of the spectators regarding how it will unfold.

(2) The production, or staging (the French term *'mise-en-scène'* is also used) is a particular artistic arrangement and interpretation of the text with a high degree of stability. It includes the set design, the lighting plot, usually the same actors performing the moves they have learned. Cuts to the text and questions of casting such as doubling roles or cross-casting all belong to the realm of the production or staging.

(3) The performance is what spectators actually see on any given night. It is a particular version of the production, and is unrepeatable.

How can we determine the relationship between play, production and performance? This is the question that drama and theatre semiotics posed towards the end of the 1960s. Although considerable progress was made towards clarifying some of the problems, it would be optimistic to claim that consensus was reached. It is also important to note that we are talking here about the status of the text within theatre studies. In other disciplinary contexts, it must be posed differently.

A problematic consequence of the notion of the unitary performance text is the assumption – either implicit or explicit – that the performance layer must demonstrate *loyalty* to the play or text layer. The function of the production, the *staging*, must be to transform authorial intentions set out in the text as precisely as possible into performance.[2] This is still a widely held idea among spectators and theatre makers alike (although less prevalent with the latter). It is an argument used to combat what are regarded as the excesses of director's theatre, where the latter's vision would appear to overwrite and distort what the dramatist intended. But what did the author intend? As we have seen with the two versions of *Hamlet* discussed above, both authors provide few explicit instructions regarding setting, costumes or intonation. This is different with Ibsen, but even here, only the most ardent advocates of loyalty to the text would insist on a one-to-one scenographic realization of the stage directions. To do so would in fact be to relegate the work of director and designer to non-artistic managerial activities. If directors and designers are expected to interpret the text, then it is difficult to limit this activity, especially in the case of open texts such as Shakespeare or postdramatic writing.

One way of resolving this contradiction, at least partially, is to reformulate the relationship between text and production or performance. Instead of regarding the drama as a performance text, it might be more profitably seen as a text *to be* performed. Although the difference between 'performance' and 'to be performed' might seem to be marginal and somewhat sophistic, an important distinction is at stake here. Following Keir Elam, we might regard the relationship between text and performance as an example of *intertextuality*. Because theatrical texts are usually written with performance in mind, the performative aspect has already determined the text either consciously or unconsciously, although the exact determinants are extremely difficult to identify: 'What this suggests is that the written text/performance text relationship is not one of simple priority but a complex of reciprocal constraints constituting a powerful intertextuality' (Elam 1980: 209). Elam argues that the relationship between the two layers is multi-faceted and not simply unidirectional, and is thus describable 'in terms of facile determinism' (Elam 1980: 209).

The complex relationships between theatrical text, production and performance can be represented schematically (see Fig. 5). Two main aspects of this diagram must be stressed. Firstly, the relationship between text and production is not to be read as a set of normative rules. Rather, it should be seen as a set of possibilities that we can identify in theatrical texts at certain times in history.

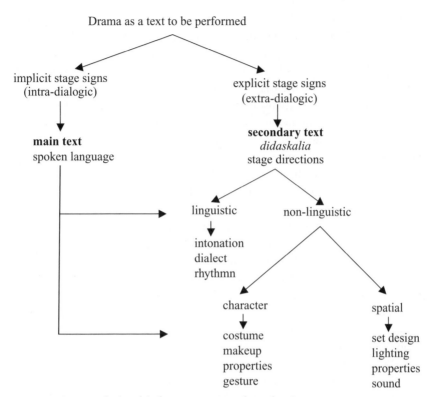

Fig. 5. Relationship between text and production.

Secondly, the interaction between explicit (secondary) and implicit (main text) stage signs is similarly historically contingent.

The stage directions of an Ibsen drama contain, as we have seen, numerous details regarding stage setting, costume and even remarks on characters' physical appearance. This textual material transcends what is absolutely essential for a theatre performance, and seems to be directed at the expectations of a reading rather than viewing public. It should be noted that Ibsen's dramas often appeared in print before they were seen on stage. Shakespeare's *Hamlet* contains only implicit stage directions, deducible from the spoken text, whereas the opening scene of Heiner Müller's *Hamletmachine* contains neither implicit nor explicit stage directions: there appears to be little in the text that alerts us to the realm of stage performance.

What are the implications of such theoretical categories and distinctions for the discipline of theatre studies? Firstly, they are terminological: if the relationship between text and performance is defined as a form of intertextuality this leads ineluctably to a problematization of the concept of 'drama' in its accepted sense. This would mean that any kind of text can be used for performance, as Müller's *Hamletmachine* illustrates. The wider term 'theatrical text', which subsumes drama but is not coterminous with it, can logically be best determined after the act of performance: if it has been or is intended to be performed, it can be defined as theatrical.

The terminological expansion that contemporary postdramatic writing brings about raises important questions regarding the activity of analysis or interpretation. While an old-style 'stagecraft' analysis of a Greek drama or a play by Shakespeare will indeed render observable manifold inter-relationships between a text and the theatrical conventions of the time, and a semiotic analysis will highlight details of communication structures, neither will provide much elucidation or commentary about the text's content, nor its relationship to the world. There are, of course, examples of theatrical texts that were never performed in the author's lifetime – such as Georg Büchner's *Woyzeck* (1837) – but which have attained classical status on the modern stage. Because they were never performed in the author's lifetime, their relationship to the theatre of their time is tenuous. It could be argued that every theatrical text, even one that explicitly distances itself from the existing theatrical system, is still linked to that system and its conventions. Dramatists write for, with or against the pre-existing theatrical code.

While the 'stagecraft' approach may certainly be productive for theatre historians, it is only of limited use for contemporary performance analysis. The past 'theatrical reality' encoded in a play should be seen as an object of research *sui generis* but not as a precondition for performance analysis, because then it threatens to become a normative interpretation. Whatever intended theatrical reality dramatic texts may contain, this constitutes an independent field of research, but it certainly does not explain the complicated and often highly contradictory relationship between literary text and theatre reality. One should certainly not construct an implied or even normative ideal production from such a perspective.

How should one then read a theatrical text in the context of performance analysis? As we shall see, there is no simple recipe or formula; the text is just one of several sign systems that must be analysed within the larger framework of the complex task of performance analysis to which we shall now turn.

Further reading

There are numerous books on dramatists studied from a 'stagecraft' point of view, which contain close readings of particular works in relation to their conditions of performance. For Greek drama, see Taplin (1977) and Revermann

(2006); for Shakespeare, see Brown (1966), Styan (1967) and Jones (1971). For more systematic approaches to the relationship between text and performance, Williams (1972) remains the most theoretically nuanced, together with Styan (1963), the two texts that pioneered the field. Beckerman (1970), a much quoted study, proposes a proto-structuralist approach to analysing drama, by replacing intrinsic textual divisions such as 'act' or 'scene' by a notion of 'segmentation', which more closely corresponds to human perception. Styan (1975) represents a shift in focus towards drama as 'communication', and attempts to bring in media theory in order to better understand the function of the audience. The most systematic treatment of drama as communication is Pfister (1988), first published in German in 1977. Although its terminology is sometimes daunting, and today somewhat dated, it remains an important contribution to understanding how dramatic texts function and 'work' trans-historically.

The field of semiotics, to which Pfister especially is indebted, has provided a new vocabulary for analysing drama, and is especially interested in the relation between text and performance. Elam (1980) introduces the field for English-speaking readers, although his book places much more emphasis on text than performance. A more balanced (and readable) introduction to semiotics is Aston and Savona (1991). For detailed applications of the semiotic approach to specific texts and performances, see Issacharoff and Jones (1988).

For students interested in exploring the changing function and status of the dramatic text as a material object, Peters (2000) is essential reading; Dillon (2006) clarifies these questions with respect to the Early Modern period in England. For a discussion of the status of drama as an object of academic and theoretical study, see Shepherd and Wallis (2004), who provide an excellent genealogical survey from the Early Modern period to contemporary postmodern performance.

Chapter 8

Performance analysis

Performance analysis constitutes a central field of study and research for theatre studies. Whether historical or contemporary, performances are what theatre scholars analyse, and they form the one part of theatrical culture that they alone are responsible for. It is the special area of expertise that distinguishes theatre scholars from other disciplines that concern themselves with theatre. For this reason, students will be expected to familiarize themselves with the techniques and methodological problems attendant on analysing performances.

As a first step, it is necessary to differentiate between the two terms 'production' and 'performance', which are often used loosely or even synonymously. As we saw in the previous chapter (p. 127), a play in performance is made up of three discrete levels that in the act of perception are difficult to distinguish: the text, the staging of the text and the performance. The performance is the unique event witnessed. It includes, to a large degree, audience involvement, whether this is manifestly evident or not. Any performance is made up of complex patterns of interaction between stage and auditorium. The performance is therefore characterized by ephemerality; it is transitory and its analysis will tend to emphasize the event and its impact on the spectators at a particular point in time. Because of the extremely complex cognitive, aesthetic, emotional and interpersonal processes that are at work, even during an intellectually undemanding performance, an analysis that seeks to take account of the actual eventness of a performance might be as much sociological or psychological as it is hermeneutical in orientation, and might fall more properly in the realm of audience research (see Chap. 2).

Because of the manifold non-aesthetic dynamics at play during a performance, which most theatre scholars are not trained to analyse in a scientific way, performance analysis tends to concentrate on the level of 'production' or 'staging'. The term 'production' can be ambiguous in English, and refers to the administrative and financial organization as much as to artistic content. Because of this confusion, the term 'staging' or its French equivalent *'mise-en-scène'* are used in theatre studies to refer to the aesthetic structure of a production or, in semiotic terms, to its arrangement of signs. Throughout this book, the terms 'staging' and '*mise-en-scène*' will be used interchangeably and synonymously. The staging is the result of the artistic endeavour of the director, designers (including lighting and sound) and actors; it is most usually an 'interpretation' of a drama but, as we saw in the previous chapter, need not necessarily be so. The production might equally arise from improvisation and devised work. The object of analysis is therefore, in the first instance, an aesthetic product resulting from an intentional organization of signs.

It must be stressed that this terminological distinction between 'performance' and 'production' is by no means standardized, although most scholars recognize the importance of the differentiation. The generally accepted term is 'performance analysis', even if in most cases production analysis is carried out. This means that the focus is usually on the more-or-less constant features of the production (set, costumes, performance space), whereas the variable aspects, such as changes in a specific actor's performance, are less frequently examined.

Despite the aforementioned terminological slippage, consensus can be found that the following three levels should be distinguished, even though they may be differently labelled.

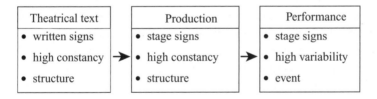

Theatrical text	Production	Performance
• written signs	• stage signs	• stage signs
• high constancy	• high constancy	• high variability
• structure	• structure	• event

An artistic team transforms the theatrical text consisting of written language into organized stage signs (the production), which could also be termed, somewhat old-fashionedly, a 'theatrical work of art' (if it indeed aspires to such status). The realization each evening of the production produces an individual performance with its special eventness. Strictly speaking, it is only the performance that is directly accessible to the spectator. At each level, specific dimensions are added, which are difficult to isolate during the performance event. This important distinction presents us with the somewhat paradoxical situation that we can only analyse a production via its performance, which renders only a partial view of the full potentiality of the play in production. In most cases, it is not especially difficult to negotiate between the different levels. Most professional repertory theatres place great emphasis on ensuring the maximum consistency between performances, i.e. in manufacturing realizations of the productions with a minimum of variability. Although theatre history abounds with anecdotes highlighting the aspect of variability, to over-emphasize this aspect would have severe methodological implications. It would lead to an aesthetics of the aleatory (the moment of chance), which has its own special history in theatre and performance but is still the exception rather than the norm. We speak of and presumably want to study Peter Brook's *Dream*, Peter Stein's *Three Sisters*, Giorgio Strehler's *Tempest*, and so on. To be able to refer to such important and internationally-viewed productions as points of orientation assumes a degree of consistency across the many hundreds of individual performances. Only then is any kind of intersubjective exchange between scholars possible; this itself represents an important precondition for the existence of a discipline. In the final analysis, however, it makes little sense heuristically to insist on a rigid distinction. When we engage in *performance* analysis, we will probably emphasize the *production*, but at the same time include observations on specific examples of audience or acting behaviour witnessed at a given showing.

Some scholars insist on the uniqueness of the individual performance, on its non-repeatability. There are, indeed, some performances that are by definition unique, or that integrate variability into the structure of the event. Early performance art was predicated on the principle of singularity. For example, in his work *Shoot*, the American performance artist Chris Burden had himself shot in the arm by an assistant. The 'event' was photographed and filmed but, understandably perhaps, not repeated. An example for the second category comprising structurally inherent variation would be improvisational theatre. In this type of theatre, text and action are created anew each night. What remains constant is the general format and the types of scenes employed. Such examples remain, however, exceptions. Most productions, even those that belong to the category of postdramatic theatre, reveal a high degree of *consistency*, and can therefore be analysed as 'works' in the sense of having an organized aesthetic structure.

Notation and documentation

Until relatively recently (the last two to three decades), performance analysis was regarded as a practical impossibility because of the difficulties involved in notating the performance. It was one thing to define the performance as theatre studies's central object of research; it was quite another to produce a textual version of the ephemeral stage work for study. It was considered essential to produce, as it were, a 'work' for both mnemotechnical and systematic reasons. Such a need to fix the transient and complex interplay of theatrical signs in written form was a response to a philological conception, according to which aesthetic objects had to be made available for study in material form. Because it is next to impossible to render a performance in textual form, the whole undertaking of performance analysis was regarded as doomed to failure.

Although notation techniques are well established in dance choreography and also in prompt copies of playscripts, there they fulfil a practical purpose of ensuring repeatability of stage action, and do not represent an autonomous work. Notation in the context of performance analysis is supposed to render a multi-media work of art into textual form. The problem was 'solved' by a combination of technological and academic developments:

- *technological*: the development of accessible video technology meant that theatre performances could be more easily recorded. A video recording can capture myriad details for which written notation would require numerous visits. Video recordings are, however, problematic sources. The camera always produces only a partial view of the action, which can be further distorted and manipulated by post-production editing. Professional television recordings are especially fond of close-ups to simulate a televisual experience to the detriment of other things happening on stage. Nevertheless, for most aspects of staging, video recordings remain the best approximation of the live event, and certainly enable analysis of many aspects of the staging (De Marinis 1985).

- *academic*: the development of video technology during the 1970s was paralleled by the rise of theatre semiotics and its flexible concept of 'text'. Semiotics remains a science devoted to explaining how signs generate meaning and how these meanings are decoded. This meant that semiotics focused its interest on the 'text' of the production, the relatively invariable aspect of performance, that could in fact be reliably captured on videotape and studied.

Despite the availability of video, theatre students should still practice notation in the form of notes made during or immediately after a performance, because it remains an important part of performance analysis. Such notes are an important mnemonic for later analysis, and they represent a record of one's own perception. It is, however, difficult to produce reliable and useful notes from just one visit. The most productive notes are produced after two or more visits to a production.

Recent developments, particularly in the UK, towards practice-as-research have led to an increased awareness of the notation/documentation problem. In this case, students' own work, usually at MA or PhD level, is by necessity the subject of the documentation. The students' own artistic activity must be made available in other media so that it can be assessed and examined. The new possibilities offered by DVD technology are being used to create complex documentations including video recordings, photographs and written texts, often linked together by hypertext. Notation and documentation are not, however, strictly, the same thing, as notation is usually applied to situations where students are not in control of the artistic production.[1]

Tools of analysis

On the basis of the previous theoretical and terminological reflections, we can draw the following provisional conclusions. Performance analysis is carried out usually by drawing on the following sources:

- on the basis of notes made during one or more visits to a performance. If the production is of a play, it can be useful to prepare a prompt copy, where one records important moves, lighting changes and scenographic devices. The aim here is not to produce a meticulous record of all moves and changes in intonation, etc. but to provide a selection of striking differences that point to significant interpretive decisions made by the directorial team. The 'significance' is usually only recognizable on the basis of very good prior knowledge of the text.
- on the basis of a video recording. Here the same criteria pertain as to notation-based analysis. It is important to contextualize and supplement video recordings with other source material such as reviews and photographs.

While notation and video recordings remain the two most important sources for performance analysis, a number of other documents can be included where available. They can be divided into production and reception sources (see Table 5).

Table 5. Tools for performance analysis

Production	Reception
prompt books	performance notes
programmes, outreach materials	theatre reviews
interviews with artists	photographs
set and costume designs	video recordings
rehearsal observations	questionnaires

This list demonstrates that, in some respects, performance analysis, depending on the types of sources used, is very close to theatre historical research (see Chap. 6). From an epistemological viewpoint, the two activities are very closely allied, even analogous, as Erika Fischer-Lichte has argued (Fischer-Lichte 1994). In a strict sense, every performance analysis writes about a past event that could be termed 'historical'. In practice, of course, the questions and hypotheses that we pose in relation to contemporary or near-contemporary productions will be different to those relating to a production of, say, Vsevolod Meyerhold or Max Reinhardt.

If we look more closely at the types of sources, it is difficult and not even fruitful to establish a hierarchy beforehand. The relative importance of the sources utilized is determined first and foremost by the questions or hypotheses being asked of the production (see the analytical steps below). In most cases, however, direct observation (and the notes resulting thereof), in combination with a video recording where available, constitute the best sources. Because there are different types of video recordings – they range from short demos or archival tapes produced by the theatres themselves to professional multi-camera productions for television – they can be regarded either as production or reception documents. For elements of staging such as movement, proxemics (the distances between bodies) and gesture, a video recording is almost essential.

Production-related documents and sources

The prompt book, acting edition, or director's copy of the text can be very useful for clarifying questions of detail. Although there is seldom standardization of notation used in such texts, and they are very seldom published, they almost always exist and contain information on blocking, sound and lighting cues. Such texts also indicate cuts to or rearrangements of the text that demonstrate crucial interpretive decisions by the production team regarding characterization, narrative and the directorial concept in general.

Programmes are another source available for performance analysis. Their analytical value is disputed, however, and highly dependent on the information contained. Apart from cast lists and advertising, programmes sometimes include statements by the production team. With the growing importance of dramaturgy, outreach, audience development and education, programmes, education packs and similar publications have become important mouthpieces for the concept of a production. What used to be called the 'director's note' is being replaced by essays, associative images and interviews with the cast and team. As sources, programmes are, of course, highly mediated. They probably convey the conception of the production intended by the directorial team, and their use and interpretation must be measured against other sources.

Interviews with artists and technical staff associated with the production can also produce much useful information illuminating production-relevant aspects. They are particularly important for analyses concerned with the processual elements of a production (its genesis and development).

Set and costume designs often provide the most immediate indication of the directorial concept. They are usually conceived in close collaboration between set and costume designers, often even by the same person. Set and costume may anchor the production – especially of a classical text – in a particular time and place, or conversely seek to deliberately obscure such direct references. Because of their visual and relatively immutable nature, semiotics offers a very useful and precise method for analysing such references (see Chap. 5).

Rehearsal observations can provide illuminating insights into a production concept, especially its evolution, although they cannot be taken for granted. Rehearsals are a complex and often intimate process where non-participants are not always welcome. The observer at rehearsals becomes a kind of participant-observer in an ethnographical sense, and should therefore be prepared to invest considerable time. In recent developments towards practice-as-research, the rehearsal process is a crucial aspect of the production, and is documented in considerable detail. Here, artist and researcher are often one and the same person. For an example of an extended rehearsal process observation, see David Selbourne's account of Peter Brook's *A Midsummer Night's Dream* production for the Royal Shakespeare Company (Selbourne 1982).

Reception-oriented documents and sources

Reception-oriented documents and sources can be divided into two categories:

(1) documents produced by the student, either in the form of notes made during the performance or systematic enquiries such as questionnaires (see below)
(2) documents made by others such as reviews, web blogs, etc.

Performance notes are the impressions jotted down either during or immediately after the performance. They are especially important if there is no video recording available, as it is exceptionally difficult to memorize the plethora of impressions generated by any theatre performance for a long period. Such notes are by definition highly subjective, but this is no different to responses generated by any other aesthetic object, except that the transient nature of theatre demands – more than, say, a poem or painting – that these responses be fixed in some way. It is especially useful to note important proxemic relationships (the spatial distances between bodies on stage), as these are perhaps the most ephemeral of the signs generated by a performance.

Theatre reviews are important for a number of reasons. They provide an important point of comparison with one's own perception and observation. What does the professional critic see (or not)? Reviews are most useful when several can be studied for comparative purposes. Sometimes strikingly different opinions and readings are articulated. In such cases, the task of analysis is not to choose the 'right' one but to discuss why a production or certain scene might give occasion for such dissent. Most critics do not engage self-reflexively with their own judgements and opinions in the sense that they do not question their own premises. Although reviews are by definition somewhat tendentious, they can serve as a point of departure, often in disagreement, for one's own hypotheses.

Production photographs belong to what Patrice Pavis terms 'supplementary documents' (Pavis 2003: 40). Depending on how they are used, they can be both productive and problematic. They are useful in as much as they make accessible for study visual aspects of a production such as set design and costumes, as well as certain physical aspects of gesture, facial expression and, of course, masks, if used. The problematic nature of photographs resides in their own aesthetic qualities. A good professional photographer will not attempt to merely 'document' a production but to produce images that are themselves products of an artistic process. Although the medium-specific aesthetic strategies of such photographs do not automatically diminish their documentary value, it must be remembered that theatre photos are produced for any number of reasons – most importantly advertising – but certainly not to serve the purpose of performance analysis.

The same circumspection required for analysing photographs should also be applied to video recordings. As mentioned above, it is important to distinguish between tapes made by the theatres themselves for archival and documentary purposes (for restaging productions, for example) and professional recordings made for television or as commercial DVDs. The latter can be divided into three subcategories depending on the degree of adaptation:

(1) live recordings during a performance
(2) studio recordings
(3) adaptations by the director or choreographer for film or television.

The three forms represent different degrees of distance from the original theatre production, which must be reflected in the analysis. When examining video recordings, it is crucial to be aware that they are not just *documents* of a performance but *monuments* in their own right, i.e. autonomous artistic products with special qualities not present in the theatre production (see De Marinis 1985 for the distinction between documents and monuments). Video recordings, depending on their type, always mediate the original performance, and the difference between recording and original must also be taken into consideration.

The rapid development of digital technology has created improved possibilities for recording performances. In comparison to the older VHS technology, digital video cameras provide an inexpensive way to capture performances and furthermore to edit the material on a computer. Independent theatre groups especially are required to produce demo DVDs for festivals and other venues as well as full-length documentations of productions. This material provides, of course, potential source documents for students and scholars. More recently, some groups have even begun to produce DVDs with the special features employed in Hollywood films such as directors' comments, multiple angle shots, extra material and so on.[2]

Questionnaires, otherwise known as systematic audience surveys, can also be used for performance analysis, especially when they are combined with more hermeneutic interpretations as discussed in Chap. 2 (see p. 45). In the late 1980s, scholars began to develop questionnaires to help students structure their impressions immediately after attending a performance. In his study of performance analysis, Patrice Pavis reviews three different questionnaires, including his own. The latter, first published in 1988, has been translated into several languages and is regularly revised by the author. A slightly abridged version is reproduced here.

Questionnaire for performance analysis (after Pavis 2003: 37–40)

(1) General characteristics of the *mise-en-scène*
   (a) What holds the elements of the performance together (relationship between systems of staging)?
   (b) What are the contradictions or coherencies between the text and *mise-en-scène?*
   (c) Can you identify general aesthetic principles?
   (d) What disturbs you about this production? Which moments are strong, weak, boring?
(2) Scenography
   (a) Relationship between audience space and acting space
   (b) Systems of colours, forms, materials and their connotations
   (c) Principles of structuring/organizing space
      (i) Dramaturgical function of the stage space and its occupation
      (ii) Relationship between on-stage and off-stage

      (iii) Connections between the space utilized and the fiction of the dramatic text

      (iv) Relationship between what is shown and what is concealed

      (v) How does the scenography evolve? To what do its transformations correspond?

(3) Lighting system: nature, connections to space and actors

(4) Objects: nature, function, relationship to space and body

(5) Costumes, makeup, masks: function, system, relationship to body

(6) Actors' performances

    (a) Physical description of the actors (movements, facial expression, changes in appearance)

    (b) Construction of character: actor/role relationship

    (c) Voice: qualities, effects produced, diction

    (d) Status of the performer: past, professional situation

(7) Function of music, noise, silence

(8) Rhythm of the performance

    (a) rhythm of various signifying systems (dialogue, lighting, systems of gesture)

    (b) Overall rhythm of the performance: continuous or discontinuous, connection with *mise-en-scène*

(9) Reading the plot through the *mise-en-scène*

    (a) What story is being told? Summarize it. Does the *mise-en-scène* recount the same story as the text?

    (b) What are the dramaturgical choices? Coherence or incoherence of reading?

    (c) What are the ambiguities in the story and how are they clarified in the *mise-en-scène?*

    (d) What is the genre of the dramatic text according to this *mise-en-scéne?*

(10) The text in performance

    (a) Choice of version for staging: what are the modifications? Translations?

    (b) Role given to the dramatic text in the *mise-en-scène?*

(11) The spectator

    (a) Within what theatre institution does the production take place?

    (b) What expectations did you have of the performance (text, director, actors)?

    (c) How did the audience react?

(12) How to record and remember the performance.

    (a) What escapes notation?

    (b) What images do you remember?

(13) What cannot be put into signs and meaning (semiotized)?

In comparison to sociologically oriented questionnaires that aim to gauge spectators' reactions and impressions or to gather demographic statistics, this one is intended to help students of theatre studies notate their reactions to a performance. The order of the questions corresponds broadly to the way we experience a performance aesthetically, i.e. the oscillation between making sense of the overall meaning (the question of the 'directorial concept') and decoding smaller units of meaning (a particular costume, gesture, etc.). Pavis points out that this and all such questionnaires provide only outlines and guidelines with which to focus and structure our viewing. It should help us to pay attention to aspects of a production that may otherwise escape our notice. With repeated usage, it should ultimately help students to expand their awareness for the ways performances generate meaning and function aesthetically. Above all, it should be seen as a tool and not as the goal of analysis; it provides a means to an end and not the end in itself.

Goal of analysis

What is, then, the point of analysis? If we take the word 'analysis' literally, then we mean the examination of something by breaking it down into its constituent parts. If we 'analyse' a sentence grammatically, we are looking at the way the different elements fit together to produce meaning. If we analyse a poem, we are taught to identify key images, metaphors, conceits, etc. as a means to making sense of the poem as a whole. Any form of analysis will try and relate parts to the whole, assuming that the whole is not fully comprehensible without an understanding of its constituent parts, and vice versa.

How does one analyse a performance? There is, of course, no single answer to this question. In a sense, each production will throw up different questions, which the analysis must address. First of all, we can make distinctions between three broad approaches:

(1) *process-oriented* analysis focuses on the way a production is created, and tends to have a strong social-science or cultural studies bias. Here, we would be looking at the genesis of a production: the interaction of the team as they create the *mise-en-scène*. In this kind of approach, first-hand observation and interviews will play a more important role than decoding signs from the spectator position. The cinematic equivalents of this type of analysis are the popular 'making of' films available on DVDs, where, in the better examples, director, designers and cinematographers explain how they arrived at a particular style or artistic decision. The fact that the majority of artists, cinematic or theatrical, will emphasize 'truth' as the ultimate category of intuition marks the limits of these kinds of interpretations. Process-oriented analysis will often follow a production as it changes over time, especially if it is performed in different cultural contexts. Examples of this approach can be found in Harvie (2002), on

a production by DV8 Physical Theatre, and Balme (1993), an analysis of Giorgio Strehler's *Faust* project.

(2) *product-oriented* analysis focuses as a rule on aesthetic questions from the same perspective as the normal spectator, without the help of inside knowledge. It regards the production as a finished aesthetic product, and the analytical terminology will probably make use of semiotics to some degree.

(3) *event-oriented* analysis emphasizes the process of the performance on a particular night; it will focus on interaction between auditorium and stage, and is particularly interested in the contributing factors leading to variations between performances.

These methods are, of course, by no means mutually exclusive. Analyses can integrate all three approaches, although usually one or the other will dominate.

Methods and models

In the face of such diversity, the next important question is to determine which methods and steps should be applied. It is clear that the student must be aware of basic choices at his or her disposal. Although there are few recipes or models, we can initially distinguish two general approaches, which we can call *transformational* and *structural* analysis.

Transformational analysis proceeds from the text to performance. It begins with an analysis of the text and attempts to compare the choices made in a particular production with the options the text would seem to provide. A detailed example of this approach can be found in Chap. 9 of Aston and Savona (1991). *Structural analysis* is followed in Pavis (2003) and Fischer-Lichte (1992). It proceeds invariably from a selection of a particular signifying system or level of segmentation such as character, plot and space. Whereas transformational analysis tends to follow the narrative line of the text, Fischer-Lichte proposes for structural analysis a more flexible approach. Neither the choice of signifying system nor the point in time is predetermined: 'it is completely arbitrary which step is taken first and which element of the text is then chosen for examination' (Fischer-Lichte 1992: 246). According to this method, one could select the text as a point of departure, but this is by no means assumed. Fischer-Lichte argues that one should try and follow the way a particular performance arranges the signifying systems. Pavis is more prescriptive in his structural approach. He states unequivocally: 'Performance analysis should begin with the description of the actor; for the actor is at the center of the mise-en-scène and tends to be the focal point drawing together the elements of a production' (Pavis 2003: 55). This may indeed be the case in most productions, but there are always exceptions to confirm the rule, so the Fischer-Lichte argument for flexibility would seem to be the more circumspect one.

Table 6 provides a schematic illustration of the two different approaches. The following points should be noted. It is not intended that the one approach be contrasted in evaluative terms, i.e. as superior to the other, but primarily to illustrate the different analytical steps that could or should be taken when applying one or the other. Aston and Savona (1991) provide a transformational analysis of two film versions of Samuel Beckett's *Krapp's Last Tape*. The first version, directed by Donald McWhinnie and featuring Patrick Magee, was first staged in 1958 but not filmed until 1972. The second version was a videotaped version directed by Alan Schneider for television in 1971, with Jack McGowran in the title role.

If we look at the preparatory steps of both methods, we see very clear differences. Transformational analysis proceeds from an analysis of the text. Very often it will consult literary criticism and scholarly research in order to frame the questions with which to approach the production. Structural analysis, on the other hand, tends to emphasize a set of procedures – the choice and ordering of sign systems – rather than an interpretation derived from the text. The work of a director like Robert Wilson highlights the limitations of transformational analysis. Even when directing a canonical text such as *King Lear*, Wilson's point of departure is not an interpretation of the text. Rather, he would appear to bring to it a predetermined artistic practice. Wilson's *Lear* is rather an addition to Wilson's oeuvre; any analysis of it must take into account this characteristic of Wilson's productions. In this respect, it is a quintessentially intertextual staging situated in the aesthetics of postdramatic theatre.

In this and the previous chapter, we have discussed the term 'postdramatic theatre', where performances usually do not proceed from a pre-existing dramatic text but meaning that new works are usually created using a collaborative working method known as 'devised performance'. Although the term 'postdramatic theatre' encompasses a broad range of work going back to the 1970s and is largely coterminous in the early period with performance art, now it is a much broader phenomenon. From the point of view of analysis, such performances, Lehmann argues, defy semiotic interpretation because they emphasize evanescent qualities such as energy, presence and, very often, the spectators' reactions. They aim to elicit responses beyond the intellectual and which are thereby often difficult to verbalize. They explore the realms of performance that cannot be semiotized, i.e. translated into signs. Very often, postdramatic performances challenge the fine line between reality and fiction and, in the work of Jan Fabre for example, test how much reality the spectator can bear. Time becomes an aesthetic experience in itself when Marina Abramovic, in her

Table 6. Models of performance analysis: dramatic theatre

Transformational analysis	Structural analysis
Krapps's Last Tape by Samuel Beckett. Royal Court Theatre 1958, Director: Donald McWhinnie; film version 1965, Director: Alan Schneider. Source: Aston and Savona (1991: 162–77)	*King Lear* by William Shakespeare. Frankfurt 1990, Director Robert Wilson. Source: Fischer-Lichte (1997)

(1) Preparatory steps
   (a) analysis of dramatic text to identify points of focus
   (b) emphasis on disjunction and undermining of habitualized reading strategies
	(1) Preparatory steps
	   (a) discussion of earlier Wilson productions
	   (b) remarks on Wilson's refusal to interpret

(2) Analysis
   (a) space
   (b) objects
   (c) actors
   (d) cinematic aspects
	(2) Analysis
	   (a) structure of production: description of opening scene; use of leitmotif
	   (b) space
	   (c) figures: costumes, gesture, diction, arrangements

(3) Results: demonstrates how film adaptation applies Beckett's strategies of destabilization of theatrical and dramatic conventions to cinematic viewer	(3) Results
	   (a) performance as kind of rite of passage
	   (b) alters perception of time and space
	   (c) link to avantgarde traditions
	   (d) production is a variation on the theme of life and death but does attempt a particular 'reading' of the play

performance *Lips of Thomas* (1995), lies naked and bleeding on a cross made of melting ice after cutting herself by breaking a glass filled with red wine, or when Forced Entertainment invites spectators to participate in the six-hour performance *Quizoola* (1996), to say nothing of their twenty-four-hour *Who Can Sing a Song to Unfrighten Me?* (1999). Clearly, there are many other things happening in such performances besides the experience of time, but the experiential rather than semantic quality of temporality is crucial. When the performers in Jan Fabre's work *History of Tears* (2005) actually pass water on stage, we are invited, perhaps, to think semantically about the significance of water for our body and mankind, but more probably we are challenged viscerally by the public exhibition on stage of an act normally reserved for private or public lavatories.

Postdramatic performance is exceptionally diverse in its themes, devices, spaces and use of language. It may be text-heavy or entirely non-verbal, low-tech or employ complex digital technology. In terms of analysis, neither trans-formational nor structural approaches are applicable. For the former, there is usually no script from which to work, and most postdramatic performance is enacted only by the creator(s). Structural analysis may prove too limiting because the performance may be less about the 'structure of signs' on stage than about spectatorial experience of space or experiential confrontation with a bleeding or urinating body. For these reasons, it is not possible to estab-lish a fixed structure of steps. Each work will require a different approach; it will probably demand a different theoretical framework, and may require an emphasis on the text, the space, the performers' bodies, the media technology employed (see Chap. 12) and so on.

Further reading

Despite the importance of performance analysis, the number of books in English devoted to the subject is actually very small. Pavis (2003) remains the most thorough treatment to date, although it is not ideal as a first introduction to the subject. It represents the summation of twenty years' thinking and writing by one of theatre studies's most influential scholars. Part 2 of Fischer-Lichte (1992) presents a systematic introduction to and application of theatre semiotics as a method of performance analysis. The German original was first published in 1983, so some of the semiotic terminology is now clearly dated. The article cited above (Fischer-Lichte 1997) gives a better and more pragmatic idea of how semiotic performance analysis works in action. Part 2 of Aston and Savona (1991) provides a less technical and more accessible introduction to semiotic performance analysis. Martin and Sauter (1997) provides a thorough discussion of many theoretical issues, and offers six analyses, one of which (Fischer-Lichte 1997) is referred to in this book (p. 145). The journal *Theatre Research International* (*TRI*) has published two special issues on performance analysis: 22(1) (Spring 1997) and 25(1) (Spring 2000). Since 2002, *TRI* publishes performance analyses in each issue.

Chapter 9

Music theatre

In this and the next chapter, we shall apply some of the principles discussed in the previous chapters to music and dance theatre. From the perspective of traditional dramatic theatre, we may be entering *terra incognita*. Yet, gradually, there is an increasing awareness that these aspects of theatre should be integrated into theatre studies, as we emphasized in the introduction. This broadening of perspectives is especially urgent in light of the challenges posed by postdramatic theatre forms, which often cross traditional genre boundaries. The following pages will outline a number of points of contact – author, text, theatrical context, staging – that have already been discussed in reference to dramatic theatre.

Elements

As pointed out in the introduction (see p. 5), the term 'music theatre' is used here to refer to three main theatrical genres: opera, operetta and musical. From a theatre studies perspective, the analysis of these genres poses the same set of problems as any other kind of theatrical text, except that the musical 'track' (the score) adds an extra expressive dimension, and with it an additional degree of complexity. In music theatre, we find the same basic division between a written text (the score and libretto) and the staged work. We also encounter the same initial questions: what 'work' are we talking about: the text or the production? How can the relationship between the work and the production be grasped analytically? We shall begin by approaching the two levels – text and staging – separately, in order to point out particular features specific to music theatre.

Like dramatic theatre, the textual level of music theatre (the score and the libretto) is historically a problematic one. The operas that have entered the canon are often the product of many factors. Exigencies of genre, changing authorial status and theatrical conventions have worked together and against each other to produce the existing canon. If we are analysing music-theatre texts from a historical perspective for a dramaturgical adaptation for a production (as is often the case), these factors need to be kept in mind.

The question of genre, for example, is crucial for understanding under what conditions particular works were written and for whom they were staged. Over its 400-year history, opera has produced a number of specific genres, and with them generic conventions that influenced the composition. Examples include *opera seria, opera buffa, tragédie lyrique, opéra comique, grand opéra*, etc. whose conventions determined both content and form of individual works. We need also to include 'subaltern' genres such as operetta and musical, which also developed highly specific formal characteristics and theatrical conventions. The historicity of genre conventions should be understood but not regarded as binding for the analysis of the works when performed.

A second important question is that of author function. The Elizabethan theatre was dominated by authorial teams, rather than the single individual. In opera too, we usually have a double author function because of the division between composer and librettist. There are notable exceptions, such as Richard Wagner or Hector Berlioz, where both functions were combined, but they remain the exception. Today, it is usual to equate the author function of an opera with its composer, and the work of the librettist to that of a subordinate 'service' role. Yet, this is by no means historically accurate. For example, the dominant figure of eighteenth-century *opera seria* was not a composer but an author of libretti, Pietro Metastasio (1698–1782), whose texts dominated European opera for several decades and were highly esteemed for their literary value (although they are seldom read today for their own sake). By the mid nineteenth century, this relationship had changed. In comparison to Metastasio, Francesco Maria Piave (1810–67) was little more than a scriptwriter for Verdi and without public literary ambitions, although he worked for a number of other composers. Verdi's relationship with his different librettists casts an interesting light on the very special relationship between composers and writers. Composers such as Verdi and Puccini worked extremely closely with their various collaborators, as is documented in the extensive correspondence of both. These written exchanges provide valuable documents where the controversial area of authorial intention is made explicit. Both composers were centrally concerned with dramaturgical as well as musical questions, and the enduring popularity of their works testifies to the successful marriage of music and drama within the conventions of their times and beyond.

Since the twentieth century, the relationship between composition and text has become more complex. Beginning with Richard Strauss's setting to music of Oscar Wilde's drama *Salome* (1905), composers increasingly began to take existing works or arrange textual collages as the basis for composition. Alban Berg's *Wozzeck* (1925) (based on Georg Büchner's *Woyzeck*) or Wolfgang Rihm's *The Conquest of Mexico* (1992) (a collage of texts by Antonin Artaud and others) are prominent examples that challenge the traditional relationship. From Metastasio to contemporary collage, the textual track of music theatre, known somewhat inexactly as the libretto, has now become an area of research in its own right.

Music dramaturgy

How do music and text work together and structure action, characters, space, time and all those elements that we associate with dramatic texts? This inter-relationship can be termed 'music dramaturgy', a concept that is not clearly defined but is increasingly common. It means that the music in opera fulfils specific semantic functions related to characterization and the organization of dramatic action, as well as the stylistic ones it shares with other musical forms. The term derives from the German *Musikdramaturgie*, where it has various meanings. In its most extreme definition, the term implies that, in opera, the music determines all aspects of a work, including its staging. The famous opera director Walter Felsenstein (1901–75) regarded the score as a kind of prompt book, a perspective that is entirely consistent with his directorial style. This perspective certainly finds confirmation in the work of some nineteenth-century composers such as Richard Wagner, who attempted (more than most of his contemporaries) to regulate the modalities of performance in the composition. We find both detailed stage directions and almost mimetic compositional passages that seem to constrain and direct the performers in their moves. In *The Flying Dutchman*, for example, the first entrance of the eponymous title figure sounds as though every single step is set out in the music, which at the time may have been intended as assistance for a theatre practice that scarcely knew the idea of prepared blocking. Today, it sounds more like the first moves of Frankenstein's monster, as more than one music scholar has remarked. This kind of exact paralleling of music and movement is known pejoratively as 'mickey mousing', a clear indication that contemporary staging, even in a relatively conservative form such as opera, has little interest in simply doubling musical and/or textual signs in movement.

Music dramaturgy should therefore be understood in a more flexible sense than just as a set of prescriptions laid out in the score. A music-dramaturgical approach to opera does mean that – in comparison to opera studies within musicology – theatre-related aspects form the focal point of scholarly interest. In place of considerations of style or compositional development, the operas (score and libretto) are regarded primarily as works created for the stage. The task of research then is to elucidate this relationship both in the past and present. This kind of research can be seen as analogous to the 'stagecraft' approach to dramatic texts discussed in Chap. 7, and is indeed directly influenced by this tradition. Like its progenitor, the stagecraft method, a music-dramaturgical approach can be a productive method of examining the relationships between text and stage, but should not be applied in a normative mode with the aim of ascertaining the 'accuracy' of a particular production.

Is it possible to examine more closely the respective functions of the two textual levels of score and libretto? In both cases we can speak of special functions. Neither libretto nor score is absolute or autonomous; a libretto is seldom read as a drama, and an opera score is seldom performed in its entirety as a piece of concert music. A central function of operatic music – up until the mid twentieth century at least – has been to represent the emotions (or passions, to use the rhetorical term). The development of opera during the Baroque period meant that it was closely allied to the ruling artistic doctrine of the passions that dominated aesthetic theory and practice across the arts (see p. 19). The aria was the part of the operatic action that was given over to representation of the passions, and in the early period at least can be seen as analogous to the monologue in dramatic theatre, where gestures and facial expressions were cued to specific emotional states (passions).

The fact that passions need to be expressed directly on stage both acoustically and visually has had important repercussions for the way operas are constructed, both dramatically and musically. In comparison to spoken drama, opera is dependent on the direct stage representation of all dramaturgically important moments, or, put another way, only those events that can be represented theatrically are included in the action. This means that opera tends to avoid so-called analytical structures, i.e. stories where the uncovering of past events is of crucial importance, such as *Oedipus Rex* or most of Ibsen's later plays. Only plots that were conducive to direct representation on stage were considered fit for operatic adaptation. A famous confirmation of this opinion is the story of Puccini's discovery of the *Madame Butterfly* subject. His inspiration came from witnessing a performance of the David Belasco melodrama on the same subject in London. Although Puccini understood hardly any English, he was moved to tears by the stage action alone, which conveyed itself in all essential details by pantomimic means.

Music theatre structures its stories around a recurrent set of conventions and units of action. In opera, the two main building blocks are:

(1) aria: an extended vocal, lyrical piece performed by one singer and accompanied by the orchestra, and usually expressing a situation of emotional agitation;

(2) recitative: the text is sung in a way that the rhythms of natural speech are imitated with little orchestral accompaniment.

There are also more complex musical and dramaturgical forms such as duets, chorus and ensemble numbers, which provide for a greater variety of character interaction than is usually found in dramatic theatre. Where arias or duets tend to emphasize sustained moments of emotional expression and thereby suspend the progression of the story, recitatives, which substitute for spoken dialogue, function to move the action forward. The building blocks of aria and recitative meant that until the mid nineteenth century, operas had a flexible dramatic structure whereby arias, duets and ensemble pieces could be removed, substituted or adapted. It was this 'kitset' principle known as the 'number opera' that Wagner so vehemently opposed with his new conception of 'music drama', which replaced individual 'numbers' with a seamless integration of text and music.

Another important factor to consider for the historical and contemporary analysis of opera is the relationship between character and singing voice. The division of singers into soprano, tenor, baritone, etc. not only marks the range and type of voice but has dramaturgical implications as well. Just as dramatic theatre made use of set character types until well into the twentieth century (some of which go back to the stock types of the *Commedia dell'arte*), so too did opera establish conventions whereby the heroine would invariably be a soprano, the hero a tenor and the male antagonist a bass-baritone.

An interesting variation on the connection between role and voice type are the roles created for the castrati. Many male title roles in the seventeenth and eighteenth centuries were composed for the extremely flexible range of the castrato, who in some cases could cover three octaves up to the highest registers. Many of the male title roles of Handel's operas, such as *Giulio Cesare in Egitto* (*Julius Caesar in Egypt*) or *Ariodante*, were composed with particular castrati in mind, and the central arias require a voice capable of singing in very high registers. As conventions changed, so too did the musical presentation of his operas. By the early twentieth century, the title roles had to be transposed for tenor or baritone so as to fit in with nineteenth-century vocal conventions. Recent Handel productions have tried to go back to the original scores, so the leading male roles are now sung by countertenors or even by sopranos. This flexible approach corresponds to Handel's own practice. If a suitable castrato was not available, he did not hesitate to cast a male role with a soprano.

Text and staging

It is important to keep in mind the changing nature of operatic conventions when analysing productions of operas. Perhaps in no other theatrical form is the 'work' considered so sacrosanct, and alterations or adaptations met with such suspicion or downright rejection. The great operatic composers – from Monteverdi to Handel, from Mozart to Wagner – are considered to be geniuses whose every note enjoys a similar status to holy writ. The opera-goer is, in general, a very competent spectator, usually having seen many versions of his or her favourite works and having heard even more. The task of the directorial team is therefore not an enviable one. While it is not unusual to cut or even adapt a Shakespeare play, such a practice is highly controversial in opera production (and, of course, much more difficult because of the score).

On closer inspection, however, the immortal masterpiece may prove to be more variable and much less sacrosanct than the average opera-goer might imagine. We have already seen that the vocal parts of Handel's operas were quite freely transposed in accordance with prevailing concepts of role and voice type, and that, for Handel himself, vocal range and not gender determined casting. In sum, we can say that it is not just the ingenious idea of the composer but also the prevailing production conditions that determine the form of the work. Changing production conventions, the exigencies of casting singers, the technical possibilities of theatres and, above all, the changing taste of the public meant that, throughout their history, operas were being continually rewritten, cut and recomposed.

Analysis: *La Bohème* and *Ariodante*

For the analysis of an opera or any other genre of music theatre, the same set of problems pertains as with dramatic theatre. We find the same three levels of concretization:

theatrical text → production/staging → performance.

The *theatrical text* consists of the score and libretto in the chosen version or adaptation. The choice of versions can, of course, influence the production. In the case of *Madame Butterfly*, the version will determine whether the opera will be staged as a doomed cross-cultural love story in an exotic setting; as an anti-American, anti-colonial parable; or even as a reflection on the Vietnam war – as was done occasionally in the 1970s.

The level of *production* or *staging* corresponds in all respects to the criteria discussed in Chap. 8 for dramatic theatre (p. 133). It can be seen as a structured system of choices regarding casting, set design, costume, makeup, movement, etc. These are the elements that remain more or less stable throughout the life of the production. As opera productions tend to remain for a long time in repertoire, these elements can be studied using the tools developed above (Chap. 8, p. 136) in particular semiotic categories. An important exception is casting. Because operatic performance is highly reliant on star singers, considerable fluctuation amongst the leading roles is not unusual. Opera houses often invest considerable sums to attract important singers for the first few performances, but they will often be replaced by second-tier singers for the rest of the season.

The singers, of course, play a crucial role on the level of *performance*, the event itself. In addition, we have the performance of the orchestra and conductor, who, for a certain section of the audience, may be equally or even more important than the singers or the staging. The performative achievements of singers, orchestra and conductor on any given night cannot be described or analysed using semiotic terminology. Semiotics are interested in the way meaning is generated, whereas the vocal achievement of a singer on a given night is a highly subjective impression that has little to do with semantics. Although the importance of *mise-en-scène* is undisputed in opera production today, it is still rivalled by the virtuoso singer and conductor as a deciding factor in conditioning audience response.

Despite these peculiarities on the level of performance, the analytic procedures remain the same when approaching an operatic production in terms of its staging. If we are going to analyse a production of *Madame Butterfly* or *La Bohème*, works that in their time attempted to reflect contemporary social reality, then the approach will probably be different to that of a Baroque opera by Handel. While most productions of *Madame Butterfly* tend to emphasize the Japanese setting (whether past or present), it makes little sense to start from considerations of space or costume, as these elements in the stagings often simply replicate the textual signs.

Two productions will serve as examples for analysing opera productions from a transformational and a structural perspective (see Table 7): *La Bohème*, directed by Baz Luhrmann for The Australian Opera, and Handel's *Ariodante*, directed by David Alden for the English National Opera. Both are readily available on DVD. Both have achieved recognition beyond their original place of performance.

Table 7. Models of performance analysis: music theatre

Transformational analysis	Structural analysis
La Bohème by Giacomo Puccini. The Australian Opera, Sydney 1993. Director: Baz Luhrmann. Design: Catherine Martin and Bill Marron. DVD: Image Entertainment, 2002	*Ariodante* by George F. Handel. English National Opera, London 2000. Director: David Alden. Design: Ian MacNeill. DVD: Arthaus Musik 2000

(1) Preparatory steps
  (a) analysis of theatrical text to identify points of focus; consultation of secondary literature
  (b) ascertain any changes to established version
  (c) consult reviews of production
  (d) information on Luhrmann: previous films and productions
  (e) hypothesis: production
	(1) Preparatory steps
	  (a) identify possible analytic approaches
	  (b) consult reviews of production
	  (c) information on Alden and revival of Baroque opera in 1990s
	  (d) hypothesis and focal points: set design and figures

(2) Analysis
  (a) focus on characters and performers; youthful casting
  (b) focus on period setting: 1950s
  (c) compare observations with reviews
  (d) discuss production in connection with Luhrmann's films: *Strictly Ballroom, Romeo + Juliet, Moulin Rouge*
	(2) Analysis
	  (a) set design: stage-within-a-stage
	  (b) figures
	    (i) casting (woman in title role)
	    (ii) costumes
	    (iii) blocking

(3) Results: Discussion of hypothesis in relation to points 2(a) to (d)	(3) Results: production is a self-reflexive treatment of the Baroque

La Bohème

Puccini's *La Bohème* is, like *Madame Butterfly*, one of the most popular operas in the international repertoire, and hence needs little introduction to opera-goers. Any production, therefore, can be measured against well-defined expectations regarding story, casting, setting, etc. The opera, first performed in 1896, is based on an 1846 autobiographical novel by Henri Murger, *Scènes de la vie de Bohème*, which reflects the author's own experiences in 1830s Paris. Like the novel, Puccini's opera is set in Bohemian Paris of the 1830s. Most productions tend to emphasize a nineteenth-century setting, although there have been, of course, many updates. Luhrmann's production is set explicitly in Paris in the late 1950s.

Although the DVD recording was made in 1993 at the Sydney Opera House, with the original cast, the production continued to be performed with different casts until 2003. It transferred to Broadway and other American cities in 2002 where it was performed with four alternating casts but in the same design concept.

Two main features of Luhrmann's production will dominate analysis: casting and setting. The casting of young singers whose ages almost exactly tally with the ages of Puccini's characters could also be termed 'the ideology of youth' and is constitutive of meaning for two reasons. Firstly, the two leading roles – Rodolfo and Mimi – are among the most famous and demanding in the operatic canon. For this reason they are often performed by mature singers, often decades older than the starving, consumptive youngsters of the story. Luhrmann's decision to sacrifice vocal virtuosity for maximum identification between singer, character and, by extension, audience was motivated in part by the requirement of the Australian National Opera that he 'reinvestigate' the opera and make it interesting for a younger audience:

> We spent a good six months investigating, and eventually coming to this revelation that when Puccini wrote 'La Bohème,' opera wasn't even the film of its time, it was the television – it was that popular [. . .] So our mission became . . . how then to take it away from this kind of distant, hallowed, highly-revered art form back to what it was, which was something sort of like cinema, just very popular and broad and able to connect with all kinds of audiences.   (Priromprintr 2004: n.p.)

Secondly, apart from casting the leads with young, attractive singers who no doubt offer greater potential for sympathetic identification than Luciano Pavarotti and Mirella Freni, Luhrmann directs his singers with extreme verve – their physical interaction has an almost naturalistic vitality and informality, quite unlike popular conceptions of static singers, who concentrate more on their vocal production than emotional verisimilitude.

The second central focal point of analysis must be the transferral of setting from 1830 to 1957. This choice was also a careful result of 'investigation' and circumspect modernization. Rather than attempt to Australianize the story, it remained in its original spatial setting but received a temporal update. Paris of

Plate 8. The artists' garret in Baz Luhrmann's production of Puccini's *La Bohème* (1993).

the late 1950s provided a background that was still economically deprived but at the same time close enough to resonate with the audience. Rodolfo's friend, the painter Marcello, makes action paintings in the style of Jackson Pollock. Otherwise, Luhrmann follows Puccini's settings with the exception of act 3. The original takes place outside the gates of Paris, where workers are demanding entry. In Luhrmann's production, the scene is set at the French-Belgian border before high fences, barbed wire and watchtowers. This scene would suggest that the world of concentration camps and prisoner-of-war camps is still close. Today, it resonates more with images of 'Fortress Europe' as a buttress against illegal immigration. Despite this discreet modernization, the original and the Lurhmann production remain in close contact and certainly do not represent any kind of 'hostile takeover'. The period also suggests the mood of existentialism and the absurd characteristics of the 1950s, but also that the bohemian lifestyles of the nineteenth and twentieth centuries are astoundingly similar. In the first act, the set is constructivist in its stylized representation of the artists' garret. Its main feature is a large neon sign 'L'amour', which alludes to the visual branding of Coca-Cola on the one hand, and is a further variation of a favourite Luhrmann stylistic device on the other, whereby key words in the text are given direct visual form (see Plate 8). This emblem also recurs in the 2003 film *Moulin Rouge*, which resonates in several ways with the opera production. Although Luhrmann directed this production before he became internationally known as a film director with his first film *Strictly Ballroom* (1992), the staging has a number of elements in common with this and the other two films in his Red Curtain Trilogy: *Romeo + Juliet* (1996) and *Moulin Rouge* (2001).

Ariodante

In comparison to the familiarity of story and setting that characterize Luhrmann's 1950s *La Bohème*, David Alden's production of *Ariodante* proceeds from an almost reverse set of preconditions.[1] Until the 1980s, Handel had practically disappeared from the operatic stage (although not from the recording studio). It is symptomatic that in his popular opera guide *Festival of Opera* (1960), Henry W. Simon only included one work by Handel: *Giulio Cesare*. He voices profound misgivings about the suitability of Handel's operas for the stage, and doubts whether his operas will regain their original popularity. This is due to the problem of casting the lead roles (see p. 151), but more especially the libretti: 'they are based on pseudohistory, classical mythology, or romantic subjects so badly out of tune with our own times that it is impossible to read them without smiles soon suffocated by boredom' (Simon 1989: 237).

Handel's triumphant return to the operatic stage in the 1980s is linked without doubt to a postmodern sensibility, indifferent to verisimilitude and rejoicing in pastiche and multiple levels of citation, which then created an aesthetic disposition open to a more playful approach to Handel's operas. In fact, one could say that it is precisely those elements (which are anathema to Henry Simon) that make them so attractive to contemporary audiences.

Because the story of *Ariodante* (1735) is a 'romantic subject . . . badly out of tune with our times', there is not a strong case to be made for a transformational analysis. Because Alden and designer MacNeil create around the libretto seemingly autonomous worlds, determined largely by visual images, a structural approach is more productive. The story itself is drawn from Ariosto's epic Renaissance poem *Orlando Furioso*, and is set in a mythical, not historical, Middle Ages, a period as distant from Handel's audience as it is from our own time. The story is one of love, deception and betrayal, in which the King of Scotland's daughter, Ginevra (Guinevere), is treacherously accused of infidelity by her promised husband (Ariodante). Tragedy is averted only at the very end when Ariodante's rival, Polinesso, confesses his misdeeds on his deathbed.

The key to understanding the production is its design concept, although it is possible to attempt a psychological reading of the characters, as Alden himself has suggested; a kind of society without values in which emotional exploitation and deception are the preferred forms of social intercourse. The setting itself alludes to the palace of Versailles with its mirrors and associations of courtly intrigues. However, the design concept does more than just suggest specious parallels between 1735 and 1995. MacNeil's stage design revolves around the principle of transformation. It alludes to the Baroque stage, which relished spectacular effects, but MacNeil's stage remains essentially one setting that is varied and added to in all sorts of ingenious ways. The core spatial element is a kind of decaying Baroque hall of mirrors. Above it hangs a section of a ceiling fresco (see Plate 9). At various points in the action, reflective surfaces are lowered that function variously as translucent curtains, which distant the actions behind them, or as mirrors, which allow the audience to see themselves dimly reflected. The back of the stage opens occasionally to create a small stage-within-a stage, to provide vistas of distant mountains. The second act – specified in the libretto simply as 'classical ruins' – is represented by lowering the ceiling fresco onto the stage so that it literally becomes a piece of a ruined building that has fallen to the ground. The courtly world of the first act has literally crumbled. This becomes the setting for the deadly intrigue with its destructive dynamics that take the main characters to the brink of destruction. The multiple settings of the third act are represented by the reflective surfaces that are at once mirrors but also the dividing walls of the jousting ground

Plate 9. Ian MacNeill's set design for the opera *Ariodante* by Handel, Bavarian State Opera (2000). We watch the action through reflective surfaces; hanging above the stage is the remains of a Baroque ceiling; in the background is a stage within a stage.

for a duel between knights in heavy suits of armour: a perfect image for an anachronistic method of solving romantic disputes. The elegance of the Baroque court and the atavistic world of medieval knights are present in one and the same image. It is this principle of simultaneous visual layering that defines best the aesthetic strategies of the production. When we see a Handel opera, we are generally confronted with a complex problem of negotiating between at least three temporal levels which the directorial team have made the central principle of their production. The diegetic time (Middle Ages), the Baroque (time of composition) and the time of performance are evoked simultaneously.

In sum, we can say that both productions provide enough material for analysis independent of purely musical considerations. Although musical knowledge is, of course, important for understanding the aesthetics of opera, it should not be forgotten that opera is also theatre, and it makes use of the same staging procedures as dramatic theatre. Productions are based on interpretations of pre-existing texts that are transformed in the sign systems of performance: movement, images and sounds.

Further reading

Although operatic production continues to produce some of the most challenging stagings in contemporary theatre, there are few studies devoted to the analysis of music theatre production. Lindenberger (1984) and Kerman (1988) attempt to bridge the gap between the specialist and non-specialist. Groos (1988) and Levin (1993) are targeted at a more specialist audience. The periodical *Opera Quarterly* regularly includes analyses of operatic productions.

Chapter 10

Dance theatre

The analysis of dance, whether it is classical ballet or contemporary movement theatre, can be approached using some of the same tools that we have explored for dramatic and music theatre. This is especially the case for those forms of dance theatre that align themselves either explicitly or implicitly with principles of dramatic theatre. However, for those dance forms that place the body and its expressive possibilities at the centre of interest, which has been increasingly the case over the last century, dance-specific tools and methods are necessary. An analysis of George Balanchine's neoclassical ballets or of modern dance in the tradition of Martha Graham require, for example, a more formalistic dance-specific approach than that needed for works created in the context of contemporary movement theatre. Like other forms of theatre, dance can draw on long and varied traditions. To analyse dance, as with analysing opera, some knowledge of these traditions is essential in order to appreciate the aesthetic processes at work. Like all art, dance forms and particular choreographies are always suspended in a dialectic between reference to the world and self-reference, the former being more easily accessible to a wider audience and the latter requiring specialized knowledge of dance history, styles and choreographers.

Elements

Developments in dance theatre often stand in close connection to parallel trends in other art forms. Before 1900, dance theatre meant ballet, and it was usually integrated into operatic performance. The innovations introduced by the exponents of free dance and the international successes of the Ballets Russes and their close co-operation with leading visual artists signalled the complete autonomy of dance as a theatre form. Since this time, dance has been regarded as an innovative theatrical genre, often more in touch with avantgarde trends than other forms of theatre.

The analytical method required to study a work of dance depends entirely on the dominant aesthetic code employed by the choreographer and dancer(s). As we shall see in the examples to be studied, both historical and contemporary dance can structure works around elements such as character and action just as drama and opera do. However, when works are strongly self-referential, as is often the case in postmodern dance, there is often little point in searching for elements that are either entirely absent or present only in a rudimentary form. It makes more sense to concentrate on formal questions such as proxemics (the relationship of body and space), citationality, corporeal codes, etc.

The term 'work' is not so easily defined in dance. In dramatic and music theatre, we have seen that the norm remains the staging of a pre-existing theatrical text, which possesses an autonomous aesthetic status independent of the performance: *Hamlet* as a drama, *Madame Butterfly* as score and libretto. This relationship cannot be easily defined in dance theatre. Instead we find the following three variations:

(1) Score, libretto and choreography form a unity and exist in a written form. This is the case for most ballets in the classical repertoire, which are staged more or less according to the original choreography.

(2) Only the musical score is used as the theatrical text, which is choreographed in a new way. Stravinsky's score of *The Rite of Spring* exists in many different choreographies (e.g. by Vaslav Nijinsky, Léonide Massine, Mary Wigman, Kenneth MacMillan, Maurice Béjart, Pina Bausch or Royston Maldoom (see Chap. 11), of which none is canonized. Such works are by definition highly intertextual because they implicitly or explicitly refer back to previous choreographies.

(3) The choreography is completely new. The choreographer chooses the music, which has usually been composed for other purposes, and creates a new series of moves for the dancers. This is the norm in contemporary dance practice.

Each of these definitions determines a different analytical approach. The analysis of a classical ballet based on an original choreography by Marius Petipa will probably concentrate on the achievements of the solo dancers and *corps de ballet*, and perhaps on the subtle variations of a familiar work. The second variation corresponds to the relation between text and staging we know from dramatic and music theatre. Even if an existing choreography is not explicitly used, knowledge of previous choreographies on the part of artists and audiences can still be assumed as a point of intertextual referentiality. The analysis will have to take this relationship into consideration as well as concentrate on elements such as movement and dance styles (neoclassical, modern, postmodern, etc.), figure and story, scenography and costume. If a completely new work is to be analysed, the approach will be largely intrinsic. Points of departure might include other works by the same choreographer or other treatments of the same subject matter.

Until the end of the nineteenth century, the authorial function in dance theatre resembled that in music theatre. A writer would draft a scenario (an outline of the story), often in close collaboration with the choreographer, which would then be passed on to a composer. The choreographer would then transform this combination of musical and linguistic texts into the 'language' of movement. These 'corporeal texts' would then be written down in a special form of notation and become reproducible by other companies. Dividing the authorial function between different artists is of particular importance for the analysis of dance theatre, in as much as the romantic notion of an originary 'creator' in this case is difficult to identify. With the rise of free dance forms around 1900, this problem became simplified to the extent that, with the exception of the music, one and the same person often created the scenario and choreography and was the principal dancer. Important representatives of this movement such as Isadora Duncan, Loïe Fuller, Ruth St. Denis and Mary Wigman were thus not just dancers but authors as well.

Movement analysis: notation, semiotics and ideology

Irrespective of the type of work to be analysed, a central factor will be an interpretation of the movement used. Whatever else choreographies might be trying to do or say, they will express it primarily through the body (although it is nowadays not unusual for language to be used in dance theatre). Dance studies have developed different discourses to write about the body. Initially, the question of notation was paramount. The oldest forms of choreographic notation go back to the fifteenth century, where it functioned as a form of mnemonic for dancers and choreographers. The academic study of dance in general and movement in particular, however, is not much older than a century. Although notation techniques were developed to study dance, with some modification they can also be used to examine movement in general, also in dramatic or postdramatic theatre. As we have noted several times, the growing importance of postdramatic theatre has led to a critical reassessment of the assumed centrality of language and a corresponding focus on the body as an alternative expressive factor.

During the first half of the twentieth century, the German choreographer and movement researcher Rudolf von Laban (1879–1958) developed a method of recording movement that is known today as labannotation. Its basic principle is the relationship between body and its surrounding space (*the kinesphere*), which refers to the position of the body in space and the way it uses this space. The kinesphere is defined spatially as the area reachable by the extremities of the body without a shift in stance. In addition to these spatial qualities of movement, Laban also identifies the dynamic quality of corporeal expression, which he defines as flow, space, gravity and time. These categories define locomotion. Labannotation is a precise, if somewhat technically complicated, way to describe how movement functions; it does not, however, offer a means to analyse the semantic dimension of the body in motion.

In order to further systematize the analysis of movement and, above all, to account for how body movement generates meaning, it is necessary to revisit semiotics. As in all forms of semiotic description, semiotic vocabulary is more useful for specifying *how* meaning is made than in explaining *what* a specific meaning may be. Structural semiotics distinguishes between syntax and semantics. The former refers to the way elements are joined together to create coherence, the latter to the realm of meaning generation.

If we turn first of all to the level of syntax, we can, following Janet Adshead (1988), distinguish between two main options or levels of analysis:

(1) A *synchronic* perspective will focus on particular moments of a performance and try to 'freeze' these, as it were, in order to relate bodies to space and to each other and to study specific figurations.

(2) A *diachronic* perspective will study how types of corporeal signs or particular qualities – for example a leap, a specific effort or figuration – relate to each other throughout the course of the performance. Diachronic analysis will focus on the relationship between pattern and alteration.

It should be emphasized that these two perspectives are not mutually exclusive but should be used in combination. In fact, any form of performance analysis will need to find the right balance between synchronic and diachronic analysis.

Turning now to the *semantic* dimension, we find in Susan Leigh Foster's study, *Reading Dancing: Bodies and Subjects in Contemporary American Dance* (1986), the notion of *modes of representation*, which she introduced to dance analysis. Foster identifies four fundamental modes: imitative, representative, metaphoric and reflexive. These four modes refer in turn to different semantic levels on which bodies can produce and spectators can deduce meaning. As with the two syntactical levels, a performance will never restrict itself to just one mode of representation but it may define one as dominant:

- The *imitative* mode is based on agreement between a particular movement and the action being represented. The movement is an iconic representation of the action danced or performed by the character.
- The *representative* mode highlights specific characteristics of corporeal signs. This is done by repetition or other forms of focalization, which results in the generation of meaning; i.e. we recognize certain movements as having particular significance.
- The *metaphoric* mode does not try to imitate or represent indexically or iconically. Instead, it creates its own symbolic frame of reference. Particular movements or actions attain semantic importance because they do not conform to patterns of everyday meaning.
- The *reflexive* mode pertains when movement or movements are themselves the point of reference in the performance. In such cases, dance seems to be about dance; there might be allusions to previous dance styles such as classical ballet.

The approaches and tools looked at so far have emphasized formal aspects of performance. This is not surprising considering the semiotic terminology applied by many scholars. Like all other forms of performance, dance, because it is so centred on the body, can and does stress how bodies transgress and critique social codes. The body is certainly a highly coded entity: it is determined by gender and ethnicity, by age and history. It is therefore not surprising that, for the past decade or so, dance researchers and artists alike have applied the discussions of critical theory (see Chap. 5) to the phenomenon of dance. An acquaintance with these discussions is crucial for understanding contemporary dance, although the latter has split up into many smaller trends and developments, which only dance experts can really accurately survey. At its most experimental, dance theatre is hard to distinguish from some performances in the area of postdramatic theatre.

The aspect of dance (both historical and contemporary) that has attracted considerable attention is that of gender. Driven by the burgeoning discussions in feminism and then gender theory, dance scholars have explored the gender divide in this art form as well. While attention was focused initially on the female dancer and its central icon, the ballerina (see Hanna 1988), the increasing sophistication of gender theory led to a more nuanced discussion of gender differences. Burt (1995) focuses attention on the male dancer as the 'other' in a dance historiography that either obliterated gender difference in its focus on formal questions or set the female as the norm. Whereas classical ballet and modern dance in the Martha Graham tradition tended to essentialize gender differences, much contemporary dance engages critically with gender stereotypes and exposes their constructedness in much the same way as gender theory has done philosophically.

Analysis: *Petrushka* and *Enter Achilles*

The two works selected for analysis – *Petrushka* and *Enter Achilles* – represent the classical and the contemporary repertoire respectively (see Table 8).

Table 8. Models of performance analysis: dance theatre

Structural analysis	Ideological analysis
Petrushka (1911): A burlesque in four scenes. Scenario by Alexandre Benois and Igor Stravinsky. Choreography: Michel Fokine. Music: Igor Stravinsky. Design: Alexandre Benois. Setting: Shrovetide fair in St Petersburg, 1830. Source: Choreography of Paris Opera Ballet. DVD: Paris Dances Diaghilev (1990)	*Enter Achilles* (1996) by DV8 Physical Theatre. Choreography: Lloyd Newson. Screen adaptation by Lloyd Newson and Clara van Gool. Music: Adrian Johnston. Design: Michael Howells. Film director: Clara van Gool. Source: VHS Dance Videos or compilation DVD of three DV8 works, Arthaus

(1) Preparatory steps. Obtain information
  (a) about genesis of ballet
  (b) on Fokine's dance reform
  (c) on the figure of Petrushka
	(1) Preparatory steps
	  (a) description of action
	  (b) read reviews (see DV8 homepage: www.dv8.co.uk, last accessed 29 February 2008)
	  (c) read literature on masculinity

(2) Analysis
  (a) break down action into scenes and subscenes
  (b) divide characters into groups and types according to appearance and movement
  (c) discuss relationship between puppet world and real world
	(2) Analysis
	  (a) on basis of critical response analyse selected scenes in terms of movement, interaction and images
	  (b) compare own analysis with critical response
	  (c) discuss possible intertextual connections with *Petrushka* (settings, puppet)

(3) Results: discussion of time-space coordinates; relationship to Modernism, especially symbolism	(3) Results: exploration of male group behaviour; comment on male dancer and dancing in dance history

Both are accessible to students without highly specialized knowledge of dance because they follow, on a narrative level at least, recognizable elements of dramatic theatre. Both works contain dimensions of character as well as narration, although they are employed in extremely different ways. Because there is no space here to develop detailed analyses of either work, the following outlines are intended as guidelines for students to gain access to the works, but not necessarily to provide incontrovertible answers.

Petrushka

Petrushka was one of the key works of the Ballets Russes, and belongs to the established repertoire of classical ballet, even though it differs in many ways from the popular nineteenth-century repertoire. For this reason, it is easy to obtain basic information about its genesis. Of crucial importance is the way it was created by a team of important artists: the choreographer Michel Fokine, the designer Alexandre Benois and the composer Igor Stravinsky; the latter two also collaborated on the scenario. All this information is readily available in any ballet guide or on the internet. One should also consult scholarly writings such as Beaumont (1981) and Baer (1988). Because the version performed by the Paris Opera Ballet essentially follows the original designs and choreography, the analysis is intrinsic rather than transformational. Although there are transformational aspects to the Paris Opera Ballet version, they are not substantial and are certainly not relevant for an introductory analysis.[1] Intrinsic means, in this case, an elucidation of the aesthetic concepts behind and within the work. It focuses on internal elements such as spatial and temporal concepts and symbolic functions of place and characters. Of particular relevance to this work are Fokine's ideas on ballet reform, which he outlined in a famous letter to *The Times* in 1914.[2] Here he specifies how his choreographies for the Ballets Russes seek to break with the older traditions of classical ballet. Essential points are the relationship between individual movement and the dramatic action and a reduction of conventionalized gestures in favour of individualized movements, which reveal the influence of Stanislavsky's naturalistic theatre reform. At the heart of Fokine's reform is a rapprochement between dance and dramatic theatre, which is one of the reasons that some of his choreographies are easily accessible to non-dance specialists. Finally, one should be aware of the meaning of the title figure. In Russian, Petrushka is a puppet, not unlike Punch, with links to the *Commedia dell'arte*, and is a popular figure of the fairgrounds. He is grounded in popular culture and at the same time has wider artistic resonances.

For analysis, if we begin with the basic structure of the work, we find that it follows the course of a day at the St Petersburg Butter Market, a celebration around carnival time. The action begins with crowds at the market. The first scene culminates with the appearance of a magician figure (the Charlatan) and his puppet booth where his three puppets – Petrushka, the Ballerina and the Moor – perform for the bystanders. The second scene takes place in Petrushka's room, the third scene in the Moor's room, where we see rivalry between Petrushka and the Moor for the affections of the Ballerina. The fourth scene takes place at the market again where the struggle between the Moor and Petrushka is continued and culminates in Petrushka's death. The ballet ends with Petrushka reappearing on the roof of a building taunting the Charlatan.

The figures can be divided into two main groups: the crowd at the market square, who are also differentiated into individualized and collective groups: individual figures such as an organ grinder, a policeman and a dancing girl (who are clearly identifiable both musically and choreographically), as well as the three puppets, with the Charlatan functioning as an intermediary figure between the two groups. Each puppet has clearly distinguishable characteristics marked by the music, by movements and by costume and makeup. Each puppet-figure has a movement style indicating marionette-like movements. In Fokine's choreography, Petrushka dances '*en dedans*', his arms and feet turned inward creating an awkward, stumbling gait. The Moor dances '*en dehors*', with his limbs splayed outwards. The Ballerina encapsulates the classical ballet dancer, fixed on her tiptoes and able to perform only mechanical movements. Her dance becomes a kind of meta-commentary on the conventionalized movements of the classical ballet dancer.

The ballet has a complex spatial and temporal structure. Scenes one and four form a frame within which scenes two and three take place. The framing setting is a puppet booth at the market square, so we have a meta-theatrical situation. Because the second and third scenes take place within the booth and the rooms of Petruschka and the Moor respectively, the work immediately takes on a second level of reality – the empirical world of the Butter Market is not commensurate with that of the puppets.

The rooms of the puppets are quite different. Petrushka's is sparse, resembles a prison cell and is dominated by a picture of the Charlatan who commands them. The Moor's room, however, is sensual, symbolized by the bed and the exotic fruit and palms decorating the walls. Although these two rooms are quite different, they are also connected, at least in Fokine's original choreography. At the end of the second scene, Petrushka jumps through the window in his cell and lands in the Moor's room. This jump establishes an interesting temporal connection between the two scenes that defies empirical time because the end of scene 2 and the beginning of scene 3 would appear to be not continuous but almost parallel to one another. This unusual staggered time structure is continued in the transition from the third to the fourth scene. The latter would seem to be unfolding parallel to the second and third scenes. The struggle between Petrushka and the Moor breaks out in the third scene and erupts into the real world of the Butter Market in the fourth. *Petrushka* shows not the contrast of a real and unreal world with clear lines of demarcation between the two, but rather an uncanny overlapping of the two worlds. Just as Petrushka's reappearance at the end of the ballet causes us to question the distinction between real and unreal, puppet and human, animate and inanimate, so too do the blurred spatial and temporal coordinates of the four scenes force us to reconsider our patterns of perception. This quite radical representation of non-linear time and non-Newtonian space is reinforced by a comment made by Stravinsky, who stated that *Petrushka* should observe the dances of the fourth scene through a hole in his cell, and the spectators should also watch events from the perspective of his cell. The spatial and temporal relationship between these two worlds provides a key to the fascination that *Petrushka* continues to exert, and marks it as a modernist work of considerable sophistication.

Possible conclusions of the analysis would include a discussion of *Petrushka* as a modernist work. The fascination with puppets marks a central theme of symbolist theatre, which we find in the theatre of both Maurice Maeterlinck and Edward Gordon Craig. It would also stress its use of characterization through highly individualized movements, including members of the crowd scenes. Further modernist elements include the meta-theatrical setting and the multi-perspectivalism created by the shifts between empirical and puppet worlds, so that, finally, *Petrushka* can be read as an essay on the nature of theatrical illusion itself.

Enter Achilles

'[*Enter Achilles*] is more than dance, it is a fascinating piece of theatre, brilliantly staged and performed.'   Sunday Telegraph

DV8 Physical Theatre, founded by the Australian dancer and choreographer Lloyd Newson in 1986, has become one of the pre-eminent UK-based dance theatre groups. Over the past twenty years, it has produced fifteen works and several films and has helped define the genre of 'physical theatre': in the words of one dance critic, 'a meeting between dance and drama which confuses those who like their arts clearly labelled' (Watson 1995). It is this 'confusion' that makes the work of DV8 Physical Theatre accessible to non-dance specialists, and therefore relevant for performance analysis. *Enter Achilles* is one of the group's most successful works to date. First staged in 1995, it was restaged in 1997 and 1998. The film version, produced for the BBC in 1996, won a number of awards. The analysis is based on the film, not the stage production.

Before you start your analysis, watch the film. Attempt to note a basic structure according to the settings and the exits and entrances of the characters. It may be useful to produce a descriptive table of the action keyed to the timer on the VCR or DVD player. This is often employed in film studies, but our table would place its main emphasis on movement and interaction rather than camera angles or purely filmic devices. The degree of description is dependent on the type of analysis to be undertaken:

Time in minutes	Location	Action
00	non-specific	Shadowy male figures look in a window.
01	bedroom	Man in bed with an inflatable sex-doll.
02	bedroom	Woman's voice on answering machine; man turns on radio to drown out the voice.
03	pub	Man enters and grooms himself before mirror. More men enter.
04	pub	A man, Liam, starts to sing karaoke; he is rudely interrupted by loud jukebox music and taunted.
05	pub	Two men dance a duet around the pool table; movement consists of horseplay, wrestling and virtuoso leaps and catches.
06	pub	Duet with beer glass.
...		
11–13	pub	Stranger enters. Music changes from rock to a waltz rhythm; group dances to new music and ignores stranger, who is wearing orange shirt and trousers.
14	pub	Stranger is taunted by Ross, who makes obscene gestures; holds a beer glass in front of his pelvis; indicates breasts.
15	pub	Stranger is attacked by other men; he frees himself and removes shirt and trousers to reveal a Superman costume.
16	backyard	Stranger/Superman is carried outside by the other men and tossed over a wall.
...		
40–42	backyard	Liam appears with Ross's doll and throws it to the other men who play with it.

Time in minutes	Location	Action
43	backyard	Play turns into sexual abuse and finally the doll is raped with a beer bottle.
44	backyard	Ross is left cradling the punctured doll; the others leave over the wall slowly, singing lines from 'Jerusalem'; Ross screams at them.
45	backyard	Another doll's head appears over the wall; the melody of 'The Impossible Dream' is heard. The stranger is seen walking on the roof of the pub. END

DV8 Physical Theatre maintains an excellent website (www.dv8.co.uk, last accessed 29 February 2008). Information on *Enter Achilles* can be found in the archive, which includes a number of full-text reviews. On the basis of these reviews, one gains an indication of critical response. Are there clear points of agreement or disagreement? Some critics accused Newson of creating anti-female stereotypes (the only 'woman' present is the inflatable doll). There is also disagreement regarding the stranger figure. Is he clearly marked as a gay man?

Since the piece is very clearly an exploration of masculinity, especially in its less savoury, alcoholized manifestations, questions of gender construction will obviously feature prominently in the analysis. This means that our approach to the work will broadly follow an ideological-theoretical framework. As elaborated above, recent dance scholarship (Hanna 1988; Burt 1995) has focused on the shifting gender stereotypes manifested in dance in the twentieth century. Burt's study, *The Male Dancer: Bodies, Spectacle, Sexualities*, includes reference to Newson and DV8, and is an essential orientation for approaching *Enter Achilles*. Another possible influence is the study by the psychologists Bletcher and Pollack, *In a Time of Fallen Heroes: The Re-creation of Masculinity* (1993), where the authors argue that modern males use the wrong heroes as models, such as Achilles, who can no longer provide orientation in the modern world. The DV8 website makes explicit mention of Jonathan Rutherford's study, *Men's Silences: Predicaments in Masculinity* (1992).

If we proceed from the hypothesis that the work is an exploration of masculinity (which it very clearly is), it would make sense to study the interaction of the men in social rituals of the all-male pub. It should be made clear, however, that the work should not be regarded as an intentional embodiment of a particular study. Rather, the latter can serve to sharpen our awareness of the

Plate 10. DV8 Physical Theatre: *Enter Achilles*. Pub setting as the environment for masculine power games.

wider psychosocial issues as they were being discussed at the time of the work's genesis.

The original production elicited a degree of controversy regarding the portrayal of women and homosexuality. These debates, which are documented on the DV8 website, provide a useful starting point for analysis. Although one can approach such a work fresh, especially if one has never seen it before, a scholarly analysis should take account of the fact that it has already been defined and commented on: even a relatively new work has a 'history'. This critical history focuses on two main scenes: the first entrance of the stranger into the pub, where he is 'mobbed' by the other men (Plate 10); and the 'rape' of the sex-doll at the end of the performance. The dance critic Judith Mackrell wrote in the *Guardian*:

> One man at least is covertly gay but he tries to be one of the lads. The first time they turn against him he fulfils every boy's dream by whirling around and trouncing his attackers, his clothes falling off to reveal his Superman suit. But the next time is for real, with ugly fighting and even uglier mimed rape. The same violence is unleashed against a plastic doll which gets beaten up in brutal pantomime sex and mutilated with a broken bottle. The hatred of women, of bodies, of physical affection is wound to a terrifying pitch. These, says the show, are the feelings and fantasies men store up to take home after a night at the pub.
>
> (Mackrell 1995)

In his reply, Lloyd Newson takes issue with Mackrell's assumptions:

> Mackrell's penchant for generalisation and reinforcing stereotypes is clearly demonstrated when she describes one of the characters in *Enter Achilles* as 'the token vulnerable gay man'. Why gay? Because he, in contrast to the other characters, dances lyrically and wears bright colours? At no point in the piece is it ever suggested that this man is sexually attracted to other men. Her assumption, that men are gay if they behave outside the realm of acceptable 'male' behaviour, is precisely the tragedy explored in *Enter Achilles*. By taking her own opinion as fact and dismissing the character so readily, Mackrell indicates that she may have more in common with the other men in *Enter Achilles* than she would like to imagine. Elsewhere in her review, Mackrell suggests that an inflatable sex doll used in the piece represents women and its destruction is therefore representative of 'the hatred of women'. I find this reading remarkable from a critic because of its simplicity: it takes the whole incident of the doll's destruction out of context. One man destroys the doll in order to get at another man, who adores it, and the ultimate object of the attack is the other man, not the doll or women.
>
> (Newson 1996)

A possible analysis could take this controversy as a point of departure. It would need to study in detail the sequences 11–15 and 40–45. In both texts, the vocabulary used is psychological, and the question an analysis needs to address is to what extent movement without language can convey 'complex' characterization or psychological processes. Mackrell assumes the Stranger is gay but gives no evidence. Newson himself provides some possible answers – 'he dances lyrically and wears bright colours' – but negates them at the same time. The key event – the transformation into Superman – cannot be construed as typically gay behaviour, and should therefore be interpreted outside the framework of a gay-versus-straight debate. Because the stranger is integrated into the group later on, it might be more useful to study the scene on a more fundamental level, as an example of psychosocial dynamics whereby newcomers are initially always excluded, perhaps humiliated, and then integrated, not unlike initiation rituals at schools and universities.

The second example – the attack on the doll – is equally complex, and its interpretation is by no means exhausted by Newson's explanation that the object of the attack is the man, not the doll. Because the scene involves little 'dance' movement in any technical sense, it can be interpreted using the semiotic tools that would be applied in other kinds of performance analysis, except that there is no linguistic sign system to help contextualize the scene. First of all, it is important to observe how the attack unfolds. The first character to attack is the stranger, who appears thereby to seek acceptance from the group; the group, however, turn on him, take down his trousers and stage a mock rape with the doll, suggesting that they still question his manliness and indicating his non-acceptance. The use of an inanimate surrogate for a woman raises interesting questions with respect to the doll's semiotic function. Because the doll is clearly marked as female – obviously so in the light of its intended function as a sex toy – it can be read as a generalized sign for women, especially women as objects of male abuse. By using a kind of puppet, the performance explores aesthetically (not ideologically) the same questions of humanity that *Petrushka* does. Indeed, there is a case to be made that the performance contains intertextual references to the Russian work. The theme of violence, the somewhat obscure spatial and temporal relations between the bedroom and the pub, and finally the reappearance of the doll at the end and the image of the stranger on the roof explicitly evoke *Petrushka*. While it would be reductive to interpret *Enter Achilles* exclusively from an intertextual perspective, such references demonstrate that *Enter Achilles*, like most complex works of art, maintains a dialogue with its artistic tradition, as well as making a statement about the world – in this case images of masculinity.

One could argue that *Enter Achilles* is an exploration of male group behaviour, especially the dynamics of inclusion and exclusion that can be found in many male-dominated social spheres such as all-male schools, clubs and the military. In this sense, *Enter Achilles* can be read and analysed on the basis of its narration and identification of changing configurations. It is not in the first instance an exploration of gay gender questions, although these have featured prominently in DV8's earlier works. A further argument could be made that on an aesthetic level it engages with dance discourse in its citation of dance styles and conflation with everyday movement. The possible intertextual references to *Petrushka* also situate the work in a history of dance theatre.

Further reading

Most of the key works for an introduction to dance theatre have already been introduced in the course of the chapter. Essential reading are Foster (1986), Adshead (1988) and Burt (1995). Carter (1998) is a wide-ranging reader that covers in more detail the issues touched on in this chapter, and many more besides. For a stimulating discussion of contemporary border-crossing choreography, and in particular its engagement with the visual arts, see Lepecki (2005).

Part III

Theatre studies between disciplines

Chapter 11

Applied theatre

The old didactic theatre must be replaced by, let us say, pedagogical theatre.

(Augusto Boal, *Theater der Unterdrückten*)

A true image of necessary theatre-going I know is a psychodrama session in an asylum.

(Peter Brook 1968: 148)

Examples of applied theatre

Scene 1: Berlin, Germany

In January 2003, 250 young people, mostly aged between eleven and seventeen, performed Igor Stravinsky's ballet *The Rite of Spring*, accompanied by the Berlin Philharmonic, which was conducted by Sir Simon Rattle. The performance took place in the huge 2,000-seat Treptow Arena by Berlin's industrial harbour. The performers had been drawn from a number of Berlin schools and dance studios, a third of whom had a non-German background, and included twenty-five different nationalities. They had been trained over a three-month rehearsal period by a team led by UK-based choreographer Royston Maldoom, who has undertaken similar dance projects all over the world. The project has been documented in a remarkable film entitled *Rhythm Is It!* (2004), directed by Thomas Grube and Enrique Sánchez Lansch.[1] The film profiles three protagonists: fourteen-year-old Marie, a Berlin-born teenager with learning problems; Martin, a nineteen-year-old middle-class boy from a small provincial town with severe inhibitions; and sixteen-year-old Olayinka, a war-orphan from Nigeria, living in a hostel. The focus is not on the performance – the film only shows brief scenes from the actual 'final product' – but on the changes the three teenagers undergo in the three-month project. While not claiming any kind of therapeutic value for the process, the main protagonists – Maldoom and Rattle – repeatedly emphasize the transformational effects of dance and music. Referring to his own discovery of dance, Maldoom states: 'You can change your life in a dance class.' His aim is less to train budding dancers than to instil in the participants values and skills such as discipline, seriousness, focus and attention.

Scene 2: Plymouth, Massachusetts, USA

Visitors to the Plimoth Plantation in Massachusetts can walk through a re-creation of a 1627 English village. The website describes what they may expect to see:

> The people you will meet are costumed role players who have taken on the names, viewpoints and life histories of the people who actually lived in the colony in 1627, popularly known as the 'Pilgrims' today. Each one has a unique story to tell. Learn about the colony's difficult beginnings or discover the gossip of the day. Ask about religious beliefs, medical practices or relations with the local Wampanoag People. Talk to a housewife and learn what a 'pottage' is, or see how a duck or bluefish is cooked on the hearth. Help a young colonist pull up a few weeds in a cornfield, mix daub with your feet for a house under construction, or just relax on a bench enjoying the unique atmosphere of 17th-century New Plymouth . . . Do not be afraid to walk in on colonists as they eat, question them as they work, or join a lively conversation in the street . . . You needn't be an expert in the language of Shakespeare to pose a question, either. Just ask and see what happens – you may be called upon to define 'bathroom' or even explain what a 'Pilgrim' is![2]

Scene 3: Tembisa, Johannesburg, South Africa

> It's evening rush hour at the railway station in Tembisa and a train from Johannesburg has just deposited hundreds of commuters onto the platform. The sound of raised voices and signs of an impending scuffle persuade many of them to linger for a few moments. A circle forms around the drama unfolding in this most public of public places. The voices belong to a man and his wife and two other men. The man is accusing his wife of having an affair with a colleague accompanying her on the train. He knows this to be true, he yells, because last night she asked him to use a condom. The man moves threateningly toward his wife, but her friend blocks him and the two men start shoving each other and exchanging insults. The crowd starts to look uncomfortable; some laugh nervously, others mumble disapproval, but no one steps forward to intervene. Finally, some spectators become irritated by the

commotion and break up the crowd. There is no time to inform them that the scene they just witnessed was a performance and the participants were actors.

The young performers belong to EngenderHealth's partner, the Youth Channel Group (YCG), a Tembisa-based nongovernmental organization that uses 'ambush theater' to educate and mobilize their local community on issues revolving around HIV and AIDS, domestic violence, and gender inequities. The goal of the performance was to spark a discussion with the onlookers about condoms and gender-based violence. But part of the nature of ambush theatre is its unpredictability. 'It went well, except we didn't have a chance to distribute the condoms', commented one of the performers.

Undeterred, the troupe of actors and facilitators moved down the road and re-enacted the scene in front of an all-male hostel. This time, the actors had time to freeze the action and reveal that the scene was fictional. Some of the onlookers felt deceived and moved on, but others lingered to engage in debate with the YCG group and to accept the free condoms they handed out.   (Siegfried 2007)

Although highly diverse in terms of scale, budget and degree of celebrity involvement, the three projects sketched here pursue methods and goals used throughout the world and which are today grouped under the broad term 'applied theatre'.

The term itself is relatively new and links together a number of theatrical practices that might not necessarily regard themselves as affine. In the words of Judith Ackroyd:

> Many of those who would fall under the umbrella title of Applied Theatre may not be familiar with or even aware of those with whom they huddle. The dramatherapist sees her work as distinctly different from that of the group who employ drama to enhance the skills of a company sales team. The prison theatre practitioner will not necessarily relate to those using drama to support the elderly. The practitioners in each group will see themselves working with specific skills appropriate to their work and not therefore the same as those in other fields.
> (Ackroyd 2000: n.p.)

What links together these forms of theatre (and others besides such as theatre in education, community theatre and psychodrama) is their concern to use theatrical techniques to facilitate change of some kind. Applied theatre is understood to mean forms of theatre that engage directly in social praxis, whether it be the closed group of a psychodrama session, the open context of a performance about AIDS in a South African township or the historical role-playing employed at heritage sites: in all cases we are outside the framework of traditional Western aesthetics in the sense that art should be non-instrumental. Applied theatre is always theatre for a specific purpose. The interest for practitioners and scholars alike lies in the power of theatrical concepts and techniques to achieve these purposes.

Although the practitioners may regard their activities as being highly specialized, applied theatre research (as opposed to its practice) tends to look at its common historical origins and theoretical paradigms. In the context of this book, applied theatre can be seen as a significant development within the field of theatre studies, which has evolved, on the one hand, a high degree of autonomy in its practice, while on the other hand retaining close links to mainstream theatre studies in its theoretical questions.

The term 'applied' immediately implies the question: to what? The answer is usually: to the participants in the theatrical process. In applied theatre, the emphasis shifts from spectators involving themselves via detached aesthetic observation to their being active participants in a process, which may or may not end in a production. This does not mean that aesthetic engagement is eliminated from applied theatre. On the contrary, it is just as crucial as it is in 'art theatre', but is redirected into a more immediate corporeal and cognitive form accessible only through direct action. Applied theatre can, however, also comprise a performance before spectators who have not been involved in the process but they will either be drawn in through discussions, questions and answers or have some kind of community or familial link to the performers. The project *Rhythm Is It!*, introduced above, combines both approaches. Its primary aim was large-scale involvement of young people in a performative process, which culminated in a high-profile performance for invited spectators, many of whom were either related or known to the performers.

The following forms of applied theatre can be identified:

- dramatherapy
- theatre in education (TIE)
- theatre for and with special groups (e.g. in prisons or with the mentally impaired)
- interactive theatre at museums and heritage sites
- community theatre
- theatre for development (TfD).

Rather than discussing each form in detail, I shall outline some of the common historical and theoretical factors linking these practices and which constitute a common field for research.[3]

Historical trajectories

The use of theatre for pedagogical and therapeutic purposes is by no means an invention of the twentieth century. There are hints contained in ancient Greek medical treatises that mental disturbances can be addressed by role-playing. Early modern texts also contain indications of curative performative practices, whereby the boundaries between psychological treatment and religious rites are not always clear, as the rite of exorcism demonstrates. The Jesuit order made extensive use of theatre for both linguistic and propagandistic purposes. The achievement of the past century has been to redefine an old relationship and focus it in highly specific ways.

Around 1900, we find a revival of interest in theatrical performance as a therapeutic or pedagogic tool. The rise of Freudian psychoanalysis is clearly one of the crucial factors behind this resurgence, but a rekindling of interest in spontaneity and improvisation is the other. Children were the first guinea pigs for the Rumanian-born psychiatrist and founder of psychodrama, Jacob Levy Moreno (1889–1974), who organized theatre games for children in Viennese parks during World War I. After the war, he turned his attention to adults, and founded a theatre based entirely on improvisation, The Theatre of Spontaneity (Das Stegreiftheater), where neophyte actors such as Peter Lorre and Elisabeth Bergner allegedly gained early stage experience. Although short-lived, Moreno's attempt to create spontaneous performances formed the basis for his concept of 'psychodrama', which he developed in the USA after his emigration there in the late 1920s.

Moreno's point of departure is Freudian psychoanalysis. In contrast to the one-on-one relationship between analyst and patient and the highly introspective subject-centredness of psychoanalysis, Moreno's thinking highlighted interpersonal interaction. Moreno was convinced that most problems resulted from an individual's interpersonal relationships, and that they needed to be made explicit. He also criticized Freud's word-centred approach, and emphasized instead the importance of body-language as both a diagnostic tool and a therapeutic medium.

The best means to make dysfunctional interpersonal relationships explicit is through a carefully designed and monitored improvised performance practice that Moreno termed 'psychodrama'. The goal of the performance is to dramatize and expose the interpersonal conflict to such a point that the protagonist experiences a cathartic response. Moreno developed these techniques in the 1930s and 1940s, along with other methods of group psychotherapy. Psychodrama has gone on to provide one of the foundations of dramatherapy, which is used in many different kinds of institutional settings. Because of its highly specialized, interventionist nature, dramatherapy is often regarded as a separate area of applied theatre. Some of the scholarship on applied theatre avoids the area entirely, which is certainly justifiable in terms of current practice, but not so from a historical perspective.

A second line of development can be found in different kinds of pedagogical theatre, which were developed in the USA, the Soviet Union and Germany in the early twentieth century. Here, children also provided an initial focus for the development of a theory and techniques aimed at empowering through play and, in a more explicitly political variation, at 're-educating' the individual for life in a postcapitalist society. Of central importance in the USA was the Hull House Project in Chicago, where a number of socially committed women such as Jane Addams (1860–1935) and Neva Boyd (1876–1963) experimented with new forms of educational, vocational and artistic training for the socially disadvantaged (Jackson 2001). Neva Boyd's experiments with children's games and the performing arts had a direct influence on her arguably most famous pupil, Viola Spolin (1906–94). Spolin's development of improvisational theatre, initially under the auspices of the WPA's (Works Progress Administration) Recreational Project during the Great Depression, when it was directed at disadvantaged groups, evolved later into a hugely influential system of theatre games for actor-training. Her book *Improvisation for the Theater*, has been continually in print since its first publication in 1963. There are very few forms of applied theatre that do not utilize improvisational techniques and share Spolin's conviction that all human beings are innately spontaneous and capable of creative expression.[4]

The next step towards combining theatre and pedagogy in a political sense can be found in Brecht's idea of *Lehrstück*, learning or teaching plays, which he wrote between the mid 1920s and the early 1930s. The central idea of the form is that it dispenses with the usual actor–audience relationship. The *Lehrstück* teaches by being performed, not by being seen. In principle, the *Lehrstück* does not require spectators, although they can of course be present. In its most radical form, the *Lehrstück* and its theory represent nothing less than a negation of the theatrical contract. The plays are intended to be performed by amateurs (young workers, apprentices, etc.), not by professional actors. The participants are supposed to gain insight into the implications of certain actions or attitudes or, more broadly, to understand that society is not immutable but can be changed. The Brechtian *Lehrstück*, whose function is to demonstrate or create an awareness of complex political questions, is designed to instruct young people about Marxist ideology. The most controversial of these, *The Measures Taken* (1930), depicts a group of revolutionaries who have to decide to sacrifice a comrade for the good of the party. The point of the play is less the actual act of sacrifice than the decision-making and consciousness-raising process that it elicits.

The *Lehrstück* is exemplary for much applied theatre because it is directed at the participants and not at a 'passive' audience. If spectators are present, then it is expected that they will engage in discussion with the performers. The roles can also be reversed. The spectators can provide suggestions, which may then be taken up and played through. In this sense, the *Lehrstück* anticipates the principles of an emancipatory pedagogy that today's applied theatre usually associates with the work of Augusto Boal.

The work of the Brazilian director Augusto Boal brings the historical account up to the present, although Boal's work goes back to the mid 1960s. His approach combines both therapeutic and pedagogical-political imperatives. Although he began work as a dramatist and director in the 1950s, it was the repressive policy of Brazil's military dictatorship (1964–85) that forced Boal to abandon conventional theatre and develop new forms, which he termed the 'Theatre of the Oppressed'. This is also the title of his famous book, which was first published in the mid 1970s and has since been translated into many languages. Along with Peter Brook's *The Empty Space* (1968) and Jerzy Grotowski's *Towards a Poor Theatre* (1969), it is one of the most influential theatre manifestos of the post-war period. Under the rubric 'Theatre of the Oppressed', Boal subsumed a number of interventionist techniques, some of which continue to play a central role in applied theatre techniques today. They include invisible theatre, breaking repression and forum theatre.

Of the three, invisible theatre is the most explicitly political in an interventionist sense. Scenes from daily life are staged without the knowledge of passers-by who witness the scenes. The action follows a predetermined scenario, but because the reactions of the bystanders cannot be calculated, much of the action and interaction is improvised. This is a form developed specifically for theatre under a dictatorship where freedom of speech and artistic licence are severely curtailed. The AIDS education performance by the Youth Channel Group in Tambisa, South Africa (introduced at the beginning of this chapter) utilizes the same technique for educational rather than political purposes, under the term 'ambush theatre'.

In contrast to the street-theatre context of invisible theatre, the technique Boal calls breaking repression resembles in many ways the structure of a psychodramatic session. It is predicated on the notion that oppression – whether on the basis of class, gender or age group – is omnipresent. A participant is asked to remember an incident in which he or she felt oppressed; they then include other members of the group in the re-enactment of the incident. The scene is performed again, but this time the participant is required to resist the repression. The overall aim is 'to pass from the particular to the general, not vice versa, and to deal with something that has happened to someone in particular, but which at the same time is typical of what happens to others' (Boal [1979] 1985: 150). Although he developed them in Latin America in situations of poverty and extreme political oppression, Boal has also applied his methods in European countries.

Arguably the most influential of the many techniques popularized by Boal is forum theatre. Like breaking repression, it combines a clear political agenda with the psychodynamic techniques of dramatherapy. In forum theatre, a 'model scene', which thematizes a social or political problem, is performed before an audience in at least two versions. After the first version the spectators are given the opportunity not just to make suggestions for alternative solutions but to actually intervene as performers and replace the trained actors. The aim is not just to raise consciousness but also to activate the desire for real-life invention. In Boal's words: 'Forum theater . . . instead of taking something away from the spectator, evoke[s] in him a desire to practice in reality the act he has rehearsed in the theatre. The practice of these theatrical forms creates a sort of uneasy sense of incompleteness that seeks fulfilment through real action' (Boal [1979] 1985: 142).

Boal's techniques, especially forum theatre, have experienced international success. By the mid 1990s, Joe Winston noted that Boal had a fundamental influence on British teachers of drama at all levels, and that forum theatre 'is now a standard strategy in the classroom' (Winston 1996: 191). Perhaps the most widespread application has been in the movement known as theatre for development (TfD). As early as the 1970s, theatre began to be used in developing countries as a tool within wider developmental projects. Different forms have evolved:

- information dissemination employed in the many anti-AIDS campaigns in African countries, where theatre has been used in lieu of printed media;
- projects that thematize complex social or ethnic problems. Here Boal's techniques have been particularly successful.

Theatre for development is an important area of research within theatre studies in general and applied theatre in particular. In countries with a high level of analphabetism and poor technical infrastructure, theatre is often the most effective medium for transmitting content because it can often be integrated with indigenous cultural forms more effectively than technical media. From its inception, theatre for development stood in close dialogue with academic study and research. In most countries where it is utilized, theatre for development projects are designed at universities, usually at local drama departments in consulation with NGOs (non-government organizations) or government organisations. This has meant that the theatre projects have usually been subject to close evaluation through research. This question is discussed in more detail below in the section on research methodologies.

Of similar international impact is the movement known as community theatre, which has its origins in the 1970s in England and the USA, and emerges from the same counter-cultural impulse that motivated many other artists and movements discussed in this book. 'Community' is, of course, an extremely slippery concept. Some theatre theorists would argue that every audience is in some way a community, albeit a short-lived one, by virtue of sharing a particular experience – the performance – in a given time and place. The idea of *communitas* is often linked to those forms of modern theatre that deliberatively seek to re-invoke theatre's supposed ritual beginnings by creating an extremely intense, even orgiastic experience (Fischer-Lichte 2005). In the context of applied theatre, however, community theatre or drama refers to a set of practices whereby artists work in an existing social community – a town, village or neighbourhood – and create with the inhabitants a performance that usually reflects either an important historical event or current burning issue. Community theatre projects usually develop a playscript or performance scenario in co-operation with local people, although a professional writer is often involved. The performers are primarily locals, although, again, professional performers may be integrated as well.

In the UK, community theatre of this kind, which is known more accurately as the community play movement, was first initiated by the dramatist Ann Jellicoe, who demonstrated how a small group of professionals could harness the energies of large groups of people. The 'rediscovery' of community underpinning the ideology behind Jellicoe's work (and that of many others who followed) emerges out of counter-cultural thinking, which identified alienation, social disintegration and social mobility as deep-seated problems of industrialized society. There is doubtlessly something romantic about going back to small communities in an effort to investigate their forgotten past. Helen Nicholson has questioned the correlation between community and locale, arguing that, today, communities can emerge outside a shared space and are becoming increasingly deterritorialized: 'drama projects that focus on straightforward constructions of local identity, shared histories and ideological unity to the exclusion of difference and diversity, are likely to reinforce the more conservative images of "otherness" sometimes associated with localism' (Nicholson

2005: 84). Although there is certainly a danger in over-emphasizing the historical dimension of community, in terms of theatrical practice it is extremely difficult to operate outside a notion of shared space, unless one harnesses the possibilities of the internet. There is no doubt, however, that diasporic communities do exist in a complex configuration of modern communication technology, relatively cheap air travel and actual lived propinquity. Such diasporic communities may coexist spatially with other groups with whom they have only a minimum of direct social intercourse. Their real affective and cognitive community may be located thousands of kilometres away.

Theoretical paradigms

The historical sketch of applied theatre indicates that, despite its clear instrumental aims, the forms – whether therapeutic, educational or political – share in common a number of central theoretical concerns, which in turn intersect with the wider field of theatre studies. These theoretical paradigms include notions such as catharsis, ethics and, inextricably related to the latter, the status of spectatorship.

As we have seen in Chap. 4, 'catharsis' is the term most commonly used to discuss questions of impact and effects of theatre. It is not surprising then that the theoretical debate on impact in applied theatre takes as its point of departure this contested concept. Its main point of reference is, however, less often the terse and highly ambiguous reference in Aristotle's *Poetics* than the more detailed discussion in his *Politics*. In Book VIII, Chap. 7, Aristotle discusses the positive effects music can have on people, especially in a theatrical context:

> Some people are particularly . . . affected by religious melodies; and when they come under the influence of melodies which fill the soul with religious excitement they are calmed and restored as if they had undergone a medical treatment and purging [catharsis]. The same sort of effect will also be produced on those who are specially subject to feelings of fear and pity, or to feelings of any kind; indeed it will also be produced on the rest of us, in proportion as each is liable to some degree of feeling; and the result will be that all alike will experience some sort of purging, and some release of emotion accompanied by pleasure.
>
> (Aristotle 1995: 315).

In this much-cited passage, Aristotle argues that harmful – today we would say socially dysfunctional – emotions can be alleviated by actually experiencing them when applied in homeopathic doses. Not only is this an argument in favour of the performing arts (as opposed to the Platonic opposition to them), but they are placed in an explicit therapeutic context. This passage proves a central point of reference for theoretical writing on the beneficial effects of the performing arts.

Throughout the twentieth century but also before, catharsis is discussed and disputed as a curative technique as well as an aesthetic experience. In 1803, the German medical professor Johann Christoph Reil (1759–1813) demanded that all asylums be equipped with a theatre, and that the staff be trained in acting to ensure their expertise in a variety of roles. In his asylum-theatre, patients would have 'their imaginations strongly excited in a purposeful way; their prudential awareness awakened; contrary passions elicited; fear, terror, amazement, anxiety, and tranquillity excited; and the fixed ideas of madness confronted' (Richards 1998: 720–21). Moreno's theory of psychodrama hinges on a notion of catharsis on both an individual and group level. For Moreno, catharsis is achieved more through a flash of insight – and it can be both on an individual and group level – than through a profound emotional response, although he by no means discounts the latter. Moreno's central metaphor is the mirror: a psychodramatic performance reflects back to the protagonist the objects of his fears and desires. He explains the effect of embodiment in terms of primitive magic: when the protagonist embodies the figures of his hallucinations, then not only do they lose their power and their magic over him, but he acquires these powers for himself. Moreno terms this reconstitution of the personality by role-playing a 'catharsis of integration'. The group catharsis can be achieved when the other participants react to the performed situations by comparing them to their own experiences (Moreno 1972: xiv).

Catharsis in particular and Aristotelian philosophy in general is a recurrent theme in Augusto Boal's theoretical writings. In his early more explicitly political phase, catharsis forms the foundation of what Boal terms Aristotle's 'coercive system of tragedy', in which the spectator is required to empathize with the tragic hero whose 'tragic flaw' (*harmatia*) is purged in the spectator. This assumes a stable social system and is incompatible with the revolutionary state Boal demands: 'the spectators purge themselves of their tragic flaw – that is, of something capable of changing society. A catharsis of the revolutionary impetus is produced! Dramatic action substitutes for real action' (Boal [1979] 1985: 155). In this reasoning, cathartic response functions to prevent insight into oppression and thus mitigates against any kind of instrumental function for theatre. In more recent writings (Boal 1995), which explicitly frame his method within a therapeutic paradigm, Boal proposes a more differentiated approach to catharsis, which he subdivides into four types: the medical, Aristotelian, 'Morenian' and that used in the Theatre of the Oppressed.

Because of the centrality of the concept, it is not surprising that 'catharsis' continues to be discussed within the scholarly field of applied theatre. Its proximity to or associations with excessive emotionalism (the idea of cathartic release would seem to imply this, if not explicitly require it) has made it a controversial term within applied theatre, particularly in the more educational and didactic forms where the emotional component of theatre often stands in an uneasy relationship to the requirement to impart cognitively comprehensible 'messages'. The drama educationalist Joe Winston, for example, has argued for a reconsideration of catharsis against the background of the philosopher Martha Nussbaum's reassessment of the term. In this reading, catharsis should be seen more as cognitive illumination through emotions than in terms of excessive affective purging bordering on the irrational. Winston concludes that catharsis in this revised understanding 'stresses the cognitive aspect of emotion and suggests that drama's educational potential centres around its capacity for illumination' (Winston 1996: 194).

A second theoretical discussion concerns the *ethical* implications of applied performances. This is particularly the case in those forms of applied theatre operating in broadly educational contexts, such as TIE and TfD. Researchers have observed a tension between, on the one hand, an attitude of ethical openness, even transgressiveness, that we expect from theatre and performance, and, on the other, the requirement to impart attitudes in keeping with the institutional and cultural values where the performances take place, such as schools, prisons or village communities. This tension can manifest itself within performance processes where the 'rules' of rehearsal and workshopping may diverge quite markedly from those pertaining to a normal classroom or institutional setting. It can also present itself on the fictional level of the story, where, in order to appear credible to the audience, morally questionable actions may need to be portrayed.

If we look at one of our opening examples again, we can find illustrations of this predicament. In *Rhythm Is It!*, a 'crisis' arises when the choreographer Maldoom excoriates the pupils for their lack of commitment and discipline and threatens to discontinue the project. The observing teachers intervene on behalf of their pupils against Maldoom, whom they accuse of being too demanding. The question here is how far can non-professional performers be pushed and subtly manipulated psychologically for the 'higher good' of Maldoom's values? In a Birmingham-based TIE production entitled *Changes*, which deals with sex education, the main difficulty was to find a balance between believable characters and institutionally acceptable values. In *Changes*, the actors needed to establish attitudes to sexuality credible to a teenage audience but most probably at odds with the prescriptions laid down by the Department for Education and Skills in the guidelines to sex and relationships education. As

Winston defines the conundrum: 'Reasoned, reasonable and safe theatre is a recipe for dull, predictable theatre. Such attitudes are more associated with the institution of school. Unpredictable, risky and even perverse are, however, qualities characteristic of much critically successful contemporary theatre' (Winston 2005: 313). The participatory techniques of hot-seating[5] and forum theatre provide an avenue to negotiate the potential impasse.

Another theoretical issue that impacts directly on the practices of applied theatre concerns the question of *spectatorship*. If we assume that theatre invariably depends on the conclusion of a contract predicated on the 'willing suspension of disbelief' on the part of the spectators, it is clear that some of the forms of applied theatre discussed above would seem to question this contract. In the ambush theatre of the South African anti-AIDS group (introduced at the beginning of the chapter), the whole performance set-up hinges on blurring the boundaries between fiction and reality. There is no contract entered into beforehand, and bystanders may understandably reject the whole enterprise on account of feeling deceived. Many forms of applied theatre in the tradition of psychodrama assume only a thin veneer of fictionality on the part of the protagonist who, it is assumed, will be performing his or her story and its social predicaments.

Research methods

As applied theatre is integrated more and more into institutional settings and is indeed specifically required by policy makers (see Nicholson 2005: 3), so too does the pressure increase to monitor practices by means of transparent research methods. For this reason, a great deal of recent writing about applied theatre has focused on the question of developing adequate research methodologies. These questions include identifying the researchers: should the practitioners themselves monitor their own activities (a situation we find in the early phases of TIE and TfD), or should external evaluation be organized? The second main point of discussion revolves around the methodological approaches: can one use analytical techniques developed for conventional theatre as outlined in Chap. 8, or must one borrow from social sciences more empirical methodologies that guarantee 'measurable' data?

Although most of the practitioners mentioned in this chapter have also written extensively about their practice, this cannot be considered 'research' in a technical sense. An early application of research-monitored practice can be found in TfD, which began in the 1970s and gained international currency in the 1980s. Early practitioners, especially in African countries, often wrote up their activities as case studies, which were published as academic articles or even PhD theses. A major contribution to reflection on TfD is the book by Zakes Mda, *When People Play People: Development Communication through Theatre* (1993), a revised version of his PhD thesis submitted to the University of Cape Town. Based on his extensive TfD work with the Marotholi Travelling Theatre in Lesotho, Mda scrutinizes the whole problem of using media for development, especially theatrical techniques. The wider paradigm of his research is therefore communication theory, within which he investigates the communication potential of TfD. He describes his methodology as 'critical' rather than 'empirical'; that is, it is 'not concerned with the operationalisation and measurement of concepts, or with the statistical treatment of data' (Mda 1993: 3). The 'critique' is directed primarily at the top-down communication strategies employed by First World development ideology, which is predicated on a uni-directional model. In this way, traditional development practices and communication theory mirror one another. Mda argues that theatrical practices, because of their potential for interpersonal interaction, can provide a politically efficacious alternative. Mda is responding to a wider discussion where TfD has come under increasing ethical scrutiny, mainly for ideological reasons. Just as the whole top-down 'development' paradigm has come to be questioned, so too has its theatrical arm been subjected to similar questioning. One way to counter this justified criticism is to replace the top-down model with a bottom-up model, whereby the theatre groups respond more closely to needs expressed by particular communities.

Contemporary applied theatre in South Africa, such as the approach used by the group Interactive Themba Theatre to combat AIDS, is explicit about the research methodologies it uses to monitor its own work. It employs the transtheoretical model of behavioural change (TTM) developed in health psychology by Prochaska and Diclemente to explain why individuals adopt or fail to adopt new healthy behaviours in place of unhealthy ones, such as smoking or drug abuse. Without detailing the different stages involved in the model, it is important to stress that this kind of reliance on social science methodology indicates that applied theatre groups are subject to pressures of evaluation and accountability alien to more conventional kinds of theatre (see www.thembahiv.org, last accessed 1 March 2008).

Because of the external pressures placed on interventionist forms of applied theatre, there is often a fine line between evaluation conducted for the funding organizations and published academic research that not only examines the project but reflects on the evaluation methodologies as well. Although applied theatre scholars tend to almost invariably combine practice with scholarship, there is a new trend to conduct research on a purely observational and evaluative basis. A thoroughly discussed example can be found in Allen *et al.*

(1999). The authors in this case observed a TIE project and reported back to the funders. Their research methods, which they term 'data collection', combined observation and interviews. Both were directed at the actors, children and, to a lesser extent, the teachers. Both methods can in turn be subdivided into process and post-process phases. Other types of data included 'a video, a teacher's questionnaire, relevant documentation such as minutes of meetings and newspaper reviews' (Allen *et al.* 1999: 24). This type of research can be termed 'ethnographic' in the sense that it involves the observation and description of human action *in situ* to a much greater degree than it relies on numerical 'measurable' data. At the same time, the researchers were required by their contractors to provide an estimation of impact and whether they had received 'value for money'. This pragmatic requirement means that research of this kind has a 'foot in two traditions':

> The first of these is to set out the truth of a social situation or process through sensitive and accurate recordings and to make sense of these recordings through sets of organising protocols. The outcome is theory, leading to the possibility of comparison and other forms of interpretation. The second tradition involves estimating the impact on individuals or organisations of an intervention that is designed to promote change . . . The researcher has to control for all other possible influences of change in order to assess the particular influence of the intervention in question.   (Allen *et al.* 1999: 34)

For all its strengths in terms of detailed and objectified observation, this ethnographic approach may ultimately not provide the kind of quantifiable data that the 'ideology of accountability' (Allen *et al.* 1999: 34) increasingly demands. Ethnography can describe and interpret, but it cannot predict.

Such examples indicate that, in terms of its research paradigms, applied theatre has moved very much into the field of social sciences because its main fields of activities in education and remedial institutions expect these methodologies. Although the theatrical techniques and the theoretical terms used situate applied theatre firmly within theatre studies, its research methodologies require a high degree of specialist and interdisciplinary training.

Outlook

Applied theatre has established a number of well-defined spheres of activity. Its social acceptance is unquestioned, as indicated by its application in a variety of institutional settings such as schools, prisons, museums and even corporate management where, ironically, Boal's techniques are applied to great effect. Theatre techniques seem to 'work' across a broad range of social activities in the sense of increasing awareness, improving interpersonal skills and sharpening sensitivity to ethical questions of power, oppression and discrimination. Theatre allows one to see, even act out, the other's point of view, and thus gain insights through a combination of empathetic identification and cognitive reasoning.

Further reading

Because of its many subdisciplines, applied theatre is an exceptionally varied area. A number of overviews of the field have appeared in the last three years. Jackson (2007), Nicholson (2005), Thompson (2003) and Taylor (2003) all discuss the concept, but bring different emphases to bear. Of these, Nicholson provides the most systematic discussion of the theoretical issues at stake; Jackson provides the most extensive historical contextualization. Thompson's approach to the issues and his case studies are heavily informed by his extensive work in prison and theatre-for-development settings. TIE is well covered historically in Jackson (1993) and (2007). The complex area of community theatre is best surveyed in Kuppers (2007) and Kuppers and Robertson (2007). Erven (2001) also demonstrates the wide international range of theatre under this heading. The work of Augusto Boal has become an area of research in its own right. Apart from Boal's own writings, already quoted in the chapter, see Cohen-Cruz and Schutzman (1994). A recent survey of theatre for development is provided by Boon and Plastow (2004). For a discussion of psychodrama, see Blatner (2000), as well as Moreno's own writings. The area of heritage and museum theatre is covered in Hughes (1998) and Jackson *et al.* (2002). Students interested in following contemporary debates on this rapidly expanding and changing field should consult two journals: *Research in Drama Education*, published by Routledge, and *Applied Theatre Researcher*, an online journal available at: www.griffith.edu.au//centre/cpci/atr/content_journal.html, last accessed 1 March 2008.

Chapter 12

Theatre and media

As one of the oldest media, theatre has survived several epochal shifts in media technology. Whether it was the invention of the printing press or the challenges posed by the invention of cinema, radio or television, the theatre met these innovations with openness and accommodation rather than with rejection. Very often, the new medium took the theatre as its model (with respect to presenting entertainment, especially of the fictional kind (dramatic stories)) before developing other forms and conventions. The theatre always reciprocated by integrating certain elements of the new medium into its own aesthetic and even organizational forms.

Although the theatre has been exposed to competition from other media since the beginning of the twentieth century, and has certainly lost its previous dominant position as the main purveyor of fictionalized entertainment, the discipline of theatre studies has, until recently, been hesitant to seriously investigate the relations between theatre and other media. There are both historical and political reasons behind this reluctance. Historically, we can trace a gradual but steady expansion of the subject in the 1960s and 1970s. During this period one of the most frequently cited 'theoretical' statements defining the essence of theatre was Eric Bentley's famous formula: 'A impersonates B while C looks on' (see the introduction). Such efforts to 'reduce' theatre to a minimalist basic situation went hand in hand with an attitude that sought to keep other media at a safe distance from the stage.

Within the institutions themselves, there were two main reactions to the rise of the new technical media. One was a move towards separatism (departments of theatre studies concentrated on theatre and nothing else). Other departments incorporated the new media as independent additions, but seldom in the spirit of genuine integration. Instead of making the relationship between the media a subject of study, each medium was studied in splendid isolation. The reasons for this trend are complex, and some will be explored in the course of this chapter. Generally speaking, we can say that the dialogue between theatre and other media has only just begun on an academic level, and much remains to be done in the future. Recent experiments with multi-media and the growing number of conventional productions that incorporate other media mean that theatre studies must re-examine previous positions and redefine theoretical axioms to account for the ubiquity of the media.

Theatre as a medium

A fundamental problem facing scholars who wish to study the inter-relation between theatre and other media is that the term 'medium' is notoriously difficult to define. Depending on the field of application and the question being asked, any number of definitions can be used. This is by no means a special problem of theatre studies; it is equally virulent in the various fields of media studies themselves. I use the plural intentionally, because media studies itself is highly disparate and can range from strictly empirical research to hermeneutically oriented cultural analyses. Depending on the academic orientation, the concept of 'medium' will emphasize technology, function or content. For this reason it is not strictly possible to speak of media theory in any kind of way that will be generally accepted across disciplinary boundaries. In view of the many different approaches to the 'media' or the concept of 'medium' currently in circulation, we can only isolate a few fundamental distinctions. The concept of 'medium' or 'mediatization' can be understood in the context of theatre studies as:

(1) the storing, transmission and reception of information
(2) the relations between technology and the human body, or human perception
(3) exploring the relation between 'liveness' and mediatization.

Questions pertaining to the storing, transmitting and receiving of information form a traditional concern for media historians and span the whole history of mankind from the origin of writing to contemporary computer science. There have been many attempts to formalize the passage of information via a medium. The most famous communication model stems from Claude Shannon and Warren Weaver (pioneers of cybernetics), who devised a schematic representation of the way information travels from a source to a receiver (see Fig. 6).

Shannon and Weaver were mainly concerned with the technical problems associated with communicating information over long distances, and the interference and distortion that could occur at the point of the channel. IS and D are presumed to be human beings, whereas the instances T, C and R are of a technical nature and can therefore be defined, broadly speaking, as a medium,

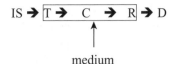

Fig. 6. Model of communication (after Shannon and Weaver).
IS: information source; T: transmitter; C: channel; R: receiver;
D: destination.

whether it be a telephone, radio or computer. Between T and R, a message is translated into a signal and then translated back again into a message.

Following this early mathematical research, linguistics and semiotics designed very elaborate models to account for myriad influences that can shape an act of linguistic communication (see Chap. 5). Because a medium is seen here primarily as a transporter or purveyor of messages, i.e. *information*, and as a means for facilitating the acts of communication between human beings (usually at some distance from one another), this concept has not usually interested scholars of theatre studies. The technological orientation of the model has also meant that it has been only of limited interest to our subject. As we have seen, theatrical communication is far more than just the exchange of linguistic messages. So where can we find and/or define the medium in theatre?

The answer most probably lies in a reformulation of the question or perspective. Firstly, the medial quality of theatre lies not in the sum of any essential characteristics (technological or otherwise), but rather in describing how it structures the flow of communication between production and reception. This 'flow' may indeed be organized by technological means, but most importantly it should be understood as a set of contingent relations structuring the interaction of space, performer and spectator. The medium of theatre should therefore be seen in relational and not in absolute terms. Secondly, a media perspective on the theatre will study how this set of relations is structured, technologically or otherwise. It will not be primarily concerned with aesthetic questions, although these can be factored in. Thirdly, it will include an anthropological perspective, because media are human inventions.

Moving on to relations between technology and the human body, or human perception, if we follow the father of modern media studies, Marshall McLuhan, and define media as 'extensions of man' (McLuhan 1964), we can reconceptualize the relationship between the medium and the human being as a complex inter-relationship between the body and the world. For McLuhan, a 'medium' is any man-made device by means of which human beings 'extend' their senses and nerves and which affect their consciousness: 'Any extension, whether of skin, hand, or foot, affects the whole psychic and social complex' (McLuhan 1964: 4). Thus, for McLuhan, a shoe or hairdo is as much a medium as the television. His best-known work, *Understanding Media: The Extensions of Man* (1964), is comprised of short chapters ranging from the spoken and written word to cinema and television (with many surprising media on the way, such as clocks and bicycles). We find here his most famous phrase: 'the medium is the message', which means essentially that we should leave behind the traditional distinction between form and content, because from the perspective of media theory, the material (technological) form of a medium is its content; it is certainly what should be studied in terms of its effects on human life. This is a concept of 'medium' which can, of course, be applied to the theatre (and McLuhan makes many references to drama – from Shakespeare to Beckett – to illustrate points).

McLuhan's thesis can be widely applied and not just when modern media are integrated into stage action (see p. 205). Even basic media such as light or costume have been integral to theatrical performance since time immemorial. McLuhan's pupil and successor at the University of Toronto, Derrick de Kerckhove, has attempted to apply McLuhan's theory to ancient Greek theatre, arguing that the Greek *theatron* played a crucial role in introducing new cognitive practices, such as the phonetic alphabet, to an audience still largely illiterate (de Kerckhove 1982). Using McLuhan's definition of medium, we can say that theatre is not distinct from, but an integral and historically important part of the study of media (if not of 'media studies').

Finally, we look at liveness and mediatization. Despite McLuhan's influence, much discussion on the relationship between theatre and media is still predicated on defining distinctions rather than inter-relationships. This discussion essentially begins with the invention of the cinema as the first new medium to seriously challenge theatre's dominant position as a purveyor of dramatized stories. The various positions of this discussion will be outlined in more detail in the following two sections. Today, as in the early twentieth century when the first debates began, theatre artists and scholars define theatre's 'non-mediated' nature through reference to its live character. Although an old discussion, the quality of 'liveness' has been the focus of a very intense debate in theatre and performance studies on the part of both artists and academics alike. It received new nourishment with the publication of Phil Auslander's book, *Liveness: Performance in a Mediatized Culture* (1999), in which the author takes issue with conventional distinctions – *mediatized* television versus *live* theatre – and the highly value-ridden judgements associated with them. He wishes to challenge those who 'reassert the integrity of the live' compared to the 'corrupt, co-opted nature of the mediatized' (Auslander 1999: 39). Firstly, Auslander argues, 'live-ness' is not an immutable given, but rather a historically contingent category that does not emerge as a distinct concept until the 1930s. One could argue, in fact, according to Auslander, that today the situation is reversed. Television dominates the market for 'liveness' with its news and sports broadcasts. He shows that television historically drew heavily on theatrical forms for its enter-tainment formats, and, of course, originally all television was live. In contrast, performance (Auslander's main example is the rock concert) is increasingly reliant on technological extensions: video screens and head mikes. Clearly, the two concepts are much more intertwined and mutually dependent than they may appear at first glance.

Auslander's argument is directed against schools of thought that try to define media through their intrinsic specificity or assumed 'essential' qualities. The term 'media specificity' refers, in the words of the film theorist Noël Carroll, to a form of 'medium-essentialism': 'It is the doctrine that each art form has its own distinctive medium, a medium that distinguishes it from other art forms . . . the medium qua essence dictates what is suitable to do with the medium' (Carroll 1996: 49). The central corollary of this theory implies or even states explicitly that the definition of medium determines notions of aesthetic value and creation. In the case of film, the aesthetically privileged films would be those that make the most extensive or innovative use of the particularities of the medium. Applied to the theatre, media specificity would imply a concentration on the basic theatrical situation that would necessarily highlight the live audience and/or a performance style not reliant on modern technology.

The concept of media specificity is, however, by no means an invention of film theory, despite its close links to that discipline. It goes back to a much older 'commonplace' of aesthetic theory that finds its first compre-hensive formulation in Gotthold Ephraim Lessing's essay *Laokoon* of 1766, where he makes a fundamental distinction between temporal and spatial arts. By critiquing the old formula of *ut pictura poesis*, which enabled one art form to be the model for another, Lessing introduced a new precept in aes-thetic theory that privileged arguments of difference and delimitation over concepts of analogy and exchange. The consequences of this perspective con-tinue into the present, and certainly provided one of the underpinnings of Modernism.

It was the modernist art critic Clement Greenberg who declared the question of medium to be the defining and distinguishing moment of art, thus effectively reversing the aesthetic doctrine of idealist aesthetic theory, which considered the material aspect of art to be the least important. For Greenberg, the search for medial purity was the ultimate goal for each and every modernist art form. In an essay entitled 'The New Sculpture', Greenberg writes:

> A modernist work of art must try, in principle, to avoid dependence upon any order of experience not given in the most essentially construed nature of its medium. This means, among other things, renouncing illusion and explicitness. The arts are to achieve concreteness, 'purity', by acting solely in terms of their separate and irreducible selves.
>
> (Greenberg 1961: 139)

Greenberg's art criticism goes back to the 1930s. By the time his famous collection of essays, *Art and Culture*, was published in 1961, the doctrine he was espousing had solidified into something approaching critical orthodoxy. It was paralleled by the same arguments in film theory. Between 1930 and 1970, numerous film and art theorists such as Béla Balázs, Siegfried Kracauer, Rudolf Arnheim, André Bazin and Erwin Panofsky expounded the dogma that the artistic nature of film – in comparison mainly to theatre – could be identified in the way it used its 'elementary material properties' (Rudolf Arnheim, *Film as Art* (1932) (2006)). The medium-specific 'property' of film was determined to be the use of the camera and montage.

With hindsight, it becomes clear that the mid-to-late 1960s saw attempts to redefine theatre in this way. Peter Brook begins his book *The Empty Space* with the famous words: 'I can take any empty space and call it a bare stage. A man walks across this empty space whilst someone else is watching him, and this is all that is needed for an act of theatre to be engaged' (Brook 1968: 11). Jerzy Grotowski's poor theatre for a few chosen spectators is a theatre bared to the basic essentials:

> By gradually eliminating what we found to be superfluous we discovered that theatre can exist without make-up, without costumes and stage settings, without a separate performance area (stage), without lighting and sound effects etc. It cannot exist without the actor–spectator relationship, a perceptual, direct living community.
>
> (Grotowski 1969: 15)

Both can be seen as attempts to formulate, both in theory and practice, the theatrical equivalent of media specificity. Both directors, in this period of their work at least, were working with a concept of theatre reduced to its basic essentials. Both positioned their concepts explicitly and implicitly in opposition to the ubiquity of cinematic and televisual media.

Theatre and other media

The need to discuss theatre in relation to other media is, of course, a product of the twentieth century, a century that has seen the invention of new media at regular intervals: cinema, radio, television and computers, all of which can compete in some way with theatre's hitherto dominant function of presenting dramatized stories. The fundamental question concerns how we can conceptualize and think about the relationship between theatre and new media, and what fields of enquiry these questions may open up. For heuristic purposes, we can propose the criteria of fictional status, media specificity and status of the performer as factors of central relevance to the theatre, and then compare their application and status in more recent media. The latter may well place their emphasis on other criteria which are, however, of less importance to the theatre.

The contents of theatre are almost exclusively fictional. This may seem patently obvious, but a media perspective needs to ask this question because media can be distinguished according to their function, i.e. whether they are primarily communication or artistic media. This almost exclusive emphasis on the fictional is, however, counteracted by theatre's liveness. The fact that spectators and performers occupy the same time and space – their physical co-presence – has been seen as a counterbalance to the fictional. There have been occasional attempts to establish theatre as an informational medium, such as the Living Newspaper movement of the 1920s and 1930s, or the theatre for development projects in 'under-developed' countries (see Chap. 11), but these remain outside the mainstream of the medium.

Radio and television, as media of mass-communication, have to balance fictional and informational content. In order to do this, certain conventions have been developed to mark the difference and transitions between the two. In the early days of cinema, when a showing might include up to seven different genres ranging from news to travelogues to comedy sketches, a live presenter moderated the shifts. There has been considerable research carried out showing how early cinema relied on theatrical conventions. This mixture of variety show and today's televisual experience later reduced itself to a weekly news film, a serial and main film, and finally, today, to advertising plus main billing. Like theatre, cinema has focused increasingly on its fictional content; even documentary films have – with a few notable exceptions – disappeared almost entirely from the cinema and re-established themselves on television.

Television has, of course, come under attack for its tendency to 'theatricalize' information. The most prominent (and polemical) critic is the media scholar Neil Postman, whose book *Amusing Ourselves to Death* is predicated on a comparison between television and popular theatre: 'when cultural life is redefined as a perpetual round of entertainments ... when, in short, *a people become an audience and their public business a vaudeville act,* then a nation finds itself at risk; culture-death is a clear possibility' (Postman 1985: 92, emphasis added). The comparison with the stage is clearly not intended to be complimentary. In Postman's view, television shares with the theatre (and cinema) a visual bias that has attracted the wrath of detractors since Plato.

The area of drama, in its broadest sense, is the domain where theatre intersects most closely with radio, cinema and television. Although each medium has its own dramaturgical conventions, they share the use of actors, directors and concepts of design. Differences (and similarities) between radio, television and stage drama have attracted the attention of researchers. Adaptations between media have a long history. What is certainly new today is a trend towards theatrical adaptations of films or television programmes, with the musical version of the animated film *The Lion King* being perhaps the most unusual and prominent example. The success of Julie Taymor's production suggests that the path between the media is very much multi-directional and in need of further research.

The most pressing issue is perhaps theatre's loss of dominance in the realm of the dramatic. Dramatic forms are much more prominent in television now than on the stage, a problem that Raymond Williams described in the early 1970s as leading to a profound shift in the function of drama. Most people are now exposed to drama in a variety of forms on a daily basis, more than ever before (Williams 1975). From being something the ancient Greeks might have experienced once or twice a year on festive occasions, drama is now integrated into the daily rhythms of our lives.

The virtual stage

The uncontested triumph of the computer as the dominant medium of the 1990s, and especially the rapid spread of the internet as a new means of communication, has reinvigorated the old debate regarding theatre and new media. As the newest of the new media, the computer has, like its predecessors, been intensely discussed within theatrical terms. Theoretically and conceptually the computer is regarded as a means of redefining the notion of performer and practically as a medium for creating new genres of performance (theatre on the web).

Current discussion of digital culture, and particularly the World Wide Web, is suffused with terms connected to the theatre. 'Virtuality', 'simulation', and 'interactivity' are all concepts with a long tradition in theatre theory. In order to describe the ever-changing dynamic interweaving of heterogeneous systems of symbols on the internet, and also the possibility of masquerading and sim-ulating other identities, in chat rooms, for example, some writers tend to refer to the new medium's 'theatricality' and 'interactivity'. The virtual role-playing in MUDs (Multi-user Dimensions) and MOOs (Multi-user Object Oriented interactive environments) harks back to older sociological discussions of social role-playing as a theatrical activity (Turkle 1995). The most cited attempt to compare theatre and digital worlds stems from the programmer and soft-ware designer Brenda Laurel. In her book *Computers as Theatre*, she outlines a possible scenario of interactive digital technologies in which theatre plays as important a role as computer science. Theatre could serve as a model for designing virtual space, since, in both media, one has to deal with concepts of characters and dramatic sequences of action, space and time: 'Designing human–computer experience . . . is about creating imaginary worlds that have a special relationship to reality – worlds in which we can extend, amplify, and enrich our own capabilities to think, feel, and act. . . . The theatrical domain can help us in this task' (Laurel 1993: 32–3).

The McLuhanesque notion of extending the human body via digital technol-ogy has recently been espoused and practised by the Australian performance artist Stelarc, who has been experimenting with prosthetic devices since the 1970s. Stelarc's *Ping Body* performance (1996–), for example, explores how the body can be seen as an interface with the flow of digital data and indeed be responsive to it (see Fig. 7). Even in more conventional theatre forms such as dance, leading choreographers like Merce Cunningham and William Forsythe are working with digital technology to expand the vocabulary of their art form.

The terms 'posthuman', 'cyborg' or 'postorganic' performance (Causey 1999) have been coined to discuss the implications of performances that seem to question certain fundamental notions of what it is to be human. Although critiques of humanist thinking can be found in the nineteenth century in philosophers such as Friedrich Nietzsche, the full consequences have only seemed to become apparent with the development of digital technology. Seen from this philosophical and ideological perspective, theatre and performance are contributing to what is clearly one of the most pressing debates of our times.

Although Stelarc's and Cunningham's experiments with digital technology still retain a live component (at some point in the process a performance takes place before spectators), recent attempts to use the World Wide Web as a performance space have redefined the notion of 'liveness' by restricting their performances entirely to the virtuality of the Web. Ever since the famous performance (in Web circles at least) of *Hamnet* in 1993 (a purely text-based

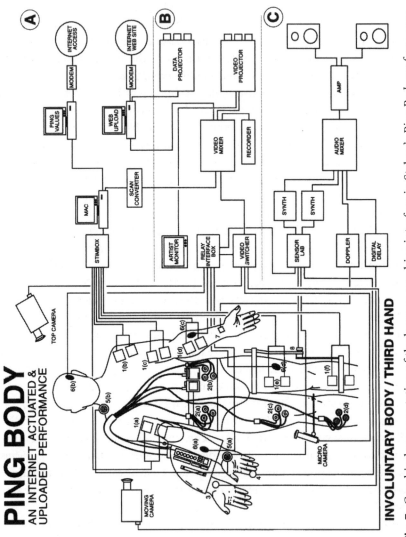

Fig. 7. Graphical representation of the human–machine interface in Stelarc's *Ping Body* performance.

parodistic re-enactment of *Hamlet*), there have been an increasing number of experiments with this medium as a 'place of performance'. As bandwidths increase (and with them the possibility to integrate sound, images and text), so too has the interest in web-based theatre (Schrum 1999). There are, of course, numerous intersections with net-based art, which in its performative variety cannot always be clearly distinguished from net- or web-based theatre (Weibel and Druckrey 2001). What links these performances is a common interest in exploring the interconnection between culture and technology; indeed in overcoming apparently insurmountable dichotomies between the two domains.

Intermediality

Although many web-theatre projects may be interested in exploring the specifics of the medium of the internet, on closer inspection it seems that the internet borrows freely from old media (like the theatre) and newer ones (such as the cinema). The increasing merger of media under the umbrella of digital technology has shown that the doctrine of media specificity discussed above is becoming obsolete, and needs to be replaced by a more integrative concept. Currently, this alternative goes by the name of 'intermediality'. The critical discussion surrounding the concept proceeds from the assumption that media specificity as defined above is at best a historically contingent phenomenon, at worst a critical and ideological construct designed to misunderstand and misrepresent much of the most interesting theatre of the past two decades. From the point of view of scholarship, we can observe a great deal of research and discussion within the humanities that is explicitly focused on the term 'intermediality', initially within the French- and German-speaking worlds but now increasingly in a broader international context. Discussion began in the 1980s with studies into the inter-relationship between text and images in surrealist and dadaist collages. This was followed by a growing number of studies into the adaptations of literature into film as a form of media transformation. Film studies has embraced the term, with the work of Peter Greenaway forming perhaps the most popular *objet de recherche*. Theatre studies has only just begun to discuss the term seriously. In English, the word is only just becoming current, although the term 'intermedia' has been around since the performance art movement of the 1960s (Higgins 1984). In 1998, a working group in the International Federation of Theatre Research (IFTR) was set up under this term. Because of the history of the term and its beginnings in literary and film criticism, there is still no clear generally accepted definition. Instead, we must distinguish three fields of application, all of which use the term. Intermediality is thus understood to be:

(1)   the transposition of diegetic content from one medium to another
(2)   a particular form of intertextuality
(3)   the attempt to realize in one medium the aesthetic conventions and/or patterns of seeing and hearing in another medium.

The first definition – the transposition of content between media – refers to older questions of adaptation – *War and Peace*: the book and the film; *Henry V*: the play and the film – of which there are any number of studies. This field of research, however, tends to base itself on a medium-specific paradigm, which asks how the different media require, on the basis of their specific requirements, certain changes and alterations to a novel or play.

The second definition – intermediality understood as an extension of the term 'intertextuality' to the relation between media products – evolved in the field of comparative literature, and was mainly applied to a specific category of text that integrated images, such as William Blake's illustrations of his own and other texts. The problem with this definition is that it is subject to the same conceptual inflation as its progenitor. Since literary theory sees intertextuality to be a basic condition of text production (there are no texts that are not intertextual, although some may be more intertextual than others), the same generalization may be applied to intermediality. If we narrow intertextuality to mean a specific strategy of explicit reference to particular pretexts, then the term becomes focused on the level of content rather than on the formal dimension of perception determined by media conventions.

It is this latter aspect – the realization of media conventions in another medium – that defines intermediality in a narrower and more useful sense.

That the exchange between media does not just proceed on the level of content but also on a deeper level of conventions and perceptions was already observed and commented on in the 1920s and 1930s. Both Walter Benjamin and Bertolt Brecht concerned themselves with this question. In 1931, Brecht published a report on the trial surrounding the film adaptation of *The Three-penny Opera*. He noted aphoristically: 'The film viewer reads stories differently. But he who writes stories is also a film viewer. The technification of literary production is irreversible' (Balme 2004). In this pithy statement, we already find some key elements of the concept of 'intermediality'. Most importantly, it shows that the question affects both production and reception: the film viewer reads stories differently, and the producer of these stories is also subject to the same influences.

When theatre becomes cinema: Robert Lepage's *Polygraph*

A particularly clear example of the use of filmic devices without actually using the medium of film can be seen in the 1989 production of *Polygraph* by Robert Lepage, which he has since made into a film. This psychological detective story consists of short scenes reminiscent of cinema, not just because of their brevity but because they are explicitly staged as film scenes. In one striking example, Lepage creates a perspective for the spectators that is otherwise only familiar in film or television:

> *Lucie uncoils from the floor to take the same position against the wall; simultaneously, the two men each put one foot on the wall, turning their bodies horizontal so as they appear to be in the classic cinematic 'top shot' of a corpse. François and David shake hands 'over' her body.*
> (Lepage and Brassard 1997: 29)

Important here is not just the perceptual perspective – we see in theatre in a way we normally only see in the cinema – but also the fact that Lepage is consciously citing and contrasting the perceptual conventions. The stage direction of the published version reads: 'they appear to be in the classic cinematic "top shot" of a corpse'. Significant here is the expression 'classic cinematic top shot'. He is staging film without film. By using very simple theatrical devices – the whole effect is achieved with a simple shift in body positions and a lighting change – we seem to be looking through a camera. In the context of the debate of media specificity or intermediality, this scene should be read not as a clear points win for the theatre but rather as a demonstration of the conventionality and historicity of all so-called media-specific forms of expression.

If we define intermediality as the simulation or realization of conventions and patterns of perception of one medium in another, we must ask in a next step: by what criteria can we recognize and study such strategies? In the case of theatre, for example, we would have to ask if the use of film, video or even slide projections is a defining factor of an intermedial approach. Strickly speaking, one could speak of multi-media theatre in such cases. The borders are, of course, fluid. Multi-media theatre may of course pursue an intermedial strategy. Examples go back to the 1920s with Erwin Piscator's use of film and slide projections, which evidence not just a use of technical media to better contextualize 'historical' background but also to contrast their various functions on a formal and perceptual level. Contemporary examples abound. Various New York-based groups and artists such as The Wooster Group, John Jesurun and The Builder's Association are, from a European perspective at least, the best-known exponents of such an approach. The French-Canadian director Robert Lepage has, since the late 1980s, explored the possibilities of intermedial theatre in productions such as *Polygraph, Tectonic Plates* and *The Seven Streams of the River Ota* (1996–8).

Further reading

Since theatre studies has been reluctant to engage with media theory, there is no one study (yet) that surveys the conjunction of the two fields. For a discussion of the concept of 'medium' McLuhan's *Understanding Media* (1964) is a useful idiosyncratic but canonical introduction to the subject. For discussion of the historical transitions between theatre and cinema, in particular the theatrical nature of early cinema, see Brewster and Jacobs, *Theatre to Cinema: Stage Pictorialism and the Early Feature Film* (1997) and Thomas Elsaesser's (ed.) *Early Cinema: Space, Frame, Narrative* (1997). 'Intermediality' is a relatively new term; two useful collections are Johan Callens (ed.), special number of *Degrés* 28 (101) (2000) and Freda Chapple and Chiel Kattenbelt (eds.), *Intermediality in Theatre and Performance* (2006), which contains many essays dealing with examples from contemporary theatre, cinema, television, opera, dance and puppet theatre. Philip Auslander's *Liveness* (1999) is essential reading for the liveness-versus-mediatization debate. Lehmann's *Postdramatic Theatre* (2006) contains extensive discussion of the use of media in contemporary experimental theatre, as does Birringer (1998). Kaye (2007) and Dixon and Smith (2007) both survey a great number of interesting projects and artists who integrate technological media into performance.

Notes

Chapter 1

1. *Verfremdung* means literally to make something or somebody appear strange or distanced. 'Alienation' is not strictly speaking an exact translation but will be used here as it is the most widely understood and used rendering of the German term.

Chapter 2

1. The emphasis will be on research that focuses on and has issued from theatre and performance studies. Because of the introductory character of the present study, the large amount of audience research conducted within media studies will not be included here.
2. This does not mean that the perception is in fact true. In his recent surveys of the economic (2004) and social (2006) impact of theatre in the UK for the Arts Council, Dominic Shellard demonstrates that the economic importance of theatre is substantial, totalling over 2.5 billion pounds annually (Shellard 2004). The social impact is more difficult to measure, but his report emphasizes, as well as the economic factor, 'changes in behaviour or improvement in skills' (McDonnell and Shellard 2006: 28). Both reports can be downloaded from www.artscouncil.org.uk/publications/.

Chapter 5

1. This essay remains untranslated into English; a discussion of its key ideas can be found in Pavis (1981).

Chapter 6

1. *Forschungen zur deutschen Theatergeschichte des Mittelalters und der Renaissance.* All translations from this work are by Christopher B. Balme.
2. See www.virtualvaudeville.com/concept.htm. Last accessed 17 February 2008.
3. Oscar Brockett and Franklin Hildy, *History of the Theatre*, now in its tenth revised edition (2007); Phyllis Hartnoll, *A Concise History of the Theatre* (1968); John Russell Brown (ed.), *The Oxford Illustrated History of Theatre* (1998).

Chapter 7

1. In ancient Greece, the *didaskaliai* were official catalogues listing the names of the winners and their plays in the dramatic festivals.
2. The question of loyality to the text poses itself differently depending on whether it is classical or contemporary. Living dramatists or their heirs (Beckett himself and the Brecht estate are famous examples) may even monitor productions and exert legal pressure to ensure conformity with the stage directions.

Chapter 8

1. A detailed discussion of documenting live performance can be found on the PARIP (Practice as Research in Performance) website under the heading 'artefacts': www.bris.ac.uk/parip/artefacts.htm. Last accessed 19 February 2008.
2. A good example of a film-style DVD is the Wooster Group production *House/Lights*, which includes multiple tracks featuring footage from different angles.

Chapter 9

1. The English National Opera first mounted David Alden's production of *Ariodante*, in 1993. It was revived in 1996 and restaged by the same team with the Bavarian State Opera Company in 2000.

Chapter 10

1. There have also been attempts to create entirely new choreographies on the basis of Stravinsky's music, such as Oleg Vinogradov's version, choreographed for the Scottish Ballet in 1989, which is clearly a political statement against the Soviet regime. It features police, and politicians, and Petrushka is represented as a political martyr.
2. Michel Fokine, 'The New Russian Ballet', letter to *The Times*, 6 July 1914; reprinted in Beaumont (1981): 144–7.

Chapter 11

1. The film is available from Boomtownmedia. See the website: www.rhythmisit.de, last accessed 1 March 2008.
2. www.plimoth.org/features/village.php, last accessed 1 March 2008.
3. Some of the areas discussed here are also of interest to other disciplines, mainly education, psychology and even political science. What will not be discussed is the

application of pedagogical techniques to the training of theatre or other arts professions, often referred to as 'performance pedagogy'. Some scholars also distinguish between applied 'drama' and 'theatre', but in this chapter the wider term 'theatre' will be used throughout. For a discussion of this distinction, see Nicholson 2005: 2–5.

4. Of equal importance in more recent years has been Keith Johnstone's book *Impro: Improvisation and the Theatre* (1979). For a comparison of Spolin's and Johnstone's approaches to improvisation, see Frost and Yarrow (2007).

5. Hot-seating is a much-used technique in applied theatre whereby an actor in role fields questions posed by the spectators.

Bibliography and other resources

Abbate, Carolyn (ed.) 1989. *Analyzing Opera: Verdi and Wagner.* Berkeley, Calif.: University of California Press

Ackroyd, Judith 2000. 'Applied Theatre: Problems and Possibilities', *Applied Theatre Researcher* 1: www.griffith.edu.au/centre/cpci/atr/journal/ article1_number1.htm, last accessed 1 March 2008

Adshead, Janet (ed.) 1988. *Dance Analysis: Theory and Practice.* London: Dance Books

Allen, Garth *et al.* 1999. 'Ideology, Practice and Evaluation: Developing the Effectiveness of Theatre in Education', *Research in Drama Education* 4(1): 21–36

Anderson, Laurie 1994. *Stories from the Nerve Bible: A Retrospective: 1972–1992.* New York, NY: HarperCollins

Aristotle 1965. *On the Art of Poetry*, in *Classical Literary Criticism*, tr. T. S. Dorsch. Harmondsworth: Penguin
  1995. *Politics*, tr. Ernest Barker. Oxford: Oxford University Press

Arnheim, Rudolf 2006 [1932]. *Film as Art.* Berkeley, Calif.: University of California Press

Arnott, James (ed.) 1977. *Theatre Space: An Examination of the Interaction between Space, Technology, Performance and Society. Contributions to the Congress* (8th World Congress, Munich, 18–25 September 1977). Munich: Schottenheim

Aronson, Arnold 2005. *Looking into the Abyss: Essays on Scenography.* Ann Arbor, Mich.: University of Michigan Press

Artaud, Antonin 1970. *The Theatre and Its Double*, tr. Victor Corti. London: Calder & Boyars

Aston, Elaine 1995. *An Introduction to Feminism and Theatre.* London: Routledge

Aston, Elaine and Savona, George 1991. *Theatre as Sign-system: A Semiotics of Text and Performance.* London: Routledge

Auslander, Philip 1999. *Liveness: Performance in a Mediatized Culture.* London: Routledge

Austin, John L. 1962. *How to Do Things with Words.* Cambridge, Mass.: Harvard University Press

Baer, Nancy van Norman (ed.) 1988. *The Art of Enchantment: Diaghilev's Ballets Russes 1909–1929.* New York, NY: Universe Books

Balme, Christopher B. 1993. 'Giorgio Strehler's *Faust*-project: Signification and
    Reception Strategies of a Work in Progress', *New Theatre Quarterly*
    9(35): 211–24
    1997. 'Interpreting the Pictorial Record: Theatre Iconography and the
    Referential Dilemma', *Theatre Research International* 22(3): 190–201
    2004. 'Intermediality: Rethinking the Relationship between Theatre and
    Other Media', *Theaterwelten* 1: www.thewis.de, last accessed 3 March
    2008
    2007. *Pacific Performances: Theatricality and Cross-cultural Encounter in the
    South Seas*. Basingstoke: Palgrave Macmillan
Balme, Christopher B., Erenstein, Robert and Molinari, Cesare (eds.) 2002.
    European Theatre Iconography. Rome: Bulzoni
Barba, Eugenio and Savarese, Nicola 1991. *A Dictionary of Theatre Anthropology:
    The Secret Art of the Performer*. London: Routledge
Barish, Jonas 1981. *The Antitheatrical Prejudice*. Berkeley, Calif.: University of
    California Press
Barry, Peter 2002. *Beginning Theory*, 2nd edn. Manchester: Manchester
    University Press
Barthes, Roland 1972. *Critical Essays*, tr. Richard Howard. Evanston, Ill.:
    Northwestern University Press
    1975. *The Pleasure of the Text*, tr. Richard Miller. New York, NY: Hill and Wang
Baugh, Christopher 2005. *Theatre Performance and Technology: The Development
    of Scenography in the Twentieth Century*. Houndmills and New York, NY:
    Palgrave Macmillan
Baumol, William J. and Bowen, William 1973 [1966]. 'Audiences – Some
    Fact-sheet Data', in Burns, Elizabeth and Burns, Tom (eds.). *Sociology of
    Literature and Drama*. Harmondsworth: Penguin: 445–70 (first
    published in Baumol and Bowen 1966. *Performing Arts: The Economic
    Dilemma*. Cambridge, Mass.: MIT Press: 71–97)
Beaumont, Cyril 1981. *Michel Fokine and His Ballets*. New York, NY: Dance
    Horizons
Beckerman, Bernard 1970. *Dynamics of Drama: Theory and Method of Analysis*.
    New York, NY: Alfred A. Knopf
Bennett, Susan 1990. *Theatre Audiences: A Theory of Production and Reception*.
    London and New York, NY: Routledge
Bentley, Eric 1965. *The Life of the Drama*. London: Methuen
Bial, Henry (ed.) 2007. *The Performance Studies Reader*. London: Routledge
Birringer, Johannes H. 1998. *Media and Performance: Along the Border*.
    Baltimore, Md.: Johns Hopkins University Press
Blatner, Adam 2000. *Foundations of Psychodrama: History, Theory and Practice*,
    4th edn. Berlin: Springer
Blau, Herbert 1990. *The Audience*. Baltimore, Md.: Johns Hopkins University
    Press
Boal, Augusto 1985 [1979]. *Theatre of the Oppressed*. New York, NY: Theatre
    Communications Group

1995. *The Rainbow of Desire: The Boal Method of Theatre and Therapy*, tr. Adrian Jackson. London: Routledge

Boenisch, Peter 2003. 'CoMEDIA electrONica: Performing Intermediality in Contemporary Theatre', *Theatre Research International* 28(1): 34–45.

Boon, Richard and Plastow, Jane (eds.) 2004. *Theatre and Empowerment: Community Drama on the World Stage.* Cambridge: Cambridge University Press

Boswell, James 1770. 'Remarks on the Profession of a Player', *London Magazine* August: 397–98; September: 468–517.

Bourdieu, Pierre 1984 [1979]. *Distinction: A Social Critique of the Judgement of Taste*, tr. Richard Nice. Cambridge, Mass.: Harvard University Press

1986. 'Forms of Capital', in Richardson, John G. (ed.). *Handbook of Theory and Research for the Sociology of Education.* New York, NY: Greenwood Press: 241–58.

Bratton, Jacky 2003. *New Readings in Theatre History.* Cambridge: Cambridge University Press

Brecht, Bertolt 1964. *Brecht on Theatre: The Development of an Aesthetic*, tr. and ed. John Willett. London: Methuen

Brewster, Ben and Jacobs, Lea 1997. *Theatre to Cinema: Stage Pictorialism and the Early Feature Film.* Oxford: Oxford University Press

Brockett, Oscar and Hildy, Franklin J. 2007. *History of the Theatre*, 10th edn. Boston, Mass.: Allyn & Bacon

Brook, Peter 1968. *The Empty Space.* Harmondsworth: Penguin

1988. *The Shifting Point: Forty Years of Theatrical Exploration 1946–1987.* London: Methuen

Brown, John Russell 1966. *Shakespeare's Plays in Performance.* London: Edward Arnold

1998. *The Oxford Illustrated History of Theatre.* Oxford: Oxford University Press

Brown, Stephen T. 2001. *Theatricalities of Power: The Cultural Politics of Noh.* Stanford, Calif.: Stanford University Press

Burns, Elizabeth 1972. *Theatricality: A Study of Convention in the Theatre and Social Life.* London: Longman

Burt, Ramsay 1995. *The Male Dancer: Bodies, Spectacle, Sexualities.* London and New York, NY: Routledge

Butler, Judith 1990. *Gender Trouble: Feminism and the Subversion of Identity.* London: Routledge

1993. *Bodies that Matter: On the Discursive Limits of 'Sex'.* London and New York, NY: Routledge

1997. *Excitable Speech: A Politics of the Performative.* London and New York, NY: Routledge

Callens, Johan (ed.) 2000. *Degrés* 28: 101 (special issue on intermediality)

Canning, Charlotte 1996. *Feminist Theaters in the USA: Staging Women's Experience.* London: Routledge

Carlson, Marvin 1984. *Theories of the Theatre: A Historical and Critical Survey from the Greeks to the Present* (2nd and expanded edn, 1993). Ithaca, NY: Cornell University Press
    1987. 'Histoires des codes', in Helbo, André and Carlson, Marvin (eds.). *Théâtre: Modes d'approche*. Brussels: Labor: 65–75
    1989. *Places of Performance: The Semiotics of Theatre Architecture*. Ithaca, NY: Cornell University Press
    1996. *Performance: A Critical Introduction*. London: Routledge
    2003. *The Haunted Stage: The Theatre as Memory Machine*. Ann Arbor, Mich.: University of Michigan Press
Carroll, Noël 1996. *Theorizing the Moving Image*. Cambridge and New York, NY: Cambridge University Press
Carter, Alexandra (ed.) 1998. *The Routledge Dance Studies Reader*. London: Routledge
Case, Sue-Ellen 1988. *Feminism and Theatre*. Basingstoke: Macmillan
Cassirer, Ernst 1955. *The Philosophy of Symbolic Forms: Vol. 2 Mythical Thought*, tr. Ralph Mannheim. New Haven, Conn.: Yale University Press
Causey, Matthew 1999. 'Postorganic Performance: The Appearance of Theatre in Virtual Spaces', in Ryan, Marie-Laurie (ed.). *Cyberspace Textuality: Computer Technology and Literary Theory*. Bloomington, Ind.: Indiana University Press: 182–202
Chapple, Freda and Kattenbelt, Chiel (eds.) 2006. *Intermediality in Theatre and Performance*. Amsterdam and New York, NY: Rodopi
Cohen-Cruz, Jan and Schutzman, Mady (eds.) 1994. *Playing Boal: Theatre, Therapy and Activism*. London: Routledge
Cole, Toby and Chinoy, Helen Krich (eds.) 1970 [1949]. *Actors on Acting: The Theories, Techniques, and Practices of the Great Actors of All Times as Told in their Own Words*. New York, NY: Crown Publishers
Collier, Jeremy 1972 [1698]. *A Short View of the Immorality and Profaneness of the English Stage*. London: Garland Reprint
Conquergood, Dwight 1991. 'Rethinking Ethnography: Towards a Critical Cultural Politics', *Communication Monographs* 58: 179–94
Cremona, Vicky Ann, Eversmann, Peter, Maanen, Hans van, Sauter, Willmar and Tulloch, John (eds.) 2004. *Theatrical Events: Borders, Dynamics, Frames*. Amsterdam: Rodopi
Davis, Tracy 1991. *Actresses as Working Women: Their Social Identity in Victorian Culture*. London: Routledge
Davis, Tracy and Postlewait, Thomas (eds.) 2003. *Theatricality*. Cambridge: Cambridge University Press
De Marinis, Marco 1985. 'A Faithful Betrayal of Performance: Notes on the Use of Video in the Theatre', *New Theatre Quarterly* 1(4): 383–89
Derrida, Jacques 1978 [1968]. *Writing and Difference*, tr. Alan Bass. Chicago, Ill.: University of Chicago Press

Desmond, Jane C. (ed.) 1997. *Meaning in Motion: New Cultural Studies of Dance.* Durham, NC: Duke University Press

Diamond, Elin 1997. *Unmaking Mimesis: Essays on Feminism and Theatre.* London: Routledge

Dillon, Janette 2000. *Theatre, Court and City, 1595–1610: Drama and Social Space in London.* Cambridge: Cambridge University Press
  2006. *The Cambridge Introduction to Early English Theatre.* Cambridge: Cambridge University Press

Dixon, Steve and Smith, Barry 2007. *Digital Performance: A History of New Media in Theater, Dance, Performance Art, and Installation.* Cambridge, Mass.: MIT Press

Dolan, Jill 2001. *Geographies of Learning: Theory and Practice, Activism and Performance.* Middletown, NJ: Wesleyan University Press

Dollimore, Jonathan and Sinfield, Alan (eds.) 1994. *Political Shakespeare: Essays in Cultural Materialism*, 2nd revised edn. Manchester: Manchester University Press

Dukore, Bernard F. (ed.) 1974. *Dramatic Theory and Criticism: Greeks to Grotowski.* New York, NY: Holt, Rinehart and Winston

Elam, Keir 1980. *The Semiotics of Theatre and Drama.* London: Methuen

Elsaesser, Thomas (ed.) 1997. *Early Cinema: Space, Frame, Narrative.* London: BFI Publications

Erven, Eugene van 2001. *Community Theatre: Global Perspectives.* London: Routledge

Eversmann, Peter 2004. 'Introduction to Part Two', in Cremona *et al.* (eds.): 133–8

Fischer-Lichte, Erika 1992. *The Semiotics of Theatre*, tr. Jeremy Gaines and Doris L. Jones. Bloomington, Ind.: Indiana University Press
  1994. 'Theatre Historiography and Performance Analysis: Different Fields – Common Approaches?', *Assaph C* 10: 99–112.
  1997. 'King Lear in Frankfurt', in Martin and Sauter: 191–211.
  2005. *Theatre, Sacrifice, Ritual: Exploring Forms of Political Theatre.* London: Routledge

Fortier, Mark 2002. *Theory/Theatre: An Introduction*, 2nd edn. London: Routledge

Foster, Susan Leigh 1986. *Reading Dancing: Bodies and Subjects in Contemporary American Dance.* Berkeley, Calif.: University of California Press

Foucault, Michel 1979. *Discipline and Punish: The Birth of the Prison*, tr. Alan Sheridan. Harmondsworth: Penguin

Fraleigh, Sandra Horton and Hanstein, Penelope (eds.) 1999. *Researching Dance: Evolving Modes of Inquiry.* Pittsburgh, Pa.: University of Pittsburgh Press

Frost, Anthony and Yarrow, Ralph 2007. *Improvisation in Drama*, 2nd edn. Houndsmills: Palgrave

Fuchs, Elinor 1996. *The Death of Character: Perspectives on Theatre after Modernism.* Bloomington, Ind.: Indiana University Press

Gebauer, Gunter and Wulf, Christoph 1995. *Mimesis: Culture, Art, Society.* tr. Don Reneau. Berkeley, Calif.: University of California Press

Geertz, Clifford 1973. *The Interpretation of Cultures: Selected Essays.* New York, NY: Basic Books
  1990. 'History and Anthropology', *New Literary History* 21(2): 321–35.
Gerould, Daniel (ed.) 2003. *Theatre/Theory/Theatre: The Major Critical Texts from Aristotle and Zeami to Soyinka and Havel.* New York, NY: Applause Books
Goffman, Erving 1974. *Frame Analysis: An Essay on the Organisation of Experience.* Cambridge, Mass.: Harvard University Press
Gombrich, Ernst 1960. *Art and Illusion: A Study in the Psychology of Pictorial Representation.* New York, NY: Pantheon Books
Gordon, Mel 1987. *The Stanislavsky Technique.* New York, NY: Applause Books
Greenberg, Clement 1961. *Art and Culture.* Boston, Mass.: Beacon Press
Groos, Arthur (ed.) 1988. *Reading Opera.* Princeton, NJ: Princeton University Press
Grotowski, Jerzy 1969. *Towards a Poor Theatre.* London: Methuen
Gurr, Andrew 2004. *Playgoing in Shakespeare's London,* 3rd edn. Cambridge: Cambridge University Press
Halliwell, Stephen 1998. *Aristotle's Poetics,* 2nd edn. Chicago, Ill.: University of Chicago Press
Hanna, Judith Lynne 1988. *Dance, Sex and Gender.* Chicago, Ill.: Chicago University Press
Harbage, Alfred 1941. *Shakespeare's Audience.* New York, NY: Columbia University Press
Hartnoll, Phyllis 1968. *A Concise History of the Theatre.* London: Thames & Hudson
Harvie, Jen 2002. 'DV8's *Can We Afford This?* The Cost of Devising on Site for Global Markets', *Theatre Research International* 27(1): 68–77
Herrmann, Max 1914. *Forschungen zur deutschen Theatergeschichte des Mittelalters und der Renaissance* [The History of German Theatre in the Middle Ages and the Renaissance]. Berlin: Weidmann
  1931. 'Das theatralische Raumerlebnis' [The Experience of Theatrical Space], *Zeitschrift für Ästhetik und allgemeine Kunstwissenschaft* (Beiheft) 25: 152–63
Higgins, Dick 1984. *Horizons, the Poetics and Theory of the Intermedia.* Carbondale, Ill.: Southern Illinois University Press
  1997. *Modernism since Postmodernism: Essays on Intermedia.* San Diego, Calif.: San Diego State University Press
Home, Henry, Lord Kames, 1762. *Elements of Criticism,* 3 vols. Edinburgh: A. Millar. Eighteenth Century Collections Online, Gale Group: http://gale.cengage.com/EighteenthCentury/index.htm, last accessed 10 March 2008
Horace 1965. 'On the Art of Poetry', in *Classical Literary Criticism,* tr. T. S. Dorsch. Harmondsworth: Penguin
Howard, Pamela 2002. *What Is Scenography?* London and New York, NY: Routledge

Hughes, Catherine 1998. *Museum Theatre: Communicating with Visitors through Drama.* Portsmouth, NH: Heinemann

Huston, Hollis 1992. *The Actor's Instrument: Body, Theory, Stage.* Ann Arbor: University of Michigan Press

Ibsen, Henrik 1923. *A Doll's House.* E. Haldeman-Julius (ed.), Girard, Kans.: Haldeman-Julius Company: www.gutenberg.org/files/15492/15492.txt, last accessed 26 February 2008

Ingarden, Roman 1973. *The Literary Work of Art: An Investigation on the Borderlines of Ontology, Logic and the Theory of Literature. With an Appendix on the Functions of Language in the Theater.* Evanston, Ill.: Northwestern University Press

Iser, Wolfgang 1978. 'Readers and the Concept of the Implied Reader', in Iser, Wolfgang, *The Act of Reading: A Theory of Aesthetic Response.* Baltimore, Md.: Johns Hopkins University Press: 27–38

Issacharoff, Michael and Jones, Robin F. (eds.) 1988. *Performing Texts.* Philadelphia, Pa.: University of Pennsylvania Press

Jackson, Anthony R. (ed.) 1993. *Learning through Theatre: New Perspectives on Theatre in Education,* 2nd revised edn. London: Routledge
  2007. *Theatre, Education and the Making of Meanings: Art or Instrument?* Manchester: Manchester University Press

Jackson, Anthony R., Johnson, Paul, Leahy, Helen Rees and Walker, Verity 2002. *Seeing It for Real: An Investigation into the Effectiveness of Theatre and Theatre Techniques in Museums*: www.plh.manchester.ac.uk/research/resources/Seeing_It_For_Real.pdf, last accessed 1 March 2008

Jackson, Shannon 2001. *Lines of Activity: Performance, Historiography, and Hull-House Domesticity.* Ann Arbor, Mich.: University of Michigan Press
  2004. *Professing Performance: Theatre in the Academy from Philology to Performativity.* Cambridge: Cambridge University Press

Jameson, Fredric 1991. *Postmodernism, or, The Cultural Logic of Late Capitalism.* Durham, NC: Duke University Press

Johnstone, Keith 1979. *Impro: Improvisation and the Theatre.* London: Methuen

Jones, Emrys 1971. *Scenic Form in Shakespeare.* Oxford: Clarendon Press

Karnad, Girish 1995. 'Introduction' to *Three Plays.* Delhi: Oxford University Press

Katritzky, M. A. 2006. *The Art of Commedia: A Study in the Commedia dell'Arte 1560–1620 with Special Reference to the Visual Records.* Amsterdam: Rodopi

Kaye, Nick 2000. *Site-specific Art: Performance, Place and Documentation.* London: Routledge
  2007. *Multi-media: Video – Installation – Performance.* London: Routledge

Kerckhove, Derrick de 1982. 'Theatre as Information-processing in Western Cultures', *Modern Drama* 25(1): 143–53

Kerman, Joseph 1988. *Opera as Drama,* new and revised edn. Berkeley and Los Angeles, Calif.: University of California Press

Kirby, Michael (ed.) 1965. *Happenings: An Illustrated Anthology*. New York, NY: Dutton
    1972. 'On Acting and Non-acting', *The Drama Review* 16(1): 3–15
Knapp, Mary E. 1961. *Prologues and Epilogues of the Eighteenth Century*. New Haven, Conn.: Yale University Press
Knowles, Ric 2004. *Reading the Material Theatre*. Cambridge: Cambridge University Press
Kowzan, Tadeusz 1968. 'The Sign in the Theater: An Introduction to the Semiology of the Art of the Spectacle', tr. Simon Pleasance, *Diogenes* 61: 52–80
    1985. 'Theatre Iconography/Iconology: The Iconic Sign and Its Referent', tr. Scott Walker, *Diogenes* 130: 53–70
Kuppers, Petra 2007. *Community Performance: An Introduction*. London: Routledge
Kuppers, Petra and Robertson, Gwen (eds.) 2007. *The Community Performance Reader*. London: Routledge
Laurel, Brenda 1993. *Computers as Theatre*. Reading, Mass.: Addison-Wesley
Leacroft, Richard and Leacroft, Helen 1984. *Theatre and Playhouse: An Illustrated Survey of Theatre Building from Ancient Greece to the Present Day*. London: Methuen
Lehmann, Hans-Thies 2006. *Postdramatic Theatre*, tr. Karen Jürs-Munby. London: Routledge
Lepage, Robert and Brassard, Marie 1997. *Polygraph*, tr. Gyllian Raby. London: Methuen
Lepecki, André 2005. *Exhausting Dance: Performance and the Politics of Movement*. London: Routledge
Lessing, Gotthold 1962. *Hamburg Dramaturgy*, tr. Helen Zimmern, new introduction by Victor Lange. New York, NY: Dover
Levin, David J. (ed.) 1993. *Opera through Other Eyes*. Stanford, Calif.: Stanford University Press
Lillo, George 1974. *The London Merchant*, in John Hampden (ed.). *The Beggar's Opera and Other Eighteenth Century Plays*. London: Dent
Lindenberger, Herbert 1984. *Opera: The Extravagant Art*. Ithaca, NY: Cornell University Press
Lough, John 1972 [1957]. *Paris Theatre Audiences in the Seventeenth and Eighteenth Centuries*. London: Oxford University Press
Loxley, James 2007. *Performativity*. London: Routledge
Mackrell, Judith 1995. 'Truly, Badly, but Terribly Manly', review of *Enter Achilles*, *The Guardian*, 22 September 1995: www.dv8.co.uk/stage/enter.achilles/press/tg_22.9.95.html, last accessed 3 March 2008
Martin, Jacqueline and Sauter, Willmar 1997. *Understanding Theatre: Performance Analysis in Theory and Practice*. Stockholm: Almqvist & Wiksell
Matthews, Brander (ed.) 1958. *Papers on Acting*. New York, NY: Hill and Wang
Mauss, Marcel 1973. 'Techniques of the Body', *Economy and Society* 2(1): 70–88

McAuley, Gay 1999. *Space in Performance: Making Meaning in the Theatre.* Ann Arbor, Mich.: University of Michigan Press

McConachie, Bruce 1985. 'Towards a Post-positivist Theatre History', *Theatre Journal* 37: 465–86

McDonnell, Bill and Shellard, Dominic 2006. *Social Impact Study of UK Theatre.* Arts Council England: www.artscouncil.org.uk/publications, last accessed 3 March 2008

McKenzie, Jon 1997. 'Laurie Anderson for Dummies', *The Drama Review* 41(2): 30–50

   2001. *Perform or Else: From Discipline to Performance.* London: Routledge

McLuhan, Marshall 1964. *Understanding Media: The Extensions of Man.* London: Routledge

Mda, Zakes 1993. *When People Play People: Development Communication through Theatre.* London: Zed Books

Merlin, Bella 2007. *The Complete Stanislavsky Toolkit.* London: Nick Hern Books

Meyer-Dinkgrafe, Daniel 2001. *Approaches to Acting: Past and Present.* London: Continuum

Meyerhold, Vsevolod 1969. *Meyerhold on Theatre*, tr. and ed. Edward Braun. London: Methuen

Moreno, Jacob Levy 1972. *Psychodrama*, Vol. I, 4th edn. Beacon, NY: Beacon House

Müller, Heiner 1984 [1977] *Hamletmachine and other Texts for the Stage*, tr. and ed. Carl Weber. New York, NY: PAJ Publications

Mulvey, Laura 1986 [1975]. 'Visual Pleasure and Narrative Cinema', in Mulvey, Laura. *Visual and Other Pleasures.* Bloomington, Ind.: Indiana University Press: 14–26

Newson, Lloyd 1996. 'Reply', *Dance Europe* 2 (February/March): 31: www.dv8.co.uk/stage/enter.achilles/press/de_3.96.html, last accessed 3 March 2008

Nicholson, Helen 2005. *Applied Drama: The Gift of Theatre.* Basingstoke and New York, NY: Palgrave Macmillan

Nicoll, Allardyce 1966. *The Development of the Theatre: A Study of Theatrical Art from the Beginnings to the Present Day.* London: Harrap

Oddey, Alison and White, Christine A. (eds.) 2006. *The Potentials of Spaces: The Theory and Practice of Scenography and Performance: International Scenography and Performance for the 21st Century.* Bristol: Intellect Books

Parker, Roger (ed.) 1994. *The Oxford Illustrated History of Opera.* Oxford: Oxford University Press

Pavis, Patrice 1981. 'The Interplay between Avant-garde Theatre and Semiology', *Performing Arts Journal* 5(3): 75–86

   1982. *Languages of the Stage: Essays in the Semiology of Theatre.* New York, NY: Performing Arts Journal Publications

   1992. 'From Page to Stage: A Difficult Birth', in Pavis, Patrice. *Theatre at the Crossroads of Culture.* London: Routledge: 24–47

1998. *Dictionary of the Theatre: Terms, Concepts, and Analysis*, tr. Christine Shantz. Toronto, ON: University of Toronto Press

2003. *Analyzing Performance: Theater, Dance, and Film*, tr. David Williams. Ann Arbor, Mich.: University of Michigan Press

Pearson, Mike and Shanks, Michael 2001. *Theatre/Archaeology: Disciplinary Dialogues*. London: Routledge

Peirce, Charles Sanders 1985. 'Logic as Semiotic: The Theory of Signs', in Innis, Robert E. (ed.). *Semiotics: An Anthology*. Bloomington, Ind.: Indiana University Press: 5

Peters, Julie Stone 2000. *Theatre of the Book, 1480–1880: Print, Text, and Performance in Europe*. Oxford: Oxford University Press

Pfister, Manfred 1988. *The Theory and Analysis of Drama*, tr. John Halliday. Cambridge: Cambridge University Press

Pitches, Jonathan 2006. *Science and the Stanislavsky Tradition of Acting*. London: Routledge

Plato 1955. *The Republic*, tr. H. D. P. Lee. Harmondsworth: Penguin

Postlewait, Thomas 1988. 'The Criteria for Periodization in Theatre History', *Theatre Journal* 40(3) (October): 299–318

Postlewait, Thomas and McConachie, Bruce (eds.) 1989. *Interpreting the Theatrical Past: Essays in the Historiography of Performance*. Iowa City, IA: University of Iowa Press

Postman, Neil 1985. *Amusing Ourselves to Death*. London: Heinemann

Priromprintr, Art 2004. 'Revitalizing "La Bohème". Baz Luhrmann Works to Make Italian Opera Relevant to a Modern Audience', *Daily Trojan Online*, 22 January, 151(6): 7–10: www.dailytrojan.com, last accessed 28 February 2008.

Pronko, Leonard 1967. *Theatre East and West*. Berkeley, Calif.: University of California Press

Rangacharya, Adya 1996. *The Nātyasāstra. English Translation with Critical Notes*. New Delhi: Munshiram Manoharial Publishers

Reid, Gilbert 1994. 'Computers and Theatre: Mimesis, Simulation and Interconnectivity', *Canadian Theatre Review* 81: 10–15

Reinelt, Janelle G. and Roach, Joseph R. (eds.) 1992. *Critical Theory and Performance*. Ann Arbor, Mich.: University of Michigan Press

Revermann, Martin 2006. *Comic Business: Theatricality, Dramatic Technique, and Performance Contexts of Aristophanic Comedy*. Oxford: Oxford University Press

Richards, Robert J. 1998. 'Rhapsodies on a Cat-piano, or Johann Christian Reil and the Foundations of Romantic Psychiatry', *Critical Inquiry* 24(3) (Spring): 700–36

Rimer, J. Thomas and Masakazu, Yamazaki (trs. and eds.) 1984. *On the Art of the Nō Drama: The Major Treatises of Zeami*. Princeton, NJ: Princeton University Press

Roach, Joseph 1985. *The Player's Passion: Studies in the Science of Acting*. Ann Arbor, Mich.: The University of Michigan Press

1996. *Cities of the Dead: Circum-Atlantic Performance*. New York, NY:
    Columbia University Press
Rousseau, Jean-Jacques 1968. *Politics and the Arts: Letter to M. D'Alembert on the
    Theatre*, translated and introduced by Allan Bloom. Ithaca, NY: Cornell
    University Press
Sauter, Willmar 2000. *The Theatrical Event: Dynamics of Performance and
    Perception*. Iowa City, IA: University of Iowa Press
Schechner, Richard 2003. *Performance Theory*, revised and expanded edn.
    London: Routledge
  2006. *Performance Studies: An Introduction*, 2nd revised edn. London:
    Routledge
Schoenmakers, Henri 1990. 'The Spectator in the Leading Role: Developments in
    Reception and Audience Research with Theatre Studies: Theory and
    Research', in Sauter, Willmar (ed.), *Nordic Theatre Studies: Special
    International Issue. New Directions in Theatre Research*, Stockholm:
    93–106
Schramm, Wilbur 1971 [1954]. 'How Mass Communication Works', in Schramm,
    Wilbur and Roberts, Donald (eds.). *The Process and Effects of Mass
    Communication*. Urbana, Ill.: University of Illinois Press: 3–26
Schrum, Stephen A. (ed.) 1999. *Theatre in Cyberspace: Issues of Teaching, Acting
    and Directing*. New York, NY: Lang
Scolnicov, Hanna 1987. 'Theatre Space, Theatrical Space, and the Theatrical
    Space Without', in Redmond, James (ed.), *The Theatrical Space* (Themes
    in Drama, Vol. IX). Cambridge: Cambridge University Press: 11–26
Selbourne, David 1982. *The Making of A Midsummer Night's Dream: An
    Eye-witness Account of Peter Brook's Production from First Rehearsal to
    First Night*. London: Methuen
Shakespeare, William 1963. *Hamlet*, First Folio edn: http://etext.virginia.edu/
    shakespeare/folio, last accessed 26 February 2008
Shellard, Dominic 2004. *Economic Impact Study of UK Theatre*. Arts Council
    England: www.artscouncil.org.uk/publications
Shepherd, Simon and Wallis, Mick 2004. *Drama /Theatre/Performance*. London:
    Routledge
Siegfried, Kristy 2007. 'Ambushing Commuters with Life-saving Messages',
    Saifaid News 11 (June): 7–8: www.safaids.net/publications/
    SAFAIDSNewe_June 2005.pdf, last accessed 4 March 2008.
Simon, Henry W. 1989. *100 Great Operas and their Stories: Act-by-act
    Synopses*. New York, NY: Anchor Books. Abridged from *Festival of Opera*
    (1957)
Singer, Millon (ed.) 1959. *Traditional India: Structure and Change*. Philadelphia,
    Pa.: American Folklore Society
Smith, Susan Valeria, Harris 1984. *Masks in Modern Drama*. Berkeley, Calif.:
    University of California Press
Sorell, Walter 1981. *Dance in Its Time*. Garden City, NY: Anchor Press
Southern, Richard 1962. *The Seven Ages of Theatre*. London: Faber & Faber

States, Bert O. 1985. *Great Reckonings in Little Rooms: On the Phenomenology of Theatre.* Berkeley and Los Angeles, Calif.: University of California Press

Stelarc 2007: www.stelarc.va.com.au, last accessed 3 March 2008

Styan, John Louis 1963. *The Elements of Drama.* Cambridge: Cambridge University Press

  1967. *Shakespeare's Stagecraft.* Cambridge: Cambridge University Press

  1975. *Drama, Stage and Audience.* Cambridge: Cambridge University Press

Sutcliffe, Tom (ed.) 2000. *The Faber Book of Opera.* London: Faber & Faber

Szondi, Peter 1987. *Theory of the Modern Drama,* tr. and ed. Michael Hays. Minneapolis, Minn.: University of Minnesota Press

Taplin, Oliver 1977. *The Stagecraft of Aeschylus: The Dramatic Use of Exits and Entrances in Greek Tragedy.* Oxford: Clarendon Press

  1993. *Comic Angels and Other Approaches to Greek Drama through Vase-paintings.* Oxford: Clarendon Press

  2007. *Pots and Plays: Interactions between Tragedy and Greek Vase-painting of the Fourth Century BC.* Los Angeles, Calif.: Getty Museum Publications

Taylor, Philip 2003. *Applied Theatre: Creating Transformative Encounters in the Community.* Portsmouth, NH: Heinemann

Thomas, Helen 1995. *Dance, Modernity and Culture: Explorations in the Sociology of Dance.* London: Routledge

Thompson, James 2003. *Applied Theatre: Bewilderment and Beyond.* Oxford: Peter Lang

Tulloch, John 2005. *Shakespeare and Chekhov in Production and Reception: Theatrical Events and Their Audiences.* Iowa City, IA: University of Iowa Press

Turkle, Sherry 1995. *Life on the Screen: Identity in the Age of the Internet.* New York, NY: Simon & Schuster

Turner, Victor 1987. *The Anthropology of Performance.* New York, NY: PAJ Publications

Vince, Ronald W. 1989. 'Theatre History as an Academic Discipline', in Postlewait and McConachie: 1–18

Watson, Keith 1995. 'From Sexual Paranoia to Bar-room Violence, DV8 Physical Theatre Explore the Terrors of Testosterone', *The Observer Review,* September 10

Weibel, Peter and Druckrey, Timothy (eds.) 2001. *Net Condition: Art and Global Media.* Cambridge, Mass.: MIT Press

West, Shearer 1991. *The Image of the Actor: Verbal and Visual Representation in the Age of Garrick and Kemble.* London: Pinter

White, Hayden 1973. *Metahistory: The Historical Imagination in Nineteenth-century Europe.* Baltimore, Md.: Johns Hopkins University Press

Wiles, David 2003. *A Short History of Western Performance Space.* Cambridge: Cambridge University Press

Wilkie, Fiona 2002. 'Mapping the Terrain: A Survey of Site-specific Performance in Britain', *New Theatre Quarterly* 70(18): 140–60

Williams, Raymond 1972 [1954]. *Drama in Performance.* Harmondsworth:
    Penguin
    1975. *Drama in a Dramatised Society: An Inaugural Lecture.* Cambridge:
        Cambridge University Press
    1980. *Problems in Materialism and Culture: Selected Essays.* London and New
        York, NY: Verso
    1989 [1975]. 'Drama in a Dramatised Society', in O'Connor, Alan (ed.).
        Raymond Williams on Television. London: Routledge: 3–13.
Winston, Joe 1996. 'Emotion, Reason and Moral Engagement in Drama',
    Research in Drama Education 1(2): 189–200
    2005. 'Between the Aesthetic and the Ethical: Analysing the Tension at the
        Heart of Theatre in Education', *Journal of Moral Education* 34(3): 309–23
Winton, Dean 1990. *Essays on Opera.* Oxford: Clarendon Press
Worthen, William B. 1984. *The Ideal of the Actor: Drama and the Ethics of
    Performance.* Princeton, NJ: Princeton University Press
    (ed.) 1999. *The Harcourt Brace Anthology of Drama,* 3rd edn. Fort Worth, Tex.:
        Harcourt College Publishers
Zarrilli, Phillip B. (ed.) 2002. *Acting (Re)Considered: A Theoretical and Practical
    Guide,* 2nd edn. London: Routledge
Zarrilli, Phillip B., McConachie, Bruce, Williams, Gary Jay and Sorgenfrei, Carol
    Fischer 2006. *Theatre Histories: An Introduction.* New York, NY:
    Routledge

Encyclopedias and dictionaries

The Cambridge Guide to Theatre. Martin Banham (ed.). Cambridge: Cambridge
    University Press 1995
The Concise Oxford Companion to the Theatre. Phyllis Hartnoll and Peter Found
    (eds.), 2nd edn. Oxford: Oxford University Press 1992
International Dictionary of Ballet. Martha Bremser (ed.). 2 Vols. London and
    Detroit, Mich.: St. James Press 1993
International Dictionary of Theatre. Mark Hawkins-Dady (ed.). Vol. I. Plays, Vol.
    II: Playwrights; Vol. III: Actors, Directors and Designers. Chicago, Ill.:
    St James Press 1992–6
An International Dictionary of Theatre Language. Joel Trapido (ed.). Westport,
    Conn.: Greenwood Press 1985
International Encyclopedia of Dance. Selma Jeanne Cohen (ed.). 6 Vols. Oxford
    and New York, NY: Oxford University Press 1998
The Metropolitan Opera Encyclopedia. David Hamilton (ed.). London: Thames
    and Hudson 1987
The New Grove Dictionary of Opera. Stanley Sadie (ed.). 4 Vols. London:
    Macmillan 1992
The Oxford Encyclopedia of Theatre and Performance. Dennis Kennedy (ed.). 2
    Vols. Oxford: Oxford University Press 2003

Pavis, Patrice. *Dictionary of the Theatre: Terms, Concepts and Analysis*, tr.
	Christine Shantz. Toronto, ON: University of Toronto Press 1998
World Encyclopedia of Contemporary Theatre. Dan Rubin (ed.). Vol. I: Europe;
	Vol. 2: The Americas; Vol. 3: Africa; Vol. 4: The Arab World; Vol. 5:
	Asia/Pacific. London: Routledge 1995–9

Bibliographies

Bibliographic Guide to Theatre Arts. Boston, Mass.: G. K. Hall 1975–
Innes, C. *Twentieth-century British and American Theatre: a Critical Guide to
	Archives*. Aldershot: Ashgate 1999
International Bibliography of Theatre. New York, NY: IBT 1985–
Performing Arts Books 1876–1981. London and New York, NY: Bowker 1981
Whalon, M. K. *Performing Arts Research: A Guide to Information Sources*. Detroit,
	Mich.: Gale Research 1976

Periodicals

Cambridge Opera Journal. Cambridge: Cambridge University Press 1989–
Contemporary Theatre Review. London: Routledge 1990–
Dance Research. Oxford: Oxford University Press 1983–
Dance Theatre Journal. London: Laban Centre 1983–
New Theatre Quarterly. Cambridge: Cambridge University Press 1985–
Opera Quarterly. Oxford: Oxford University Press 1983–
Performance Research. London: Routledge 1995–
Studies in Theatre and Performance. Bristol: Intellect 1980–
TDR: The Drama Review. Cambridge, Mass.: MIT Press 1955–
Theatre Journal. Baltimore, Md.: Johns Hopkins University Press 1979–
Theatre Research International. Cambridge: Cambridge University Press 1975–

Websites

Brockett's History of the Theatre, Digital Bibliography: www.abacon.com/
	brockett/links.html, last accessed 3 March 2003. A digital resource
	designed to provide additional information to Oscar Brockett's *History
	of the Theatre*
http://vl-theatre.com. A comprehensive resource covering more than fifty
	countries around the world, for professionals, amateurs, academics and
	students

Index

The Cambridge Introductions to . . .

AUTHORS

Jane Austen Janet Todd

Samuel Beckett Ronan McDonald

Walter Benjamin David Ferris

J. M. Coetzee Dominic Head

Joseph Conrad John Peters

Jacques Derrida Leslie Hill

Emily Dickinson Wendy Martin

George Eliot Nancy Henry

T. S. Eliot John Xiros Cooper

William Faulkner Theresa M. Towner

F. Scott Fitzgerald Kirk Curnutt

Michel Foucault Lisa Downing

Robert Frost Robert Faggen

Nathaniel Hawthorne
   Leland S. Person

Zora Neale Hurston Lovalerie King

James Joyce Eric Bulson

Herman Melville Kevin J. Hayes

Sylvia Plath Jo Gill

Edgar Allan Poe Benjamin F. Fisher

Ezra Pound Ira Nadel

Jean Rhys Elaine Savory

Shakespeare Emma Smith

Harriet Beecher Stowe Sarah Robbins

Mark Twain Peter Messent

Virginia Woolf Jane Goldman

W. B. Yeats David Holdeman

Edith Wharton Pamela Knights

Walt Whitman M. Jimmie
   Killingsworth

TOPICS

The American Short Story
   Martin Scofield

Creative Writing David Morley

Early English Theatre Janette Dillon

English Theatre, 1660–1900
   Peter Thomson

Francophone Literature
   Patrick Corcoran

Modernism Pericles Lewis

Modern Irish Poetry Justin Quinn

Narrative (second edition)
   H. Porter Abbott

*The Nineteenth-Century American
   Novel* Gregg Crane

Postcolonial Literatures C. L. Innes

Russian Literature Caryl Emerson

Shakespeare's Comedies Penny Gay

Shakespeare's History Plays
   Warren Chernaik

Shakespeare's Tragedies
   Janette Dillon

The Short Story in English
   Adrian Hunter

Theatre Historiography
   Thomas Postlewait

Theatre Studies
   Christopher Balme

Tragedy Jennifer Wallace